The Boyer Brothers
of Baseball

The Boyer Brothers
of Baseball

Lew Freedman

McFarland & Company, Inc., Publishers

Jefferson, North Carolina

LIBRARY OF CONGRESS CATALOGUING-IN-PUBLICATION DATA

Freedman, Lew.
    The Boyer Brothers of baseball / Lew Freedman.
      p.   cm.
    Includes bibliographical references and index.

    ISBN 978-0-7864-7099-0 (softcover : acid free paper) ∞
    ISBN 978-1-4766-1789-3 (ebook)

    1. Boyer, Cloyd, 1927–   2. Boyer, Ken, 1931–   3. Boyer, Clete,
1937–2007.   4. Baseball players—United States—Biography.
5. Brothers—United States—Biography.   I. Title.

    GV865.A1F69 2015
    796.357092'2—dc23
    [B]   2014046873

BRITISH LIBRARY CATALOGUING DATA ARE AVAILABLE

On the cover: (clockwise, from upper right) Clete Boyer, Ken Boyer
and Cloyd Boyer (National Baseball Hall of Fame Library, Cooperstown,
N.Y.)

Printed in the United States of America

McFarland & Company, Inc., Publishers
 Box 611, Jefferson, North Carolina 28640
  www.mcfarlandpub.com

TABLE OF CONTENTS

PREFACE

G enerations have passed since Ken, Clete and Cloyd Boyer were in their heyday, but when they were in the major leagues in the 1950s and 1960s, the fact that a trio of brothers from a small town in Missouri made it to the big time regularly gained considerable attention from sportswriters and sportscasters.

Although pitcher Cloyd's career was cut short because of arm injuries, he remained in the game for years as a coach and manager. Ken had the most glittering of resumes, an 11-time All-Star who won a Most Valuable Player Award as he became one of the St. Louis Cardinals' most popular players. Clete was a regular at third base for the perennial American League-champion New York Yankees.

As if that was not enough achievement on the diamond for one family, seemingly every other year a new Boyer brother would appear on the scene trying to fight his way through the minors to the top level of the sport. There were seven Boyer brothers in all, and all seven of them signed professional baseball contracts.

Three Boyers reached the majors and the other four gave it a shot. Rarely has any family in any sport experienced that type of success. I found the entire concept of so many brother ballplayers to be fascinating.

Part of my interest was sparked by the belief that third baseman Ken Boyer was worthy of inclusion in the Baseball Hall of Fame, yet he was not garnering many votes. My certainty that Ken was being unfairly overlooked for the Hall only solidified when Chicago Cubs star Ron Santo was selected. This is to by no means minimize Santo's accomplishments because I definitely feel Santo should have been chosen long before his own induction in 2012. However, during the same era Santo and Boyer were two of the top third basemen in the National League and I feel their achievements are virtually identical.

Originally, I was not aware that there were so many Boyer brothers, only the three major leaguers. Reading up on the family convinced me that there was a fun baseball story, and one worth telling. I found a receptive audience in Cloyd Boyer, the oldest brother, and the trend-setter for his family when it came to inking professional deals.

Alas, Ken Boyer and Clete Boyer had both passed away, but a number of brothers and sisters among the original 14 siblings were alive and well, many still residing in Western Missouri where they grew up. I made a pilgrimage to the area and spent time talking to the several members of the family who are quoted in this book.

For an author and researcher, it would have been easier if Ken and Clete had been able to speak for themselves, but that was not possible. In researching this volume I gleaned a large percentage of information from interviews with Cloyd Boyer, several other members of the Boyer family, and some former major league teammates of the big-league brothers. Except where otherwise noted, all quotations in this book come from those interviews.

In addition, given the prominence of Ken and Clete in their prime playing years there was a wealth of material about them from old newspaper and magazine stories, as well as information in books written about the St. Louis Cardinals and New York Yankees teams of that era that included passages of direct relevance to Ken and Clete Boyer.

Periodically, fathers and sons reach the majors, as do brothers, two most commonly, and sometimes three. But it's doubtful that we will ever again see a family that includes seven boys all of whom play professional baseball.

Those of a certain age with good memories will recall the slickness afield of Ken and Clete Boyer and their prominence in baseball at a time when each league had only eight teams. Yet even those good fans probably don't know that Cloyd spent half a century in the game and that four other brothers were also able to state proudly that they played baseball in the pros.

This is the untold story of the Boyer brothers, a look behind the scenes at the sport through the eyes of one American family.

INTRODUCTION

The arm didn't hold up as long as he wanted it to or believed it should. Cloyd Victor Boyer was the oldest of the seven brothers growing up in tiny Alba, Missouri, one of 14 children in all.

A right-handed pitcher born in 1927, Cloyd not only could throw a dancing fastball, he knew his stuff. And even though his arm was not tough enough to withstand the rigors of regular big league pitching for very long, his mind never stopped gathering information. He absorbed knowledge, and the result was a long career in the majors as a scout, coach and manager.

Although Cloyd was the oldest brother, he was not the most famous. The Boyer clan loved baseball. Cloyd set the example, was the pathfinder. But in all, seven Boyer brothers eventually were paid to play professional baseball at one time or another from the late 1940s through the early 1970s.

Ultimately, Cloyd's renown was eclipsed by younger brother Ken (Cloyd usually refers to him by his given name, Kenton), who became a star for the St. Louis Cardinals—the team they all rooted for, even if it was located on the far eastern end of Missouri—and Clete, who became the third baseman for the perennial World Series-contending New York Yankees. At the height of their fame Ken and Clete engaged in a showdown in the 1964 World Series with family members sprinkled around the stands busting with pride.

Cloyd was talented, inherited a sound work ethic from their father, Chester Vern, and made his own breaks. Ken was the natural athlete and many believe he should be in the Baseball Hall of Fame. Clete was the character, the funnyman, always looking to have a good time and trying to make sure that anyone visiting with him had fun as well.

Over the decades a fair number of members of the same family have achieved the ultimate dream of reaching the majors. There have been fathers and sons, and there have even been three-generation ballplayers that made it to the big-time. There have been numerous brother acts. Hank Aaron's brother Tommie played big-league ball. Gaylord and Jim Perry were outstanding pitchers. Phil and Joe Niekro were likewise tremendous hurlers. Paul and Lloyd Waner both became Hall of Famers. Joe, Dom and Vince DiMaggio made for a famous trio.

And then there were the Delahantys. Five of them played major league baseball. Ed was the big star, but Tom, Joe, Jim and Frank at least sipped from a cup of coffee in the bigs. Playing largely in the outfield and at first base between 1888 and 1903, Ed batted .346. He was selected for the Hall of Fame. Tom, Joe and Frank had fairly short careers, with limited playing time and achievements. Jim Delahanty played 13 years and batted .283.

As for the Boyers, although three of them played in the major leagues, there were four others good enough to get noticed, good enough to obtain minor league contracts, and good enough to harbor the dream of following their brothers into the majors. But overall seven brothers—seven members of the same tightly knit family—impressed scouts or baseball teams sufficiently enough with their skills that they were wooed to sign contracts.

Ken won a World Series ring with the Cardinals. Clete won two World Series rings with the Yankees. Years later, when he was the pitching coach for the 1977 Yankees, Cloyd earned his Series ring, too.

They hailed from the small community of Alba (their home is part of a small rural area where the boundary lines blurred). Now, as then, Alba is a smattering of buildings on the outskirts of Joplin, Missouri, not far from the Oklahoma state line—Tulsa is 130 miles to the west. Kansas City, Missouri, where major league ball is now played though it wasn't during the Boyers' youth, is 140 miles to the north.

When Cloyd was growing up, the population of Alba was around 350. In the 2010 census the government counted 555 residents, and there are posted signs with that figure on them. Some of those residents still are Boyers, or Boyers with married names. There are churches and a tavern, farmland, homes on a county road, and empty fields. Once, some of those were baseball fields where dreams were born and even fulfilled.

Ken passed away prematurely from cancer. Clete's death was due to complications from a brain hemorrhage. Cloyd still lives a few miles down the road from their boyhood home. So do several of the siblings.

Throughout the first half of the 20th century and into the 1960s, baseball was king in the United States. It was THE professional team sport. Just about every Missouri boy imagined that one day he could be throwing heat on the mound in Yankee Stadium in the Bronx, or taking his cuts at the plate in Sportsman's Park in St. Louis. The sandlots were jammed with youngsters playing informal games. Mostly it was play, but the best of the best always hoped they would be discovered by some backwoods scout who just happened to be driving by and was compelled to stop and study the talent arrayed before him.

It was comparable to the Hollywood dream of being discovered at Schwab's drugstore, though given that each of the 16 major league clubs either operated, or had affiliations with, a glut of minor league teams ranging from Class D upward, the odds were better for the ball players. Sometimes major league teams sponsored regional tryout camps. Essentially, they were cattle calls. Although just about everyone was welcome to try out, there were usually so many players on hand that the management had to employ quick ways to weed out the no-hopers and find the real talent.

With crowds of hopefuls, it was easy to get lost in the shuffle or be overlooked, even if you were a fine player. There were never enough coaches or scouts present to evaluate everyone completely. God forbid you got off to a slow start at the plate or made an error in the field. One little mistake could bury you, and there definitely might not be the opportunity for a second chance. You had to shine when you got your shot, or better still, you had to have a patron who knew who you were and knew what you could do.

Mostly, though, the hungry ballplayers in their late teens at these tryouts were on their own, wishing and hoping, desperate to show off skills and be noticed. Sometimes that just meant an extended tryout, getting kept a day longer after the first group was sent home. Every minute that you survived increased your chances of being a chosen one who belonged to a big-league team.

That's all the Boyers wanted—a chance. Once Cloyd crossed over, it helped open doors for the others. Baseball scouts believed in good genes. They figured if the older brother had the goods to play, then the younger ones probably could make it, too. Of course, the brother still had to demonstrate he was talented, but because of the name Boyer, at least someone was going to look them over.

1

BEGINNINGS
(Cloyd)

A tryout camp gave Cloyd Boyer his professional start in 1945. He was one of the fortunate ones who shone when the spotlight was turned on and the experts were watching. It was a St. Louis Cardinals session in Carthage.

Just down the road from Alba, Carthage, Missouri, is the county seat of Jasper County, and is called America's Maple Leaf City. The Cardinals were beating the bushes, just about literally.

For the first half of the 20th century, the Cardinals were the westernmost and southernmost team in the majors (excepting their American League co-habitant of St. Louis, the Browns). The Cards had a gigantic radio network, and 50,000 watts of sound carried their games into Arkansas and Oklahoma, many miles from Sportsman's Park. They were certainly the kings of Missouri and every boy in that state grew up wanting to play for the Cardinals. Mostly, the Browns just hobbled along, rarely winning, not drawing nearly as well as the Cards.

The tryout camp being a half-hour or so from his home was a bonus for Boyer. He had excelled on the sandlots and there were enough people around who believed he might have the right stuff to make the trip worthwhile. Yet he almost didn't even attend. When he was 17 years old, Boyer felt he was a pretty good player for his neighborhood, but had not thought for a minute that he was capable of being a professional. He was a good sandlot player, but he knew there was a big difference between being a big cheese in a small Missouri town and making money playing the game. He didn't yet have the confidence to feel that he belonged.

Today's sports world, with teenagers weaned on travel teams and being scouted from junior high on, is vastly different. Boyer said so many athletes of the 2000s have an inflated opinion of themselves and their parents feed the image, hoping it is all true so their son can earn a scholarship and be a star.

"It never entered my mind that I could play pro," Boyer said. "A lot of kids now, when they're 15 years old, start talking about going to the pros. They don't have any idea. You see a lot of that. The average person cannot judge talent. They say, 'Boy, he's a big, old 200-pounder, this, that and the other. He can throw a ball through a wall. He can hit the ball a mile.' You go and look at him, and well, you know how parents are."

It took others to convince Boyer that he might have the goods. He had to be talked into even showing up at that tryout camp. "I didn't want to go," Boyer said. "I wasn't going."

The camp was run by a scout named Clifton Ambrose "Runt" Marr. The big brass from St. Louis did not journey over to check things out. The Cardinals were famed for virtually creating the farm system and they stocked many teams at all levels of the minors. At one point the Cardinals controlled so many players that Commissioner Kenesaw Landis stepped in and ordered many of them set loose as free agents. That action did not tamper with the aspirations of teenaged boys from Missouri wanting to become Cardinals, however, and the Cardinals remained aggressive scouting their territory.

When Boyer made the pilgrimage to Carthage, his first goal was to get noticed. He wanted to become a big-league pitcher. Initially, though, he was received in a slightly off-putting way. "Runt Marr was running the thing," Boyer said, "and he wanted me to go try out in the outfield, as well. So I went out there and I guess they were impressed with my arm." That was the point of the entire exercise for Boyer, anyway, though not showing off his right arm from the outfield grass.

Like everyone else he took his cuts at the plate, but doesn't remember doing anything special on offense. Soon enough the camp operators recognized Boyer's best bet was as a pitcher. That was the philosophy of the Cardinals at the time—check out the arm strength of all of the prospects and mull over whether they might be turned into pitchers. "Later, they tried to make a pitcher out of my brother Kenny, and he hadn't even pitched," Boyer said.

The Cardinals did decide, though, that Cloyd might make a pitcher for them someday, with some seasoning. He was signed. He was still a senior in high school, but in early March, when spring training beckoned, he fled schooling early to take a train out of Carthage. His father spotted him $25 for spending money and for odds and ends, and the teenager rode the rails to St. Louis. It was as far as he had ever been away from home.

"I had a five-hour layover and I was getting homesick already," he said. "I was excited to go to spring training, but I got scared taking the trip. I was even going to quit. I thought, 'I believe I'll just turn around and go back home.'"

But he didn't. A much wider world called his name.

The Alba Boyer was leaving behind was a dot on the map. There were fields, some of them grassy, some of them scrubbed down a bit from ball playing. There were churches and schools and homes that people made in houses that were never going to be mistaken for structures in Beverly Hills. Much of Boyer's youth was spent out-running the Great Depression.

As a youngster, Boyer lived in four different houses in the area, and only one is still standing. That one house, many decades old, remains erect, though it has seen better days. Including the girl who died young, there were 14 Boyer children, seven boys and seven girls. Cloyd Boyer, who was born on September 1, 1927, was the oldest son, 25 years older than his youngest sister, a full generation's span.

Juanita, born in 1923, was the oldest Boyer sibling. Next came LeLa Thelma, born in 1925, the one who passed away as a child. Cloyd said he never knew her. Cloyd was born in 1927. Brother Wayne was born in 1929. Kenton, or Ken, the future All-Star third baseman, was born in 1931. Delores came along in 1933. Lewis Lynn was born in 1935. Clete, the other major leaguer, who starred for so long with the New York Yankees, was born in 1937. Pansy was born in 1939, Shirley in 1941, Ron in 1944, Lenny in 1946, Bobby Jo in 1948, and Marcella, the baby of the group, in 1952. When Marcella was an infant she had brothers old enough to be her father traveling the country playing baseball for a living.

"There was a gang of us," Cloyd Boyer said.

Although baseball records place the site of his birth in Alba, Boyer said he was actually born in one of the family houses that no longer exists in an area called Duval. The Boyers also lived in a house in abutting Cossville, though where the community lines merge is not easy to tell for someone not from that part of Missouri. Some of the Boyers lived in Carl Junction, too.

Mother Mabel worked full-time at child rearing. Father Chester Vern (but called Vern) worked full-time at any job that was available. Giving his oldest boy 25 bucks when he left for spring training was no small gesture in a household where luxuries were scarce and every dollar counted.

Left to right: Wayne, Cloyd and Ken Boyer when they all played for the local Alba Aces summer team (courtesy Cloyd and Nadine Boyer).

During the Depression, when President Franklin D. Roosevelt sought to put the nation back to work, Vern Boyer landed a job with the Works Progress Administration. That meant road construction and road improvements in the area. "They did a lot of good," Cloyd Boyer said.

Vern also worked in a blacksmith shop in Cossville and a grocery store, and baled hale in the summer when the farmers needed assistance with their crops. A little later he actually ran one of a chain of grocery stores populating those small Missouri towns. Still later he worked in a quarry. Cloyd joined him at that hard labor during the winters of 1946 and 1947, the baseball off-seasons.

Before Boyer boarded that train to the future he had enjoyed a family and baseball-centric existence with his friends. Boyer said he probably played his first baseball when he was five or six, just playing with the other kids outdoors for kicks. They did love it, though, and about halfway through elementary school a local man helped organize a team.

Boyer was a student at Rosebank Elementary School. The elementary school, junior high, and high school were situated in the same brick building. The structure still stands, but has been closed to students for many years. Roughly a half-dozen years ago a religious leader took control of the building and preached there for a few years. But it is locked down again now and passersby will usually observe a broken window or two. No other educational or religious project moved in. An online search for Alba High School does list Cloyd Boyer as a prominent graduate.

The area features the Wooden Nickel Tavern and some small stores. In addition, there is the Parlez Vous Café. There were no French restaurants in Alba in the 1940s. Much of the action is centered on Main Street, as it seemingly always has been in small-town America. Nearby, the old school keeps them company.

Carl Parker was enthusiastic about the sport and he was the one who organized a team for the kids, breaking some in with softball as well as hardball so that by the time they were in junior high school the experienced youngsters were a tough out for any competition in the neighboring counties.

Cloyd recalls that club losing only one game, and he more or less blames himself. Taking a reckless, foolish chance for no good reason except being a teenaged boy, Cloyd decided to fiddle with the family's new washing machine. That appliance represented a major investment for the Boyers and he was fascinated by it. Just goofing around, Cloyd got the index finger on his left hand stuck in a hole, and when he jerked his finger out it was yanked out of place and was a bloody mess requiring stitches. "It ripped the whole thing loose," Boyer said of his finger.

This would have been a greater catastrophe except for Boyer being a right-handed pitcher. There was a

Mabel and Vern Boyer had 14 children, seven boys and seven girls.

game on the schedule he was slated to pitch soon after the accident and he was rarin' to go. But mom and dad stepped in and refused to let him pitch. "I wanted to pitch that next game," Boyer said. "That was the only game we lost."

The injury healed and did not hold Boyer back, as evidenced by his success at that Cardinals tryout camp. It was news almost too good to be true, being signed by St. Louis, but the reality of the vast distances between places in the United States hit Boyer as he rolled by train across the land. People did not stay in touch via email or Facebook. There were no cell phones, and private phones in homes where a dollar was dear were not a given. Boyer was pretty much cut off from the environment and people he knew best, and the great unknown intimidated him.

Boyer hadn't yet turned 18 when he departed for his first spring training. It was much more common then for major league clubs to sign young players and move them up through the system one class at a time, one year at a time. There was also a shortage of players then. World War II had been raging with America's involvement since Pearl Harbor was bombed on December 7, 1941.

Hundreds of big leaguers went off to war, some of them among the most famous names in the sport such as Ted Williams, Bob Feller and Joe DiMaggio. And many hundreds more minor leaguers also served. From the standpoint of a teen like Boyer, the depletion of talent represented opportunity, as long as he didn't get drafted before he could show off his skills.

That chance was a big thing to the Boyer family. The Boyers were not rich. They were hard-working, regular folk with a lot of mouths to feed. Cloyd was both big brother and to some a somewhat distant figure as he passed into adulthood with some of his siblings still in elementary school—or even younger.

For an emotionally roiling Boyer, the train trip to Cardinals spring training was both adventure and eye-opening. His journey began in Carthage and he had that five-hour layover in St. Louis. Next stop was Cincinnati, with a six-hour layover.

By the time the train reached St. Louis, though, it was jam-packed. Many of the riders were soldiers coming home from the war. The number of troops in certain locations was being drawn down, and some young men were on their way home for the first time in a couple of years, out of harm's way for the first time in a long time.

Boyer was caught off guard by the huge numbers of uniformed men vying for space on the train's cars. It was a fight just to get on, like the

New York City subway today at rush hour. And then he couldn't get a seat, so he rode sitting on the floor for hours at a time.

"You had to bust it to get on," Boyer said. "People were just shoving and pushing. I just sat down on the floor with a couple of guys each time there was a change. We just talked. A lot of them had those big, old duffel bags, too, and that made it more crowded still."

The railroad tracks ran out for Boyer in Lynchburg, Virginia. It was a Cardinals minor-league spring training camp, not where the varsity roster was heading. The elite and favored group was off to Cairo, Illinois, in 1945. Adhering to war-time restrictions, major league clubs trained closer to their home cities in the first half of the 1940s.

There were five teams working out in Lynchburg, and while Boyer can't recall the names of the others sharing the same field, he was assigned to Lynchburg. The camp was scheduled for ten days leading up to April and nobody was getting paid. That's where the $25 Vern laid on him helped Cloyd survive. He nursed that money until a Cardinals check could be cashed. "I was smart enough to know that I had to make that $25 last," Boyer said. "I think I grew up a little quicker than most people."

Even then, as a 17-year-old who hadn't played his first professional game, Boyer showed maturity and wisdom in how he approached the crowded scene. When Lynchburg was off the field, instead of mainlining lemonade or fooling around, Boyer sat in the sun and watched the other players work out. When it was his team's turn, Boyer worked out hard, doing lots of running. But when the other teams took the diamond he watched and absorbed.

It made a big impression on the coaches seeing Boyer sit near the field for hours, studying the game. They even told him that they informed the front office about this laudable behavior and said just maybe he would be coach or managerial material in the coming years.

Yes, Boyer was watching the competition since he was going to have beat out some of those players for a job, and yes, he was studying the nuances of play and trying to file them away in his mind for future use. But there was one other thing that kept him rooted to the park during what could have been down time. "They didn't know I was broke," Boyer said.

It wasn't as if Boyer could find a pay phone and leave a message for his parents saying, "Please send money." That was not going to happen. He was incredulous enough that his scrimping father came up with the $25 gift in the first place. He didn't see it coming and was very grateful.

"I knew I wasn't going to get any more," Boyer said. "I couldn't believe

Dad had $25 to give me. I never forgot that. My father was proud of me and he did give me a push to get ahead. We worked in the grocery store together a little while, too. I used to help him cut wood. We'd cut wood and sell it for a dollar a rick, which wasn't very much."

Now people more often use the term "cord" for firewood. A rick of cut wood is eight feet long by four feet high. It was a packaged amount for sale. Extra money was good to obtain, but cutting wood alongside his dad made it a memorable shared experience for Boyer. Vern owned a Model T, and on Sundays he used it to drive to an area where they sawed wood and then sold it.

It might be that the profits from those muscle-testing excursions contributed to the $25 that initially kept Cloyd going in Lynchburg. After taking what might have felt like the Siberian Express for a zillion miles of train travel, Boyer found himself surrounded with many like-minded, fuzzy-cheeked teenagers who had been big-shots in their neighborhoods, but were about to experience the winnowing process as they went up against others with the same backgrounds.

One of the key ways to advance out of the herd is to be distinctive, to have someone in authority take notice of you. That happened for Boyer. He was 6-foot-1 and weighed 188 pounds, meaning his size was nothing extraordinary. He was a right-hander, as are the majority of pitchers. But whether it was something in his nature or makeup, or the way he threw, one of the managers on the scene, George Farrell, liked him. "I don't know why," Boyer said, "because I wasn't showing the ability that I had anything that special."

Boyer's money pitch was a fastball, and he threw what was then called a nickel curve. He didn't even have a change-up. It was something he was going to have to learn if he wanted to advance through the ranks. It was obvious that Boyer was not on the fast track to the Cardinals. Nor was he such a sterling prospect that he was going to be shuttled ahead to a higher classification of the minors right away.

Farrell kept Boyer around the Class A Lynchburg club. He didn't use him very much on the mound, but supervised his learning curve. Boyer did soak up the atmosphere and pick up on little things that could help him. A few times Farrell dared to throw Boyer out there against live opposition. He was not ready for that level. "He got me in a couple of games and I got wrung out pretty good both times," Boyer said.

Most players in Boyer's situation would realize they were on precarious ground. The big club didn't need players hanging out at the lowest rungs of the minors who weren't even playing. He recognized that he could

When the Boyer brothers were youngsters, they ate and breathed baseball. This photograph was likely taken in the late 1930s in front of the Rosebank Elementary School in Alba. Cloyd is standing second from left. Ken is kneeling left front. Wayne is kneeling in the middle, fourth from left (courtesy Cloyd and Nadine Boyer).

well have been cut and sent back to Alba. For some reason Farrell liked him and saw potential. "I think he's the one who saved me," Boyer said. "He kept me there, I think, just so I could get paid. Dad's $25 was long gone. He was a nice guy. He treated me very well."

Around June 20, the short-season rookie leagues started up and Boyer was optioned to Johnson City, Tennessee, where the manager was Freddy Hawn. Like Farrell, he liked something about Boyer that portended well for the future.

There was no doubt that Boyer needed seasoning and instruction. Hawn was the teacher. One thing he taught Boyer to do that later National League hitters wished was left out of the curriculum was the nuances of how to throw inside at hitters to brush them off of the plate. Boyer had no clue how to do that coming out of high school. It wasn't really necessary since he owned a superior fastball that was going to dominate the average high school hitter.

"He's the one that taught me," Boyer said of Hawn. "It was something I had to learn to succeed, but of course I never intentionally hit anyone. But I heard Freddy Hawn tell the story two or three times when he said, 'I told him about having to brush hitters back and boy, did he take it to heart.' I do look back over some of the things I did throwing."

During the summer of 1945 in Johnson City, Boyer was still very much learning how to pitch. He finished 4–7, and because rookie ball features a shorter season he went home before his 18th birthday on September 1. Boyer was sure he was going to be drafted into the Army, but decided he would probably like the Navy better, so he signed up.

"I got in just before I turned 18," Boyer said. "I don't know why I preferred the Navy over the Army. No reason. The war was close to being over when I went to sign up and it was over before I got in. I always said, when I joined, they (the Japanese) decided to quit."

Thinking ahead, Boyer wanted to serve his country, but he also wanted to get it over with while he was young. He wanted to be free to follow his baseball heart without being derailed by the draft.

2

NAVY MAN
(Cloyd)

I t was a strange time to be entering the military. Since World War II had just ended and troops were returning to their delirious families in the glow of victory by the thousands, for Cloyd Boyer it was a little like driving the wrong way down a one-way street.

Almost as soon as Boyer joined the Navy, his dad began experiencing health problems. There were many more youngsters at home and Vern was the sole support of the family. A local chaplain suggested that Boyer promptly try to get out of his military commitment, return to Missouri, and be declared the head of the household in order to work instead of serve. "He said, 'You know, I could get you discharged,'" Boyer recalled. "I said, 'I don't want it. I want to go ahead and serve my time because I want to pursue baseball and I don't want to always have to look at getting drafted.' I figured they're always going to have wars, right?"

Of course, Boyer was right about that, and within a few years the United States was embroiled in another conflict, this time in the North Korea versus South Korea showdown.

Instead of seeking an early discharge, Boyer was able to become part of an allotment program where much of his pay went directly to his father and family. So Boyer went ahead with his Navy commitment, and a check for $37.50 was regularly sent back to his dad in Missouri. He also sent his mother Mabel war bonds. That was a deal he was very proud of arranging, and it didn't have anything to do with baseball. It was a win-win situation.

The Navy first shipped Boyer to Long Beach, California, and assigned him to the battleship *Iowa*, which had a storied history. The ship was launched in 1942 and was an active vessel for a half-century. It is currently docked in Los Angeles and is a tourist destination. When Boyer hefted his duffel bag onboard, the *Iowa* was new and it was on the high seas often.

Sailing out of Southern California, the *Iowa* headed to Japan as part of the immediate post-war reconstruction. The boat docked in Yokohama Bay for three months. However, it was the trip across the Pacific Ocean that was most memorable. At sea the ship encountered a typhoon with its 100-mile-per-hour-plus winds. It was mealtime aboard the *Iowa* and the sailors were about to take their places at their long mess table when the first howling wind struck. "I was just getting ready to sit down and eat," Boyer said. "With that thing rolling, it took all our trays right down to the floor. We weren't expecting it, I guess."

The blasting wind forced the ship

Cloyd Boyer when serving in the U.S. Navy (courtesy Cloyd and Nadine Boyer).

to roll with the waves and tilt with the ocean, and simply cleared the table of everyone's food. Discipline and protocol continued during the hours of the storm, and at one point Boyer drew a watch shift. As he tried to remain standing, the boat dipped low as the sea dropped and flew high as the waves crested. It takes a violent storm to toss around a ship like a cork bobbing on the surface. "The front would go down under and then come back up and then the bottom would go down," Boyer said. "I couldn't believe it, how bad it was. The storm put a dent in the bow. It was 16 inches of steel and it put a dent in it."

Everyone survived, but eventually the boat had to return to dry dock for repairs in the state of Washington.

The shooting part of the war was over before Boyer ever set foot on land in Japan. That nation had been devastated with the atomic bombs dropped on Hiroshima on August 6 and Nagasaki on August 9, only weeks earlier, incinerating people, all life forms, and buildings for miles around. By the time of Boyer's arrival the American military's role had been transformed into more of a peace mission. Unlike some of his school chums who were a little bit older, Boyer knew it was unlikely he was going to be shot at in Japan.

Indeed, the biggest surprise he incurred upon settling into Yokohama

Bay was the enthusiastic leadership of a young lieutenant who began scouring and scouting the ranks for talented baseball players in order to form a ship team. It turned out that this officer had just transferred from another ship that had a baseball team playing in a service league, and he wanted his new ship to be represented on the diamond. Boyer had not spoken much of his own baseball prowess, and not many of his shipmates knew that he had actually played a little bit of pro ball. Nor did that lieutenant at first.

> He went around getting everyone who wanted to try out. This is one time I was kind of proud of myself. A whole group of us goes to a tryout. They started a game and I was down in the bullpen with two or three other pitchers and a couple of catchers. It was getting late in the game and I hadn't gotten in yet. I began to wonder if I was going to get in. It got into the ninth inning and finally the lieutenant had me warm up. I went into the game and struck out three guys.

Suddenly there was a lot of curiosity about Boyer's fastball. It was the start of a beautiful friendship between Boyer and the lieutenant.

> He started to quiz me about my baseball career. I said I had just played a little rookie ball and I didn't have a good year or anything, but I had signed a professional contract. He said, "Well, we've got a game in a day or two and you're my pitcher." I started pitching for the Navy team and I played great. By the time I got out the team was 9–2 and I was batting .625. My first time up I hit a home run. I can't remember how many of those games I won. I didn't pitch all of them. But I had a heck of a time there for a few days.

As young and raw as Boyer was as a pitcher, having any opportunity, at any level of the game, to play regularly was beneficial. Time on the field was essential to his growth, expanding his experience and knowledge, facing situations, facing as many batters as he could. That was all to the good, even if nobody was keeping official statistics in Japan.

When Boyer came out of high school and played his partial summer of rookie ball he was a skinny guy, not yet filled out. The Cardinals thought he could become a player, but they were viewing him as an unfinished product, a project. In the mid–1940s the closest thing to regular use of a radar gun to determine how fast a pitcher threw was a scout's 20-20 vision.

A young Bob Feller had come off of an Iowa farm as a 17-year-old, not even out of high school, to baffle and blind hitters with his extraordinary speed. There was considerable curiosity about how fast his fastball moved. Some extremely rudimentary tests were run, and the conclusion was that young Mr. Feller could crack 100 mph. The same could not be true of young Mr. Boyer.

Speaking from the vantage point of a professional lifetime coaching pitchers, Boyer looked back at his younger self and concluded that he probably threw a fastball no more swiftly than 80–82 mph when he was at the Cardinals' tryout camp. That velocity is a virtual certainty to get a pitcher sent home unless he is trying to be a knuckleball hurler.

Boyer spent just under 11 months in the Navy, his tour cut short because the U.S. was ratcheting down the numbers of men in the service. But in that short period of time Boyer gained considerable strength and muscle. He guesses that by the time he was discharged that fastball hummed into the plate in the low 90s. "I think it was because I was eating regular and sleeping regular," Boyer said. "Before that I was working a lot, chasing girls, and doing everything, so you didn't get your regular rest. I always thought that probably helped me a lot."

It was late summer when Boyer was discharged, the waning month or so of the 1946 baseball season. He wanted to find a place to play so the entire year did not slip away, so he called Joe Mathis, the Cardinals' farm director, and asked if he could join the organization's club in Carthage for the rest of the year. It was so close to home and the team played at a low level of the minors. He was hoping to be well received.

His proposal was accepted and Boyer made a nice transition from one type of uniform to another. He was barely with Carthage for more than two weeks, but was plugged into the rotation and appeared in four games. Boyer's record was 3–1, which gave both him and the Cardinals system something to think about for the 1947 season.

Since he had played ball in the Navy, Boyer wasn't rusty and he had not lost any timing or rhythm. He may well have showed better than if he had been with the team for the entire season. "It all came back," Boyer said. "I had a lot more than I had when I was in the rookie league. My fastball was better. I think it made an impression on them."

For more than a century, major league teams have loaded up their gear and traveled to the American Deep South, to warmer climes, to conduct spring training, whether it was in Florida, Arizona or Hot Springs, Arkansas. Baseball fans got used to reading the datelines from those places in their local newspapers as they alternately gazed out the window of their kitchens at piled-up snow.

Policies previously in effect during World War II which kept many teams from traveling far from their main bases had been lifted, and the Cardinals no longer congregated in Lynchburg, Virginia. In 1947, the young players were sent to Albany, Georgia. When the Cardinals signed Boyer for that season the plan was for him to play for their Columbus, Georgia, affiliate.

That connection lasted about ten minutes for Boyer. Instead of sending him to Columbus, the Cardinals brass voted to have him play that summer of 1947 in Duluth, Minnesota. One of the other passengers on the bus north was a catcher named Paul Bowa. He had a young son named Larry, who grew up to become a very good shortstop for the Philadelphia Phillies. The younger Bowa won two National League Gold Glove Awards and was a five-time All-Star. Boyer could definitely say he knew Larry Bowa forever. At the time of the journey on an old school bus, Bowa was not yet two years old and spent some of the miles sitting on Boyer's lap. "He was just a baby," Boyer said. "I carried him about all the way up there."

Some years later, in the mid–1960s, Boyer lived in Sacramento, the Bowas' hometown, about two blocks away from that family. One day, after Boyer retired from the majors and was coaching in the minors, he received a phone call from Larry. Boyer was working in the New York Yankees organization and Bowa, who was 20 at the time, was getting feelers from big league teams. He wanted to sign with the Yankees, but he wasn't getting warm vibes from them. "I was in Johnson City in my rookie league job," Boyer said. "Bowa called me and said, 'I want to sign with the Yankees.' I said, 'Well, we've got a scout out there. Has he seen you?' Larry said, 'Yeah, but he doesn't like me.' I said, 'Well, let me give a call to our farm director.'"

Boyer reached Johnny Johnson by phone and gave him a sales pitch. "I've got a kid I want to sign. I haven't seen him play or anything, but if he's any kind of competitor like his dad was, he's worth a gamble." Indeed, of all his attributes as a player, Bowa was best known for his competitiveness. But it wasn't an easy sell.

> I just said, "I'd like to sign that kid." But Johnny said, "Well, I can't." He checked over the reports the scout, whose name I can't remember, had sent in. Johnny said, "I can't do it. Our scout in that area doesn't like him." I said, "Well, I'll take the blame if he doesn't make it." I couldn't go over the scout's head. If I was cross-checking as the second scout or something, then it might have been different. So we didn't sign him.

That's how Bowa remained available for the Phillies to grab and develop him into an All-Star. Bowa broke in with the Phillies as a rookie in 1970, played 16 years in the majors and won a World Series ring with the 1980 Phillies, one of the best and most famous teams in franchise history. It was obvious the original New York scout was wrong and Boyer's gut instinct was correct.

It's a story that also illustrates the way baseball networking can play out. The Boyer-Bowa link was forged in the 1940s when Larry Bowa was a tiny child. In terms of Boyer's own professional career, it began when his own professional playing days were in their infancy. Cloyd Boyer was not yet 20 years old himself in the summer of 1947, an entire generation ahead of Larry Bowa, and then still hoping to unwrap a career like the one the younger Bowa would enjoy.

3

MOVING TO AA
(Cloyd)

C loyd Boyer's Columbus, Georgia, contract gave him entrée to AA ball, but it was swiftly decided that wasn't a good fit yet. While the money was better and it was guaranteed to him, he could still be optioned, and that's how he ended up on the bus to Class A Duluth.

The Duluth season ran from May 1 to September 1, but the higher pay commitment from the Cardinals was the equivalent of getting a couple of extra checks. Boyer was turning 20 years old just as the 1947 season ended, and his father was still in ill health.

Boyer had tried to get ahead a little bit, saving money in the bank, but his father's poor health kept him out of the job market and the Boyers' credit grocery bill was almost identical to the amount Cloyd had saved up. "So there went my money," Boyer said. "I paid the grocery bill and told mom that I had to buy a car so I would be able to go back and forth to work in the off-season."

As a young man pretty much feeling his oats, he also had other reasons for wanting wheels. It was hard to get dates if you couldn't pick up the gal and take her somewhere. So Boyer went to a finance company in nearby Joplin, Missouri, and signed for a loan that enabled him to buy a 1940 Chevrolet with payments of $54.50 a month.

Boyer was still a rather inexperienced player, but the Cardinals liked his looks in the field. Farm director Joe Mathis wanted Boyer to spend the fall in the instructional league. "It'll be worth your while," Mathis said. That was undoubtedly true from the standpoint of honing his skills and impressing his bosses. But it didn't mesh well with the family's circumstances, not with his father laid up. Boyer told Mathis, "I need to be home, helping my dad. There's a bunch of kids out there who like to eat." Mathis called Boyer two or three times, saying, "It's really gonna help you." But he wasn't going to make any money in the instructional league, just room and board.

At the time the instructional league was conducted in Lynchburg, Virginia, the same place where Boyer had embarked for his first season. It was only later that it moved around to Florida and Arizona. Finally, Boyer yielded and signed on to the instructional league for three weeks. He left his new car at home in the care of brother Wayne. Wayne definitely treated access to the vehicle as a perk. While Cloyd was gone—less than a month—Wayne put 3,000 miles on the odometer. Cloyd was flabbergasted when he returned.

"It didn't have many miles on it when I bought it," Cloyd said. "I can't remember what the number was, but I went over to the car and checked the oil and checked the mileage and said, 'Dang, you about burned the wheels off of this, ain't you?' Wayne said, 'What do you mean?' I mentioned the 3,000 miles. He said, 'What are you doing, checking up on me?' I said, 'No, but I just knew how many miles it had when I left.'"

It wasn't as if Wayne confessed to how he had been using the car—it wasn't for a long commute to a job. "I knew what he did," Cloyd said. "He was chasing women, hard, real hard. Then I still had to pay for the car and the interest and all."

Wayne was two years younger than Cloyd. At that point, the younger Boyer children still in the house included not only Wayne, but Ken, Delores, Lynn (who used that over Lewis), Clete, Pansy, Shirley, Ron, and Bobby Jo. Cloyd was everyone's big brother, but he was so much older than some of the other kids that he was almost like a second dad. He helped provide for them. Although this lay in the future, when Cloyd got married, he had a son that was born the same year as his youngest sister.

Cloyd neither shirked nor minded his role of helping his parents and younger siblings with the finances. "I had to help quite a few people out along the way, which I was glad to do," he said.

The next oldest Boyer brother was Wayne, and like all of the boys in the family he was an athlete. Baseball came naturally to all of them, but in a small school, which had limited resources and didn't add basketball and football until after Cloyd's days, everyone played just about everything. This was pretty much the heyday of the three-sport high school athlete when the boys played all sports in season, with the emphasis on football, basketball and baseball.

Being a professional baseball player, Cloyd was seldom around when his younger siblings played ball at home in Missouri. He was off chasing his dream and they were still representing the local schools. More often he caught brothers Wayne and Ken playing football or basketball during his own off-season. For a little while, though, Cloyd, Wayne and Ken did play for a town team that made the rounds, playing up to a dozen exhibition games. "We'd have crowds and make a little money," Cloyd said. "It would help everybody out, you know what I mean?" Not a bad sidelight for raising some petty cash, doing something you loved.

Wayne got his start playing ball the same way Cloyd did. He remembers the same adult, Carl Parker, getting the team started when he was in elementary school. "I started out when we were in the country," said Wayne, who unlike many of his siblings, strayed from Missouri and settled in Kokomo, Indiana. "We had a little one-room school before we moved into Alba and started going there. I graduated from eighth grade in Alba."

A favorite family photograph features the oldest three boys—Cloyd, Wayne and Ken—together with their father Vern. Dad, Ken, and Wayne are all wearing bib overalls over white, short-sleeved shirts (Cloyd is minus the overalls), and they definitely look country. Someone forgot to say "cheese" before snapping the shutter because no one is smiling. Cloyd was probably 13, Wayne 11 and Ken nine in the picture.

"My dad kind of promoted us playing baseball," Wayne said. "The interesting thing to me, thinking back, was that baseball gloves didn't cost very much then. You could buy a baseball glove for about 50 cents. Of course that dates me."

Just starting out. Father Vern, who always encouraged his sons to play baseball, stands behind Wayne (left), Ken (center) and Cloyd during their early days playing sandlot ball in their Alba, Missouri, home (courtesy Cloyd and Nadine Boyer).

One difference between Wayne and those brothers is that he was left-handed. They were righties. That was a problem for him as a youth when money was tight. When Wayne was about 11 years old Vern surprised the three oldest boys by purchasing baseball gloves for them. Vern must have spotted a bargain and bought three at once. There was only one problem. While Cloyd's and Ken's were a good fit, the new glove didn't quite work for Wayne because it was a right-handed mitt. "He forgot that I was left-handed," Wayne said. "So I learned to play baseball with a glove that was built for a right-hander. I would put it on my right hand and throw left-handed. The little finger and the thumb were actually reversed. That's the way it was for me."

Baseball was always a big thing in the Boyer family, from the time that Cloyd discovered the game. For one thing, it was an inexpensive activity for a large family with many boys itching to fill their free time. "We were a big family, a huge family," Wayne said. "And we lived out in the country, in Cossville first, which was a little, small place. A little place in the middle of town had a baseball park. It was about a half-mile from our house. We could walk to that park every day, or any time we wanted to. The people around there sort of promoted baseball."

In a later decade, perhaps the park would have featured asphalt basketball courts and playground courts, and the Boyers might have become basketball players instead. In the 1930s and 1940s, however, baseball was the National Pastime, and the one team sport that everyone cared about and talked about. That's how Wayne remembers the way it was, too, in their small, out-of-the-way neck of the woods. "It was kind of typical at the time," he said, "because baseball was, you know, really important as a game. Baseball was considered America's No. 1 sport. So we played."

In more recent decades, as baseball spread beyond the borders of the United States and became supremely popular in Latin American countries, leading to an influx of major leaguers from such lands as the Dominican Republic, Puerto Rico, Cuba and Mexico, stories were frequently told about the young Hispanic players raised in poverty making do with home-made baseball materials. It was the same for the Boyer brothers, decades earlier. They could not afford the best store-bought equipment, the splurge on the three gloves at once by their father being an exception. To play the game on the sandlot, the Boyers and their pals frequently manufactured the necessary equipment. A bat was shared, and if sadly it was cracked, it was not tossed aside, it was repaired. The bat was nailed back together. The boys made their own balls by using tape, wrapping it around and around. If fans think the Deadball era inhibited the distance a baseball traveled in the pros before 1920, by comparison a ball made out of tape was like the Wright Brothers' plane instead of a jet. According to Wayne,

> We didn't have very good equipment, but we grew up playing baseball that way and it kept us off the street. My dad encouraged us to play and sometimes he acted as an umpire. He had never really played, but when he served as an umpire he dressed the part. At the time I thought it was funny. To dress up as an umpire he used the same kind of equipment catchers used. He had a chest protector and no protection on his shoulders. I was just a kid and I thought it was funny because it seemed like every game he caught a foul ball or a pitch off a shoulder and he would get a stinger. But dad promoted us playing ball all of the way from the time I was five or six years old.

It is only speculation, but Vern had to know he couldn't give his boys much in the way of toys or tangible gifts. He seemed to recognize that they were a good fit with the nation's favorite sport, though, and he could share their experiences with them by volunteering to ump. Wayne remembers his dad coming home after working a day shift on a Works Progress Administration road project and joining him, Cloyd, Kenny and the younger Clete in the backyard on summer nights before it got dark. "He would hit us fly balls," Wayne said. "I remember, day after day, evening after evening, he'd take out a ball and hit us fly balls."

As good as Cloyd was—and he became a professional a few years later—and as solid as Wayne was, it was apparent that Kenton, or Ken as he was always known as a big-leaguer, was a better all-around athlete than his older brothers. By the time Ken was in high school Cloyd was out in the world, except for winters, and although Wayne was two years older, Ken shone as a natural at just about everything he tried. He was a star on the football team, the basketball team and the baseball team.

For a time, when Wayne was 16 and Ken was 14, they worked the local hayfields. Wayne drove a truck. They took the places of other young local lads who had gone off to war. According to Wayne,

> All of the older guys, the farm boys, were in the service. I drove the hay trucks and they grew a lot of hay. It's actually called prairie grass. The guy that I worked for had two sections of land, so we had two balers. We'd bale the hay like crazy in one section and by the time we got through the other section had grown up. Kenny was just naturally strong. He didn't have to build his muscles from baling. He was just a strong kid. At one time back home in Missouri they said he had the most perfect build for an athlete. He was 6-foot-2 and weighed 220 pounds. He was a fast runner, too. He could run from first to third as quick as anybody I've ever seen. But he had the perfect musculature.

Actually, Wayne had some similar hard farm labor experience on his resume by then. During the summer when he was 15, Wayne decided he needed to make some money and took a bus to Pratt, Kansas, for the wheat harvest. It was a bold thing to do on spec. It was about a 500-mile bus ride and when he disembarked he had nowhere to go. He asked the first lady he saw in town how to find a job, and she told him all he had to do was go out in the street and he might be picked up for farm work.

He bumped into a man in front of the county courthouse and was asked, "Are you looking for a job?" "I said, 'I sure am.' He didn't even ask me if I had any experience." Wayne was asked where he was from and when he replied Missouri, the man said, 'Most of you Missouri boys are pretty good workers.' I said, 'Well, I'm a heck of a good worker.' I didn't even know how to drive a tractor. Thinking back on it I wonder if I was crazy."

Wayne got hired, and that summer of 1945 Wayne skipped playing baseball and turned 16 in July while he was working the wheat harvest of western Kansas. Wouldn't you know it, like the cliché, he fell for the farmer's daughter, a girl almost exactly his age whom daddy wanted to keep close and put to work on the harvest, too. She drove the truck that the laborers filled. According to Wayne,

> They had a big pond on the property and on Sundays we'd go fishing and [she] had a little kissy face and she liked me. I liked her. She was the one who taught me how to drive a tractor. The tractor pulled the combine alongside it. Now they have a tractor and combine that work all together. That dates me. I stayed there all summer and worked hard. When the summer was ending, the farmer asked me if I wanted to stay on and work the next crop. I said I would because I liked what was going on there and I liked this little gal. She wanted me to stay, too, so I said OK.

The work agreed with him in other ways. The tendency among the Boyers was to turn out six-footers. Cloyd was a little taller than that. Ken was headed in that direction. But Wayne was only about 5-foot-5 when he left home. He was gone for three months, and wheat was not the only thing that sprouted in Kansas. He shot up to six feet tall on his way to his full height of 6-3. It was almost like a stranger had returned from the east when he alighted in Missouri again.

"My brothers thought there was something wrong with me because I was not very big," Wayne said. "They thought I was going to be little. But something happened and I just grew up out there. When I got home I had to have a whole new set of clothes. I came home in August just in time to finish out playing a little baseball there."

Ken Boyer was two years younger than Wayne, but from an early age he showed off a stronger arm on the diamond. They had contests to see who could throw a baseball farther, and the younger brother could best Wayne. "He had a great throwing arm," Wayne said. "We used to go out in this pasture area and see who could throw a baseball the farthest. He always had a stronger arm, even when he was a teenager."

The high school did not field a football team until after Cloyd and Wayne graduated. The squad was started just in time for Kenny to play a little in his senior year. He was the star of the team. Rarely did his older brothers have the chance to watch Ken play baseball in high school because they were both involved with their own teams in the same season, but sometimes they made it back home and were able to catch a Friday night game with the pigskin.

Boyer had come late to the sport. It wasn't as if he had much official coaching, nor had he played much football on community fields the way he and the other Boyers did with baseball. But he took to the game immediately. When Wayne returned home once to catch Ken in a high school game, he was surprised how good at it he was. According to Wayne,

> There was all kind of talk about how strong his arm was, and I knew that. But he also had strong legs. He was the best athlete on the team. When he kicked off, he kicked it clear through the end zone. A lot of guys who are professionals now don't do that. I marveled at that at that time. He was a 17-year-old kid with only that year in the sport. He could boot the ball 65 or 75 yards in the air.

As teens, Wayne and Ken played together on a summer team that was part of something called the Cardinals Junior League. During this time period Little League was just spreading from its founding place in Pennsylvania in 1939 as a three-team operation to other corners of the country. There was no Little League World Series until 1947. Babe Ruth League, for slightly older boys, did not begin until 1951.

That meant that any opportunity the Boyers had to play ball stemmed from a local operation. Ken was a budding star and just about any baseball expert that saw him by the time he was 16 recognized that he might be going places. "There were a lot of guys, coaches and people who had been around baseball a little bit and they touted him to be a great future baseball player even when he was 16 or 17," Wayne said. "You know, really, they could see him coming even when he was 14. He had a stance, you know, like Mel Ott, where he raised his leg up."

Ken was destined to become the star of the family, and Wayne said it was evident to him at a pretty young age that this brother was worthy of big-league attention. According to Wayne,

When Kenny was a kid he was strictly a pull hitter. Nobody taught him. We were just country kids. We didn't have professional coaches. The guy that coached us the most owned the grocery store. He spent most of his time in the store, not at the baseball field. So Kenny would kick that left leg up in the air and was a pull hitter, a power hitter, from the time he was an early teen-ager. Kenny was young for the Junior Cardinals and people would say he was a little bit young to be playing, but he liked the challenge. He liked the challenge in everything.

He didn't have a big background in basketball, but when the high school basketball season came around he briefly played on the team. He was a very, very good player. He had an opportunity for a basketball scholarship to go to Marquette in Milwaukee. He didn't take it because he was committed to playing baseball and wanted to play baseball out of high school. He could do anything, he was so athletic. He demonstrated it in football. He demonstrated it in basketball. And, of course, in baseball, he went all the way.

Wayne hoped to go all of the way in baseball, too, and the fact that Cloyd was ahead of him helped earn him some notoriety. Before Wayne left for his sojourn in Kansas in the wheat world, he had been primarily a right fielder. When he came back he tried a little pitching. Then, as now, southpaws were always in demand, and while it may have been awkward when he was younger and tried to stuff the wrong paw into the wrong-handed fielder's mitt, being a lefty could be an advantage now in the eyes of scouts.

Over the years, with the expansion of television, the advent of the Internet and creation of specialized websites, scouting has not only gone electronic, it makes it harder to hide a prospect and easier to find one in an out-of-the-way place. In the old days of big-league scouting, the best bird-dogs, as they were called, drove the back roads of the nation hoping to find a jewel in the rough and sign him before another team caught on to his talent.

Sometimes, though, an athlete was so superb that word of mouth carried beyond the borders of his little pond to the wide, wide ocean. The raves would be so loud that the local newspaper might write something about the phenom. A radio reporter might find him. A local coach might see him and talk him up to a scout. Ken Boyer was such a player. Wayne was a solid ball player and he had the advantage of being related to Cloyd, carrying the same last name. Decades later, scouting remains an inexact science, but teams then worried less about getting burned on a little brother if big brother had a name. The old phrase, "You should see the one back home," applied to the Boyers. At the very least Cloyd's minor success to that point warranted a look-see at the brothers. After all, they had the same genes, didn't they?

Wayne had shot up in height, but he was still slender, although he insisted he weighed 170 pounds by then. Still, his wife used to tease him when she gazed upon a picture of him at the end of high school. Her comment: "You look kind of like a sissy there."

After Cloyd, the scouts checked out Wayne. In 1946 Wayne signed a contract to play Class D ball for the Opelika Owls in the long-gone Georgia-Alabama League, or GAAL. He was a southpaw pitcher who saw action in five games, throwing 23 innings and posting an 0–1 record. It was a cameo, a brief fling. But that made Wayne the second Boyer to play professional baseball. However, he had not yet graduated from high school. He graduated early in 1947, in March, so he could go to Cardinals spring training in Albany, Georgia. Like Cloyd before him, Wayne traveled by train.

In this era of big bonus payments to prospects out of high school who are highly regarded, the bonus paid to the Boyers for Wayne's signature could not only be termed peanuts, it might not have covered the purchase of a bushel of peanuts. The Cardinals paid out $300, and not to Wayne, but to Vern. The salary was set at $150 a month.

Cloyd is fond of his brother, but as someone who spent much of his later life assessing talent, he did not bestow wide-ranging compliments on Wayne's skills. In Cloyd's mind Wayne did not bring the necessary dedication or work ethic to the playing field to turn into a long-term success. "Wayne was pretty erratic in sports," Cloyd said, "basketball and baseball. He might be real good one day and not so good the next. He was a little bit different in our family. To me it was just that he spent more energy (partying). He was very smart, though. After he quit baseball he went to school and became a dentist."

Still, in 1947, Wayne remained a hopeful when he was assigned to Lenoir, North Carolina, in the Blue Ridge League. He spent part of the season there, going 2–4 with an ugly 6.40 earned run average before shifting to Carthage, Missouri, another Class D team, but one near home— the Carthage Cardinals. He went 4–2 in the Kansas-Oklahoma-Missouri League and lowered his ERA to 4.70. So that summer ended on an upswing.

Wayne did not have a great deal of pitching experience, so he was learning on the fly. "I could throw hard and that was my main asset," he said. "But I didn't have very good control. Back then you threw a fastball, a curve, and a change-up. I had a fairly good curve, but later I saw guys come along who were much better and had great change-ups. I needed good coaching and things kind of passed me by."

In 1948, the Cardinals sent Wayne to another Class D outfit in the Georgia-Alabama League. The community has the name Tallahassee, but is much smaller and lesser known than the city of the same name that is the capital of Florida. The closest big city that held amusements for young ball players was Montgomery.

Wayne spent most of the season with that club, finishing with an 8–10 record and a 4.66 earned run average. He surrendered 138 hits in 137 innings. Near the end of the year he was used more for pinch-hitting duties. The team liked his lefty bat and so did the organization. He was promoted to Columbus, Georgia, then in the Sally League. He made some clutch hits and at the end of the campaign the Cardinals organization informed him that he had to choose between being a pitcher or an outfielder.

"It didn't make any difference to me," he said. "I just wanted to play ball." As soon as Wayne was prepared to become a full-time hitter, the Cardinals decided they had a shortage of left-handed pitchers and for the next season shipped him to Duluth, Minnesota, where Cloyd had played.

Duluth is one of Minnesota's largest cities. It is situated on the shore of Lake Superior, the nation's biggest lake and one of the biggest in the world. It is a cold-water lake and Duluth catches breezes off of Superior that often make it a cold-weather community.

"I remember a few things about Duluth," Wayne Boyer said decades later. "No. 1, it's on a hill. All the women have big legs. There are no skinny-legged women there because they're either walking up a hill or down a hill. And about every third opening along the main streets are places where they like to drink beer. Probably it isn't that way now. Anyway, I went back to pitching."

By the end of the minor-league season he was back in Missouri, and self-assessment told him he wasn't making much progress advancing out of the low minors, just being shuttled from one small town to another. In September of 1949, Wayne enrolled in college. That fall he began classes at Pittsburg State Teachers College in Kansas. Later, he transferred to the University of Missouri in Columbia and never went back to baseball.

Although Wayne did want to go to college, he got a little push. The Boyer family was well known and the local draft board lady tipped Wayne off that either he was going to have to go school or he was going to get drafted. "She called me and said, 'Either you're going to have to go to school or you will lose your 4S student exemption,'" Boyer said. "'They're going to classify you 1A and you'll be eligible for the draft.'"

By the time Wayne switched to the University of Missouri, the Korean

War had begun. He joined the Air Force ROTC program on campus. He had started school with the goal of majoring in chemical engineering, taking 37 hours of chemistry and 20 hours of math. But he received some advice suggesting that chemistry was a better major. Because of the ROTC program, Boyer also considered a career in the Air Force. But it was obvious he was not going to be able to report to spring training those years. He had to stay in school or risk being drafted.

Wayne wasn't exactly getting rich making $300 a month in Columbus, but now he had to pay for school. And Wayne missed baseball. Even if he hadn't shown much progress in the minors yet, he didn't really want to stop playing. Neither did Vern want him to stop. According to Wayne,

> I had made the decision to give up baseball and go to school, but my dad said he didn't want me to. He told me he wanted me to quit school and concentrate on baseball. I remember him telling me, "I think you've got the best chance of any of the boys in the family of making it in the big leagues." At that point I didn't agree with him. Cloyd hadn't made the majors yet. He was close to making the Cardinals. I don't know. If he had made it before I made the choice I might have stuck with it even though I wasn't making much money. There was having to go into the military, too. But if Cloyd had made it I might have said, "Well, I can make it, too." But it wasn't as if Cloyd made a lot of money his first year in the majors, either.
>
> I made the decision to concentrate on getting an education. Even then guys were saying, "Get your education." You know how important it is now. People go out and borrow thousands and thousands of dollars to get through college, and they can't even find a job sometimes.

Cloyd became the first Boyer to reach the majors, and Wayne became the first Boyer to retire from professional baseball.

4

JOINING THE CARDINALS
(Cloyd)

The big moment, the breakthrough, for Cloyd Boyer came in 1949. He got the call from the St. Louis Cardinals summoning him to the majors. Step by step, Boyer had slogged through the minors, becoming a virtual connoisseur of trains. He played here and he played there, but he was improving, gaining in savvy, throwing his fastball with more accuracy.

During the 1947 season, Boyer shined for the Duluth Dukes, compiling a 16–9 record. He led the Northern League in strikeouts with 239. In 1948 Boyer toiled for the Houston Buffaloes, the AA club in the Texas League who were often referred to as the Buffs. Things were clicking for him at a higher level and he finished with a 16–10 mark and a 3.14 earned run average in 223 innings. The Houston manager was Johnny Keane, who was involved in his long apprenticeship as a Cards minor league manager before being given the reins of the top team and leading St. Louis to a World Series title in 1964.

When he joined that club, a local publication called *The Pecan Park Eagle* published a light-haired cartoon of Boyer. A close-up facial sketch showed him as a handsome man with wavy hair. In another corner of the cartoon a stereotypical looking baseball figure portrayed him accompanied with the words, "One of eleven children, men on bases don't bother him!" It was a novel way to disclose the fact that Boyer came from a large family (some of the siblings were yet to be born), but men on base certainly did bother the competitor in Boyer. Among the other comments in the accompanying text were: "Hails from the 'Show-Me' state of Missouri—and he shows 'em a fastball that looks like a marble, when you can see it," and "Not married yet, but threatening."[1]

Slowly, but surely, Boyer was rising through the ranks of the Cardinals' farm system. During that season with Houston, the Cardinals played an exhibition game against the Buffaloes. Boyer drew the starting assignment and he beat the major league regulars, 3–1. It was a lineup that included All-Star Marty Marion, future Hall of Famer Enos Slaughter, and catcher Del Rice. Talk about coming to play at the right time. That type of victory would resonate with the brass and linger in their minds for a long time. It was one thing to have minor league managers send encouraging reports to the front office. It was quite another to excel against the players already in the majors right before important eyes.

To some extent, however, Boyer hadn't added to his repertoire. His money pitch was still the fastball. Of course it was the improved model, his post–Navy fastball, not the slower fastball from when he first signed.

> My fastball was good enough. Even in the big leagues I could get by with my fastball before I hurt my arm. I tried to change speeds. I made some changes. I learned the change-up, but it wasn't a good pitch. I found out you can get hitters out with only a fastball, but it was a lot harder. It was always nice to have it when you got in trouble in the count. You reach back and strike somebody out.

That season a team named the Tulsa Drillers made the Class AA playoffs and Boyer's Buffaloes faced them. Tulsa was only a couple of hours' drive from Alba, so Boyer's relatives, friends, and his girlfriend Nadine, whom he was soon to marry, made the trek to the larger Oklahoma city for the game. Joe Mathis, the Cardinals' farm supervisor, bought tickets for all of them to come and watch Cloyd pitch.

"He bought all of my people a ticket," Cloyd said. "It was a pretty big family outing. I pitched in the first game and lost 3–2. I hit a home run for one run and drove in the second run. Only our shortstop made an error to give the other team two runs. I could have been a big hero if I got both RBIs and we won 2–1."

It was a fine showing, and Boyer had another start in the series. That time he got the win in a 5–3 game and complemented it with a two-run triple. All of a sudden Boyer was both the Bob Feller and the Joe DiMaggio of the playoffs. He was held out of the next couple of contests by Keane with the idea that he would pitch the seventh game if necessary. Keane was confident his team could handle the Drillers. But the Buffaloes lost without a seventh game being played.

"My family was there and Nadine was there, so I packed my bags and came on home from Tulsa," Boyer said. "I got a free ride home." It saved him another train trip.

Although Boyer had one of the best records in the league with that 16–10 mark, he best remembered the losses because so many of them were close games where something happened to give him a one-run defeat instead of a one-run victory. He also did remember a one-run win that he pulled out that could have gone either way. The game was against Fort Worth, and in the ninth inning the Buffs were ahead, 5–4. Boyer had thrown a lot of pitches, and in the modern era of the game where relief pitchers flood out of the bullpen like a colony of ants, he would have been lifted much earlier.

But there he was on the mound, hanging on to a one-run lead when he loaded the bases. It seemed likely that Keane would yank him, but he never budged from the dugout. Boyer got the final out and Houston prevailed. After the game sportswriters asked Keane why he had not replaced Boyer. "Well, the next guy coming up, I figured he would either strike him out or walk him," Keane said. "If he walked him, I'd take him out. If he struck him out, we win." The Buffaloes won.

Off his 1948 successful season, Boyer was invited to the Cardinals' spring training camp in March of 1949. Not the minor-league camp, the big-league camp in St. Petersburg, Florida, the spot that had been abandoned for a few years during World War II due to commissioner's office travel restrictions during the conflict.

"It made me a pretty happy fellow," Boyer said of the invite to schmooze with and work out with the top players in the organization. The summons was a reward for the hard work he put in during his stints in the minors and showed the team thought highly of him.

Sometimes an underdog player who is supposed to be just passing through spring training has an outstanding stretch of weeks in the Florida sunshine and forces the organization to keep him on the major league roster. That's what happened with Boyer. Everything the manager and coaches asked him to do, he did. Everything he tried, he did well. The plan was for Boyer to spend the season in Rochester, but he was untouchable in spring training, and when a guy is going that well a team doesn't want to tamper with success. "I wasn't supposed to make the club at all, you know," Boyer said. "They were going to send me to Rochester (in upstate New York). But I had a heck of a spring. Unbelievable, really. I pitched 22 or 23 runless innings or something like that. It was unbelievable."

It also made him a mini-celebrity back in Alba, where everyone rooted for the Cardinals. Now they had a hometown boy with them. A local was a Cardinal. Or it looked as if he was going to be. When St. Louis broke camp for the regular season, Boyer was with the team. He was only in his early 20s in April of 1949 and he was in the big-time. However, he was not guaranteed a spot in the starting rotation or anything like that.

During that era, major league clubs could break camp for the regular season carrying 28 players instead of the general roster limit of 25. Teams could dress the three extra players for the first month of the season and then they had to make a cut. It was a thrill to be in a Cardinals uniform for Boyer, but pretty early on he realized he was going to be one of the expendable three after that month. It was easy enough to tell because he mostly sat around either on the bench or in the bullpen. Manager Eddie Dyer clearly valued other pitchers more than he did Boyer.

On April 23, 1949, Boyer made his major league debut. He was not the starter versus the Chicago Cubs that day, but he did get into a wide-open game where the Cardinals needed quite a bit of help from the bullpen. It was a slugfest that the Cubs won, 11–7. Boyer was the fifth pitcher summoned by Dyer and he didn't surrender any of the runs. Boyer pitched the final two innings for St. Louis and allowed two hits plus a walk. It was a solid outing.

Things did not improve from there. Mostly Boyer was idle, but he got into two more games and made one start. The three appearances left him with a 0–0 big-league mark, but he was hit pretty hard after that first showing. His pitching line was 3⅓ innings, five hits, four runs, all earned, seven walks allowed and an earned run average of 10.80. In his one start, Boyer was smoked.

While it was fun to be a member of the St. Louis Cardinals, Boyer didn't really think it did him much good given how little he pitched during this first three-week stretch of the season.

> Actually, I would have been better off if Dyer had sent me right out, but he let me sit around and I didn't do anything. I don't know what it was. I don't think I was scared, but I went out there to the mound and it looked as if home plate was from here to the wall. I felt like I could throw my fastball by anybody and I didn't get it by anybody. They just knocked me out. So that gave them the excuse to send me to Rochester.

Boyer pondered the harsh results at the time and has had plenty of time to think about his first days with the Cardinals in the 60-plus years since. He is certain he did not have stage fright. He might have not have been ready for the majors, but he never felt as if he got hit hard because of emotional reasons.

> It wasn't nerves. I've thought about it a lot of times because people have always blamed it, saying, "Well, your first start when it didn't go well, it was probably nerves." I don't think I ever got nervous in any baseball situation.

One guy used to always tell me, "Gee, you had ice water in your veins. Not even if you had the bases loaded and 3–0 on the next hitter with nobody out." I don't ever react too much to pressure. My theory about anything in life, especially in sports, was that you go out and do the best you can. If you get rocked, you get rocked. You can't worry about it. And if you win, don't get too excited because you've got to go back out and do it again. That's the way I think and that's the way I thought then.

Boyer, who married girlfriend Nadine on November 17, 1948 (they are still together more than 66 years later), was not crushed when the Cardinals sent him out. It was not a surprise to him when it occurred. He felt he had been earmarked for Rochester from the start, but bought this taste of life in "the Show" by starring in spring training.

After spring training I thought I might get a start or something. They had good pitching (the Cardinals finished 96–58 that season as runners-up for the National League pennant). The way I pitched in spring training I probably did deserve to be thrown into the rotation temporarily, and I never did find out why Eddie Dyer didn't do that. I suppose he had his reasons. Instead I sat around and when I got my chance I didn't pitch well. He probably figured I wasn't ready for the big leagues. He was smarter than I was.

The Rochester Red Wings were members of the Class AAA International League. There has been minor-league baseball in that city since 1877, and although the Red Wings have changed associations with major league teams (currently the Minnesota Twins), they were the top farm club of the Cardinals from 1929 to 1960. Sure enough, when St. Louis sent Boyer out he was on a train again, this time to upstate New York, but also this time accompanied by his wife.

As if they were linked at the hip, the Rochester manager was Johnny Keane. Boyer and Keane were following one another around the Cardinals chain, each hoping for the same thing, that one day they would be brought up by the Cardinals to stay. As soon as Boyer got to Rochester, the Red Wings embarked on a road trip. Nadine moved into a hotel for the duration. "I dropped her off at the hotel and said I'd be gone for about a week," Boyer said.

First stop was Buffalo, about 70 miles down the road, and Boyer started. He had a 2–0 lead going, but ended up losing, 3–2, in his first Rochester decision. He got beat by a sacrifice fly. Not even having Russ Derry, one of the most prolific sluggers in team and league history, backing him helped Boyer. Derry had a brief major league career touching on four seasons, including two games with the Cardinals in 1949, with a .224 lifetime average, but he was a minor league slugger. Derry, a member of the

International League Hall of Fame, as well as the Rochester team's Hall of Fame, smashed 42 homers for the Red Wings that summer.

The road trip continued to Toronto and Boyer got another start. He pitched a terrific game, a two-hitter, but lost, 1–0. A couple of days later, Keane inserted Boyer into a tie game, and he gave up the winning run.

"So now I'm 0–3, my wife has been listening to the games back at the hotel, and I haven't even pitched in Rochester," Boyer said. Boyer was reunited with his wife and got the chance to start a game in Rochester. Things went badly initially and he fell behind, 5–1. But the Red Wings rallied and gave Boyer a 6–5 decision. Finally he got a little bit of luck. "That made up for some of the other ones," Boyer said. "I got on a hot streak and won six in a row. A little later I had another stretch where I pitched 29 innings and I gave up only one run. Wouldn't you know, that was in a 1–0 game that I lost?"

Boyer took the loss against George Bamberger, who had a brief major league pitching career, but became more famous later as the esteemed pitching coach of the Baltimore Orioles for whom a stream of 20-game winners threw. He also managed the Milwaukee Brewers and New York Mets. Although Boyer also won two games during the midst of that stretch, he remembers the frustrating defeat more clearly.

Boyer's pitching grew sharper as the season went on, and he was on his way to a 15–10 campaign with a 3.13 earned run average. A regular rotation starter with a record like that has proven himself at AAA, leaving no minor league worlds left to conquer. Boyer believed he would be called back up by the Cardinals in September when rosters expanded, but it didn't happen.

Boyer's pitching experiences tested his equanimity that season with the ups and downs and fluke results. He lost when he pitched well, and he sometimes won when he didn't pitch as well. He learned to ride the waves emotionally. It was good training for some of his later experiences. In a different season Boyer pitched a game against the Aberdeen Pheasants, a Class C team in South Dakota, for prominent manager Paul Richards. He went nine innings one day, but the next game in the series astonished all watchers.

It was a day when no pitcher was safe, and both teams hit safely quite frequently. The score went from one tie to another, 2–2, 5–5, 7–7, and the runs kept mounting. Managers ran through every pitcher they had.

> We kept using different pitchers. We're getting close to the end of the game and I look down the bench and I'm the only guy left. Old Paul looks at me and said, "Can you pitch an inning?" I said, "Yeah," even though I pitched the

night before. So I went to the bullpen and warmed up. When I went into the game we were ahead, 17–16. It was a day when everybody pitches. I got in the game. They got a hit off me and the next guy came up. He hit a pitch so hard I thought it was out, a home run. It missed by inches going out, hitting the top of the fence in left field. When he hit it, I thought it was gone and I figured that was it, 18–17. But my guy fielded the ball, threw it back to the infield, and the hitter fell down, they got him in a rundown and got him out. Nobody scored. That's how it ended, 17–16. That was a save.

Boyer had a good year with Rochester and hoped that the next spring, if and when the Cardinals invited him to spring training, it would be with a genuine chance to make the roster. Meanwhile, back in Missouri, when Boyer ran into people they asked him what Stan Musial was really like. And what Red Schoendienst was really like. "I was asked that," Boyer said. "I had only been to spring training with them. They were good guys. But that's what everyone asked me."

Pretty soon, Boyer was sure he was going to become teammates with those future Hall of Famers, wearing the same unis with the redbirds on the front.

5

BEGINNINGS
(Ken)

From the time he was a kid, it was apparent that Kenton Boyer possessed athletic skills that might exceed those of his brothers. He had the same passion for baseball as older siblings Cloyd and Wayne had, but he was more purely athletic, with a knack for picking up other sports after little tutoring. He was physically strong and fast, talents that were always helpful in baseball, but were useful no matter what sport he undertook.

Cloyd was born in 1927 and Wayne in 1939. Ken was born in 1931. That was just enough of an age spread that Cloyd was out of the house and playing professional baseball when Ken was still in high school playing interscholastic football and basketball as well as baseball.

There were no organized youth leagues, such as Little League, but the Alba Aces was a town team and for brief periods Cloyd, Wayne and Ken all played together. Ken may have been multi-talented, but his heart belonged to baseball.

The funny part of the Alba Aces was being an opponent. The years passed, but there were still players named Boyer on the roster, coming and going, one after the other, each with a set of skills good enough to attract pro scouts. When Cloyd and Wayne moved on and moved up, they were replaced by Ken, and other younger brothers, Lynn and Clete.

Once, a long-time coach of an opposing team shook his head and marveled about the makeup of the Aces. "Every time we come to play here, seems there's always a new Boyer on the team," the man said.[1]

Ken made his ambition clear at an early age. Just like Cloyd and Wayne, he wanted to play pro ball, and, of course, being from Missouri, he wanted to be a member of their favorite team, the St. Louis Cardinals.

Clete, who was six years younger than Ken and would enjoy his own fame in the years to come, commented on his brother's goals. "It'll soon be your turn to go away, Ken," Clete said. The statement was accurate, and any Boyer who harbored the dream of playing major league baseball was going to have to leave Alba, but there was a certain plaintiveness in Clete's words, too, since it meant the family was further breaking up. Ken replied, "I sure hope so. I sure hope so, Clete. I want to play ball for the Cardinals."[2]

The attraction was mutual. To the area scout, Runt Marr, Ken had the obvious tools. The day after Ken Boyer graduated from Alba High School in June of 1949, he got word from the Cardinals to report to a tryout camp in St. Louis. This was not one of those mass come-one, come-all camps, but a targeted tryout camp where the invitees had already been scouted and were felt to have potential.

The third Boyer brother had been christened Kenton, not the more common Kenneth, by mother Mabel, who said, "I always was one to think of unusual names."[3]

From the oldest child, Cloyd, to the middle children, the Boyers had moved around in small towns in the same area of Missouri, never going too far. When Ken was a youth, they lived in a farmhouse and grew their own vegetables. It was a blessing for a family that had so many mouths to feed, a huge help. There was a garden where blackberries were grown, too, and the children helped pick them. Growing things was a big help in keeping the Boyers self-sufficient. Mabel canned them. The Boyers also had chickens and pigs on their land, and feeding them was one of the kids' chores. Those chickens, through their eggs, and then being cooked along with the pigs, helped keep the Boyers fed.

One of the boys' hobbies when Ken was young was swimming. There were no built-in pools around, but they took advantage of an old open mine that was filled with water. This "pool" was very deep, with water reaching depths of 100 feet. It was also not easily accessible. The best approach route was crossing a ledge, and boys being boys, once Wayne pushed Ken on the ledge and he suffered a pretty big gash on his bare feet. He screamed at Wayne, and when Wayne made a conciliatory gesture, reaching out his hand to haul Ken back up, Ken yanked on Wayne's arm, pulled him over and watched him sail through the air into the water. It was suitable revenge, but the brothers did not hold a grudge and made up almost instantly.

For a time before Cloyd left for pro ball, Cloyd, Wayne and Ken went door-to-door selling a local weekly newspaper. They also sold a health ointment that was supposed to cure anything, but made them sound a little bit like snake oil salesmen. Once, they all pooled their earnings and bought a bicycle, though one bike for three boys all anxious to ride it was inadequate. Their favorite pastime was playing baseball.

As the oldest, and an accomplished player, Cloyd was looked up to by his brothers. They were fortunate that Buford Cooper, owner of the local grocery store, took an interest in them. He sponsored the Alba Aces and bought their uniforms. The Boyers were mainstays of the team, but other groups of brothers from the area all helped fill out the roster. Ken was only 11 when he first suited up, and it was obvious he would not have received the chance if not for his older brothers. It took a little bit of time, but eventually Ken was the best player the Aces had. A few years later it was Cooper who informed the Cardinals' scouts that they had to come to Alba to watch Ken play ball.

The Aces played against teams from other small towns, and once Alba ran across a team from Baxter Springs, Kansas. That squad was well-turned-out and seemed to have more money backing it. But one player on that club stood out in Ken's mind and he commented on his talents at shortstop to Cooper. The player, Cooper informed him, was a young man from Oklahoma named Mickey Mantle. "They say he's a pretty good football player, too," Cooper told Ken.[4]

So was Boyer. He was good at anything he tried, the way Cloyd remembers it. "Kenny played a couple of years of football, but they dropped the sport again after a couple of years," Cloyd said. "Clete, who was younger, didn't get to play."

Cloyd never got much chance to watch Ken perform as a high school athlete. First he was away playing minor-league ball. Then he got married. He had his own life going, but he always listened carefully to the family reports of how Ken excelled at Alba High. While Ken was a big star, the other boys did very well and Cloyd felt Clete was a natural athlete at just about anything he tried as well. He would telephone home and ask how everyone was doing and be informed about the sports exploits of his younger brothers.

"They were the best, the best in the community," Cloyd said of Ken and Clete. "And especially Kenny. He just stood out." The only time Cloyd ever played with Ken when they were young was on those fall baseball teams. However, they did get to play some basketball together. One winter Cloyd accepted a job for Eagle-Picher, a battery manufacturer. He ended up playing basketball for the company team. For a while he played regularly with brother Lynn. In Cloyd's mind, Ken was the top basketball player in the brood. According to Cloyd,

Young Ken Boyer, who was a ten-time All-Star with the St. Louis Cardinals and whose No. 14 jersey was later retired (courtesy Cloyd and Nadine Boyer).

I could score 20 points when I was playing with Kenny, because he'd give you the ball just so. I always compared his passing to Larry Bird. Of course, Larry Bird was a pro, but I thought Kenny could have played pro, too. Clete was a different kind of basketball player. Clete was a shooter. When he got the ball, he was going to shoot it. Kenny was an all-around player. If we were winning by 20 or 30 points, Kenny was going to let the other guys score. Kenny would rebound, play defense and pass.

One season Cloyd and Lynn were playing for Eagle-Picher and Clete came home to spend a few days in Missouri. He asked if the team would allow him to play a few games with his brothers. The coach said it would be fine if Clete joined the club temporarily. Cloyd said Lynn was a better basketball player than he was, but they were not gunners. Clete showed up and ended up alienating the coach. According to Cloyd,

> Clete played a couple of games and the other guys were not happy. They said, "If he keeps playing, we're gonna quit because he won't ever pass to anybody. You and Lynn are so much different." I did not consider myself a great basketball player. I never thought I was better at basketball than baseball. Lynn could score a little bit better than me when he took his shots, but I would end up scoring more because I got a lot of points off rebounds. Once Lynn said, "Gol' dang, we played that whole game and I swear you didn't score over ten points. I look at the score book and I see you had 20." I was a pretty good rebounder, pretty good on defense, and a pretty good passer. But Ken, oh boy, he was just a standout.

When Cloyd was signed and embarked on his stamina-draining train ride, he was escorted to the station by his parents, Ken and Wayne. Ken had complete faith that Cloyd was going to make it big and Cloyd believed that his younger brothers would soon follow him into the Cardinals' organization. The scene at the train station as Cloyd set off to embrace a new life sounds much like a movie scene.

Mabel's comment was a simple "Don't forget to write." Vern's comment was a basic "Take good care of yourself, son." Ken talked to himself through the tears he had promised not to shed because teenaged boys didn't cry, everyone knew that, but he couldn't hold back all of his emotions. As if pledging to Cloyd, but not saying it out loud, Ken thought, "He's going to be the best darned big-league pitcher there ever was." Cloyd looked at his brothers and said, "It won't be long until you'll be taking this train, too."[5]

Cloyd was right about that. Six more brothers would book passage on a train carrying them hundreds, or even a thousand or more miles, to seek their diamond destiny. None of them would make it bigger than Ken. Everyone in the family admitted that he was the best, and his big-league record proved it. Many years later, Lynn, the brother born four years after Ken, and thus a still-at-home witness to Ken's high school athletic feats, said, "Kenny was probably the best of all of them."[6]

Still, at the time there was no baseball draft, and seeking amateur talent was more haphazard and less sophisticated than it is now. Ken received a bonus of only several hundred dollars, to the best of brother Lenny Boyer's recollection. Scouting was much more personal in that era. Teams employed area scouts and local ballplayers got to know who the guy was in their area.

Runt Marr is the one who played such a significant role in the lives of the Boyer family. Marr was born in 1891 and while he played 19 years in the minors, he never reached the majors as a player. He also managed several teams in the minors and before his death in 1981 he worked as a scout for the Detroit Tigers, Cleveland Indians, Kansas City Athletics and New York Mets. All of those jobs followed his stint as a scout with the Cardinals. Marr, who lived in Grove, Oklahoma, was the first scout to target Mickey Mantle, although the Hall of Famer eventually signed with the Yankees.

A member of the Kansas Baseball Hall of Fame, Marr was almost like a member of the family in Alba when he came around to check up on the next Boyer brother reaching maturity. According to Lenny Boyer,

> He almost lived at our house. Runt and his wife Inez were just like part of our family. Really. My dad would go to Grove where Runt was from, visit with him, and go fishing. Runt would come and visit us, just casual, not always trying to sign somebody. But they got to be friends, my dad and Runt Marr. Runt was kind of like my uncle. He was there all the time and they were really good people.

Once Marr presented a Boyer and his parents with a contract, making the player property of the St. Louis Cardinals, matters were out of his hands. He had done his job linking the talent and the organization. Now it was up to the player, the Boyer, to guide his own fate through his performance, working his way up the minors and one day, he hoped, into the lineup, playing for the Cardinals at Sportsman's Park.

Ken Boyer did make the trek across the state to watch the Cardinals in person, not a frequent occurrence in his family. It was a pretty big thrill for a baseball lover. This was his first game and he marveled at the way Stan "The Man" Musial handled the bat and came through in the clutch. Boyer studied Musial and considered him a role model, no doubt one of thousands of boys who did so, but one of the few who later became a Musial teammate.

"He's always ready to hit," Boyer felt when watching the way Musial eyed the pitcher and the way he loosened up with the bat and took his practiced stance. "You know he's in charge when he's up there. That's the way to be."[7] A left-handed hitter, Musial stood at the plate in a semi-crouch.

Sure enough, moments later, a Musial swing won the game for the Cardinals with a home run.

When Boyer got that summons from the Cardinals to go to the special tryout in St. Louis, Buford Cooper, the Alba Aces coach, predicted that he would be signed and immediately sent to a minor-league outpost to start his professional career. Bring plenty of clothes with you, he advised Boyer, not simply enough to last a few days in St. Louis.

There were between 50 and 60 invited prospects to the tryouts being held in Sportsman's Park, the home stadium of the Cardinals, not at some small, out-of-the-way field. Boyer had a man's body at six feet in height and weighing 190 pounds, and the Cardinals first thought to give him a shot at shortstop. Boyer made a good showing right away, scooping up grounders, impressing the Cardinals with his arm strength. He was patient at the plate, waiting for a good pitch to hit. When he got it, he smacked a double.

Boyer did not impress nearly as much at the plate because he liked to hit the inside pitch and he didn't like to adjust to swing at balls on the outside corner. He did very well as an infielder. The three days were long and tiring, and scouts took copious notes about the players. The young players barely had time to do anything except eat, sleep and inhabit the diamond.

Ken Boyer was the most accomplished of the Boyer brothers. The St. Louis Cardinals third baseman won the 1964 National League Most Valuable Player Award (courtesy Cloyd and Nadine Boyer).

On the third day, as things were winding down, a Cardinals representative asked Boyer to take the mound. He was not shocked, mostly because his older brothers were in the chain. Cloyd was a full-time hurler and Wayne had thrown some. One of the Cardinals observers told Ken the team wondered if he would keep growing and lose his agility at shortstop. They knew he had a powerful right arm so they wanted to see it in a pitching situation.

Boyer reared back and threw some, and to his embarrassment he was wilder that day than he had ever been in his life. He didn't look much like a professional pitcher. He looked like a kid unleashed on a mound for the first time in his life. His first pitch missed the strike zone by so much it nearly bounded over to a dugout. His second throw forced the catcher to make a diving stop. No one in the stadium was more surprised than Boyer. He had never thrown like that. What was the matter?

Ken did not feel nervous, but he couldn't understand his wildness. He had plenty of velocity, but his accuracy was non-existent. He almost laughed with relief when he threw a pitch over the plate for a strike. Boyer pitched for 30 minutes and walked off the mound hot, sweaty and depressed, feeling as if he had blown his chance to become a Cardinal.

He headed for the dugout and was greeted by a familiar face—Runt Marr. Boyer felt he had let Marr, and indeed, the entire Boyer family down. But that's not how the Cardinals saw things. Boyer sat down in the dugout next to Marr, feeling confused and defeated. But Marr perked him up fairly quickly with the news that Cardinals owner Fred Saigh was prepared to sign him to a pro contract. "The Cardinals want to make you a pitcher," Marr informed Boyer.[8]

At that point, after his ordeal on the mound, Boyer was happy the Cardinals were still talking to him. He was an all-around athlete, a ball player with many skills, and he thought he would be an infielder. But if the Cardinals wanted him to become a pitcher, he was willing. The most important thing to Ken Boyer was that he was a member of the Cardinals' organization. He had a chance to make a living playing baseball with his favorite team.

6

MARRIAGE IN
THE MINORS
(Cloyd)

T he real milestone event of Cloyd Boyer's life in the late 1940s took place away from the baseball diamond when he married Nadine. Although she was born in Idaho, Nadine's parents were from the same Western Missouri area as the Boyers, and she was two when they moved back.

Although Cloyd and Nadine were from Missouri, the ceremony actually took place in Ottawa, Kansas, between the end of the 1948 baseball season and the beginning of the 1949 season, about 140 miles from home. They originally met in high school, had been dating for a couple of years and had talked about marriage. "I'm not sure what we were waiting on," Nadine Boyer said. "Both of us growing up, I think."

During that off-season, Cloyd obtained a job in Ottawa. He had an uncle who lived there and helped him secure off-season work as a butcher in a grocery store. Cloyd was in Kansas and Nadine was in Missouri and they decided they didn't enjoy being separated and didn't want to wait any long to get married. Never mind big-league parks, Cloyd had pitched in front of much larger audiences in his sandlot days than witnessed him getting hitched. It was a crowd of four, including the bride and groom.

"It was just the two of us and his aunt and uncle," Nadine Boyer said. "We didn't have the family. We were so busy." Cloyd was working so hard he didn't even have a full weekend off to drive home and visit, just a day. It wasn't enough. "I was working six days a week and then on Saturdays we'd close at 9 p.m. and then we'd clean up until about 12," Cloyd said. "Then I'd drive home and spend Sunday."

Another reason why the couple chose to marry then was that Cloyd was making a little bit more money playing baseball after his season in Houston. It doesn't sound like very much now, but when he was earning $450 a month it seemed as if they would be able to make a go of it. To put that in perspective, when Cloyd and Nadine first started dating Cloyd was making $250 a month from baseball. When he got the boost to $450, in his mind he was making big money. He had never made anything close to that before from a job of any kind.

Although her life was about to become intertwined with baseball for many years to come, Nadine said she did not think of things that way at the time. She liked Cloyd the man, not Cloyd the ball player who was a member of the revered Cardinals organization. "I think back and that didn't impress me," she said. "I was impressed with him, but not that he was going to become a big star or anything."

Nadine didn't even hear much from Alba residents about Cloyd's playing. They didn't ask her very often about how he was doing, but followed him from afar, and she was mostly with him out of town. "When he played they probably talked to his parents more than they did to me about it," Nadine said.

Unlike many of the neighbors who lived and died with Cardinals fortunes, Nadine did not grow up a baseball fan. She began enjoying the game when she followed it more closely because of Cloyd's involvement and developed an appreciation for the sport. But the order was always Cloyd first, then baseball, for interest.

"If it wasn't for him I wouldn't have been interested in it," Nadine said. "Probably not even later when I liked it. Now I don't watch it on TV. I was interested in how Cloyd was doing and how his team was doing. I'm not a diehard baseball fan. I didn't really live and die with the wins and losses each day. Most of the time Cloyd didn't bring the game home with him. Well, sometimes if he lost."

Sitting nearby in the dining room of their home as Nadine spoke, Cloyd interrupted, which led to an admission. "I was thinking you'd tell that," he said.

One of the rituals the Boyers had after games when they were at home, and became a staple of nightly existence, especially if Cloyd or his Rochester Red Wings lost the game, was to play cards together. According to Nadine,

> When he would lose we would go home and he'd have a sandwich. We ate because Cloyd ate early before the game and he would be hungry afterwards. We'd sit there and play cards, casino. Just him and me. If he lost he wouldn't

say a word. And of course I always won at cards when he lost the ball game. He was pretty quiet when he'd lose a game. The way it worked, Cloyd came home, downed that sandwich and said, "I gotta win something. Let's play cards. I've got to get a win."

This was terrific in theory, a way to diffuse frustration, and start feeling good about himself again. Except on plenty of nights Nadine was a worthy adversary at casino and she chalked up the victory in her win-loss column. Then Cloyd got more disgusted and said, "Can't win at anything."

With so many family members still living in the Alba area and so many Boyer boys playing baseball, how they fared was the object of great interest at home. A tiny town with 350 people producing pro ball player after pro ball player was quite unusual, and it was natural for the other residents to keep a close watch on what the boys accomplished. "I think they (other Alba citizens) were real proud of that," Nadine said, "real proud of them. They were proud of Cloyd and were impressed that they knew him and that he grew up there."

In some ways Nadine married baseball when she married Cloyd and baseball helped define their lives together for years, in terms of the cities they visited and moved to, in terms of their livelihood and lifestyle. Nadine was part of the baseball world, but not fully invested emotionally, and the same is true today. She admits that almost all of the other Boyers are probably bigger fans of the sport at this point than she is.

At the time Nadine was speaking, the huge baseball news for Cardinals fans was whether or not career-long Cardinal Albert Pujols (definitely Cooperstown-bound as a Hall of Famer) would stay with his only pro team or take more money to play elsewhere. The "Pujols Watch" was all over the newspapers and television news. Then Pujols finally decided to go to the Los Angeles Angels instead of staying in Missouri. Nadine was asked if she would get over Pujols' departure.

"Oh, did he leave?" she said, laughing. It was her way of indicating that what the Cardinals of the 2000s did was not going to affect her life in the same manner as what the Cardinals of the 1940s and 1950s did. Certainly if she ever had stars in her eyes—and that is doubtful based on what she said—she did not any longer. Of Pujols, Nadine said, "It was just his job."

Cloyd loved baseball, and he wanted it to be not only his job, but his career. He was in the process of making the game his life's work with the Cardinals' organization. He had reached the AAA level, the top level of professional baseball short of the major leagues, by playing with Rochester. He was fortunate in that again his manager was Johnny Keane, with whom he already had a strong rapport.

Sometimes in the minors, when teams played doubleheaders they played two seven-inning games instead of nine innings. In one of those contests, a game that was 0–0 went to an eighth inning, Boyer took another hard-luck loss. This one was more difficult to swallow because he got beat by a line drive up the middle that he tried to stab. It did not land in his glove and the ball did not travel up the middle. Instead it smacked him on the hand.

Boyer wondered if he had broken his hand, but he shrugged off the pain, finished the game and lost, 1–0. In the minors the manager sends reports back to the main office and Boyer had such tough luck that Keane sent in a report saying he was good enough to finish 18–7 or 17–8.

At this point in his minor league career, Boyer was starting to run across players who were establishing reputations and who were on their way to the majors. Slugger Steve Bilko was one. Rocky Nelson was another.

Bilko, a first baseman, pounded the heck out of the ball in the minors, putting up huge numbers in homers, RBI and average in the Pacific Coast League, and he did have a ten-year big-league career, but with only minimal success. His lifetime average was .249 and only twice did he reach 20 homers in a season. Nelson spent parts of nine years in the majors, also batted .249, and never drove in more than 35 runs in a season.

Boyer thought those two minor-league bashers would be stars in the majors after spending time with them in the minors or watching them play. "They didn't have big years in the majors," Boyer said. "I never could figure out why they couldn't hit in the big leagues."

Following Boyer's very brief stay in the majors at the start of the 1949 season when the Cardinals took him north after spring training, he believed he would receive a late-season call-up. That summons never came, but he returned to spring training in 1950 with single-minded purpose. He felt he showed what he could do over the preceding couple of seasons in the minors and that he was ready for the big-time, a permanent place on the Cardinals' roster.

And he was right. This time the Cardinals kept him. He joined a club that at its foundation was led by future Hall of Famers Stan Musial, Red Schoendienst and Enos Slaughter. Among the other personalities were catcher Joe Garagiola, who gained much greater fame as a broadcaster, star shortstop Marty Marion, and Solly Hemus, who would later manage the Cards. Bilko and Nelson joined Boyer as minor-league escapees. Others on the pitching staff included Gerry Staley, George "Red" Munger, Max Lanier, and Harry Brecheen.

Boyer's first success was in relief of Lanier on May 1, 1950, when

Lanier was pulled for a pinch hitter. Eddie Dyer, the manager, plugged Boyer into the game for the last inning of a 2–1 contest. The Cardinals pulled it out 3–2 and Boyer had a victory—the first of his major league career. There were 11,534 people at Sportsman's Park—more, in fact, since that only represented the paid attendance. Boyer gave up one hit and no runs, and the losing pitcher was Joe Hatten.

At the time, Wayne Boyer was beginning his dental studies in Missouri. That night Wayne and Cloyd drove to Columbia where the main campus of the University of Missouri is located. "I was so excited," Cloyd said. "We went into a place and had a drink or two. I'd never been much of a drinker, usually a beer or two, and I never drank in the house or around my kids. But that night I was excited, gol' dang. I was just thrilled. I couldn't believe it happened. My first big-league win. I had waited a long time."

Boyer made another relief appearance a little later, being handed the ball in the second inning and going the rest of the way. The Cardinals won that game, too.

Boyer pined for a spot in the rotation. Finally, on July 27, it was Munger's turn in the rotation. The Cardinals were neck-and-neck with the Brooklyn Dodgers and had lost the day before by a 7–5 count with Brecheen absorbing the defeat. "Dyer came up to me and asked if could pitch tomorrow," Boyer said. "I said, 'Yeah.' I'd been waiting for that call."

Boyer got the start and the Cardinals topped the Dodgers, 13–3, at Ebbets Field. The victory gave St. Louis a four-game lead on the Dodgers and gave Boyer new status on the staff. Cloyd pitched a complete game, with the three runs allowed, and struck out nine. "So I went out and had a good game and we won," Boyer said. "That got me into the rotation. I took George Munger's place."

On August 1, Boyer was tabbed to start against the Boston Braves. He was in fine form again, winning 6–1, as Bob Chipman took the loss at Braves Field. Boyer gave up six hits and one run, striking out four. He even had a single in the game. A little later in the season Boyer had an instant-replay type of game against the Dodgers. Facing Carl Erskine this time— who was shelled—Boyer bested Brooklyn for a second time, 13–3. He permitted eight hits and struck out seven.

Perhaps Boyer's finest showing, and his best-remembered outing of the year, came late in the season at Boston. By then the Cardinals were out of the pennant race, but Vern Bickford was on the mound for Boston, seeking his 20th victory of the year. Boyer road-blocked Bickford, hurling a four-hit shutout in a 1–0 triumph. "I kept him from getting his 20th win," Boyer said. "As I was leaving the park, he passed me and came up to me and congratulated me. And there he was trying to win his 20th game."

Boyer never forgot Bickford's graciousness in defeat, especially since he had a special milestone within reach and was thwarted. Bickford never came close to winning 20 games again. Off a victory like that, a big-league shutout with a low-hit game, Boyer had good reason to think well of himself, to be proud, and to gain confidence and think that big things were in store for him.

He was just 22 years old, ensconced in the pitching rotation of the St. Louis Cardinals, and a promising career stretched out ahead of him. Boyer had every reason to believe that he could become an All-Star pitcher down the line.

7

ROOKIE YEAR
(Cloyd)

For a rookie, Cloyd Boyer made a respectable impact with the Cardinals during the 1950 season. He finished 7–7 with a 3.52 earned run average, throwing 120⅓ innings. The outlook was good as Boyer gained knowledge every time he took the mound.

At one point Boyer's record was 5–2. Then he got beat by Cincinnati's Ewell Blackwell, the right-hander known as "The Whip" for the way he fired the ball into the plate. After that, he won two more games and lost four.

Overall, things went well for Boyer until an appearance near the end of the season. Boyer is not sure how or exactly when he hurt his pitching arm. There was no distinctive tear. He remembers pitching solidly against the Dodgers one game, nursing a lead with runners on first and third and one out, with future Hall of Fame outfielder Duke Snider coming to the plate. "I figured I had to strike him out because even if I got a ground ball the odds were against getting a double play out of it," Boyer said. "I reached back for a little more to put something extra on my fastball and I struck him out. Then I got Gil Hodges on a pop up."

It was good, clutch pitching, but it was costly. The next day Boyer woke up with pain in his arm. The first person he remembers telling about the ache in his arm was Mike Ryba, who had an off-and-on career with the Cardinals and other teams and became a coach for St. Louis after he retired. Starters generally had a four-day rest between games at the time, but they had a between-starts ritual and Boyer was scheduled to throw batting practice two days after his last start. Only he couldn't do it. "I said, 'I don't believe I can throw,'" Boyer said. "'Man, I've got a catch in my arm like I've never had.'" It was a pitcher's worst nightmare. Although Boyer did not know the proper terminology at the time and even doctors rarely referred to the spot on the shoulder known as the rotator cuff, Boyer recognized he was in trouble. A little argument with Ryba followed. There was the suggestion Boyer was jaking it, not putting his all out for the team.

> He got all over me. He said, "Oh, you young kids, you get up here and you don't want to pitch." I said, "Mike, I've been in this game, how long, and even when I was a kid I never refused to pitch, if I was hurting or not hurting." So that kind of shook me up. I thought I had better not sit out batting practice pitching. They might think I was backing out and I wasn't tough enough or something. I didn't want them to think that, so I went ahead and pitched and my arm got worse.

In sports they call it sucking it up and playing with pain. It may be a foolish choice, but if you are 22 years old and your career is riding on whether or not you take your turn on the mound, you feel as if you are in a lose-lose situation. Medical care for athletes was much less sophisticated at the time, and the nurturing of baseball pitchers' arms was in its infancy, as were surgical techniques and doctors' limited knowledge of the mechanics of pitching. In addition, team trainers and doctors—either through direct orders or unspoken belief—felt it was their job to get players out on the field as swiftly as possible.

So Boyer pitched BP. When his turn in the rotation came around, he started.

> It got to where they had to give me Novocain in the afternoon for me to pitch at night. And then I would go home and my arm just hurt like the devil. I was only 22 and it was discouraging. My feeling with the manager was, well, "He's the boss." I didn't want to disagree with the boss. The whole philosophy was to pitch through the pain and it would eventually just go away. And if your arm doesn't come around, we'll get somebody else. That's the way I think they looked at it then.

Before the season ended, the team shut Boyer down. His record was sound and he could have been satisfied with that 7–7 start. But his mind and future were clouded. This mysterious arm pain put him on the questionable list heading into the off-season.

That was a very distressing time period for Boyer. He was living his dream as a major league player with the Cardinals, had worked hard for five years to progress through the minors, and now this. Frustration and pain were an ugly combination and they wore on him mentally. He wasn't alone, either, as his battle trying to return his right arm to normalcy dragged on. Two other Cardinals pitchers—Joe Presko and Eddie Yuhas— experienced similar difficulties.

> All three of us went down with bad arms. I'd take diathermy, take X-ray treatments. Even in the winter the team called me up and wanted me to go to St. Louis and have my tonsils out. They thought my tonsils might be causing an infection. My tonsils. In my mind I knew where the sore spot was. I didn't think my tonsils had anything to do with it. How could it? My shoulder's hurting. That's how much they knew about it back in 1950. I got my tonsils out.

Not surprisingly, that remedy did not help Boyer's throwing arm.

Wayne was living in St. Louis working on his dental degree, and Cloyd stayed with him. After he had recovered his full strength from the tonsillectomy, the Cardinals called him back and wanted to try something else—something up Wayne's alley, actually, though he wasn't involved. The Cardinals wanted Cloyd to have his wisdom teeth pulled, thinking maybe that would fix his pitching arm. "So I spent a few more days with Wayne and I got my wisdom teeth out," Cloyd said. "They (the Cardinals) were just grasping at straws. That's all it was."

That wasn't the end of the medical exploration, either. The Cardinals kept pondering Boyer's circumstance and advancing suggestions that they hoped would get his arm back to 100 percent so he could pitch with his usual sharpness.

> They gave me cortisone shots. You open up your arm with it facing them and that needle comes out and they jab it in a little way. They're looking for a vein or something and they say, "Is that it? Is that it?" About the third time the doctor hit the spot and boy, I came up out of that chair shouting, "Yeah!" It was sore. They gave me two or three of those treatment shots.

The needle hurt, but it didn't bring relief.

The winter off did do Boyer some good, though. Plain, old-fashioned rest helped. Boyer had posted a hopeful 7–7 record in 1950 and although the year ended with him nearly frantic from worry about his arm, when he showed up for spring training in 1951 he pitched as if he had gone to the arm store and bought a new one. "I had a heck of a spring that year," Boyer said. "It was unbelievable, really, almost like I did that other time."

Boyer wasn't about to credit the removal of his tonsils or wisdom teeth for his rejuvenation. He was just pleased that his arm didn't ache. He came out of spring training a refreshed-looking pitcher ready to take a turn with the big club again. There was a new Cardinals manager that year. Marty Marion, an eight-time All-Star as a shortstop, was named the new field boss of the Cardinals for the 1951 season. His tenure with the Cards lasted just that season, although he also managed the St. Louis Browns and the Chicago White Sox in the 1950s. When they played together in 1950, Cloyd Boyer and Marion were very friendly teammates. But their relationship deteriorated in 1951 as player and manager.

> We were just buddy-buddy. For some reason or other he got to where he didn't like me. You can tell. Then he got upset with me over a deal when we were in Boston playing the Braves one night. I was in the bullpen and he had me get up to warm up. It was early in the year and it was cold and I was slow getting warmed up. He put me in the game before I was warm and so I got hit pretty good. By the time I was loosened up and feeling pretty good, Marion came out to the mound and he was going to take me out of the game.

Boyer didn't feel it was right that he had been rushed into the game and now he was being rushed out of the game. "I said, 'Gol' dang it, Marty, I just got loosened up and here you are out here to take me out,'" Boyer said. "He said, 'Well, you didn't get up and get warmed up quick enough.' I said, 'I didn't have enough time in the first place.'"

That little discussion did not help Boyer's cause. After four more appearances Boyer was shipped out to the minors to play in Columbus, Georgia. Boyer followed orders and reported to a weak Columbus squad. But his arm was feeling pretty good, he was throwing the ball well, and he was getting the best of the hitters, although his own team did not score much.

> I was throwing pretty good. I was 2–3, but they didn't have much of a club there. The Cardinals kept tabs on me and they called me back up. I was feeling good in my first start back in the National League we were playing the Dodgers and I was winning, 2–1.
>
> I remember it was Billy Cox, their third baseman, who came up. They had a hell of a club with Jackie Robinson, Roy Campanella, Duke Snider. Cox was really the only one in the lineup who wasn't an All-Star hitter. But I hung him a curve and I got beat, 3–2. He doubled down the line with a couple of men on. That was my first game back.

(Author's note: Cox actually led off with a single, Andy Pafko doubled, and two runs scored on sacrifice flies and an error.)

That game was played on July 28, and for the rest of the season Boyer did not pitch very well. He finished 2–5 in just 19 appearances. Boyer only pitched 63⅓ innings in the majors that year. His arm didn't hurt. He didn't think he'd lost anything off his fastball. He just lost his sharpness. In that Dodgers game he went the distance, gave up only two earned runs, but walked seven in losing to Ralph Branca. Boyer's earned run average for the season escalated to an ugly 5.26. "I didn't do any good the rest of the year," Boyer said. "My arm didn't hurt. I was throwing good in Columbus. No obvious explanation. That was frustrating. I pitched good in Columbus, but I didn't pitch good up there in the majors. I had a bad year."

The Cardinals finished 81–73 that season, but Marion was not kept on board as manager. He was replaced for 1952 by Eddie Stanky. That seemed as if it would be a good fresh start for Boyer, too, under a new manager who didn't seem to have it in for him. His arm seemed healthy and he was only 24 years old, so he felt there was no reason why he could not regain his form from before he hurt his arm.

Boyer was concerned, but he had not given up. And the Cardinals had not given up on him despite his shaky season. He was invited to spring training again in 1952, being offered a chance to rebound from the disappointment of 1951. He was optimistic because his arm did not hurt. As far as he could tell, everything was fine, and if everything was back to normal he should be able to impress the new boss and spend the entire season playing for the Cardinals.

It was time to put the arm scare behind him, let loose with the hard one again, and regain his stature in the Cardinals organization. Boyer had spent parts of three seasons with the Cardinals at this juncture, counting that blink-and-you-might-miss-it three-game fling in 1949.

In 1952 he figured to be entering his prime years. If everything went well, Boyer would be in the Cardinals' rotation from April to September— and with luck in October, too, if they could win a pennant.

8

ARM WOES
(Cloyd)

Cloyd Boyer was renewed coming out of spring training in St. Petersburg, Florida, in 1952. His arm did not hurt. He had a new manager who he thought would give him a fair shake.

As a player, Eddie Stanky was a scrappy middle infielder who stood 5-foot-8 and weighed around 170 pounds. He was no power hitter, but he played the game vigorously. Stanky did the little things well and annoyed the opposition. His nickname as a player was "The Brat." He made three All-Star teams and he coaxed walks out of pitchers at a phenomenal rate, collecting more than 100 in a season six times.

Stanky was not supremely skilled, and one of his managers, future Hall of Famer Leo Durocher basically said all he knew how to do was win. In short, Stanky was the type of manager a lot of clubs looked for and hoped could spark a team with their own fiery nature. He seemed like the kind of guy for whom Boyer could play. The problem was that Stanky didn't seem to have much faith in him.

Boyer had a solid build and could run the bases well. It is said that power pitchers obtain the speed on their fastball from the strength in their legs. Boyer was both pretty fast on the mound and could run well, too.

"He (Stanky) thought I could run," Boyer said. "He liked my legs. He'd seen me get undressed and a couple of times I wondered if he was gay or something the way he stared at my legs. He came around and told me how I had nice legs and all that. He wanted to make a pinch-runner out of me."

Boyer wanted to win games for the Cardinals with his arm, and Stanky wanted Boyer to win games for the Cardinals with his legs.

Maybe Stanky thought he was being clever. Or maybe he was looking for any edge he could find, but he dragged Boyer over to the team's sliding pit and provided instruction on how to improve his base running. The sliding pit was a bunch of dirt with a base in the middle, and Stanky became Boyer's running coach. It is impossible to imagine a manager in the modern era running a young pitcher through such drills now. He would be dismissed as a crazy man jeopardizing talent. The goal was to make Boyer a slicker base runner who could avoid pickoff throws.

Time after time Stanky had Boyer should dive back into the bag, simulating a move avoiding a pitcher's throw over to first.

> He'd be my coach. He'd yell, "Get back! Get back!" And I had to dive back. I kept diving back to the base and dang if my arm didn't start hurting. Stanky didn't have any sense about hurting somebody. I think that's where I hurt my arm the second time, just jumping back to the base and landing on my arm. He wanted me to stretch a lead as far off the base as I could and then dive back when he yelled "Get back!" I was diving on my arm.

It was pointless to rebel against the thoughtless activity in a time period when a manager enjoyed dictatorial power, but even then Boyer felt the drills were foolish. When he was older and had been around the sport longer, Boyer marveled at the heedless risks young pitchers were forced to take because coaches and managers didn't think things through.

> I don't know why they wouldn't be more careful with pitchers. I look back over my career and the things that happened when I was young, and not only to me, but to other young pitchers the way teams would hurt a pitcher's arm. They just figured they'd go get another one if he couldn't pitch anymore. That's kind of the way they looked at it.

Although Boyer came to spring training with an arm he felt was sound again, as a young player of 24 he didn't feel he had much say-so to resist Stanky's pinch-running plan, even if he thought it was cockamamie. "When you're that age and you're in the big leagues, you want to stay there and do anything they tell you to do," Boyer said.

The sliding pit action did its job on Boyer's arm and he had to tell the Cardinals he had pain again resulting in him being "babied a little bit." For a little while, including after the season began. He didn't spend half of his life in a whirlpool or anything, and when the pitchers were in the outfield shagging fly balls Boyer was with them.

One day Stanky wandered past Boyer and fellow pitcher Gerry Staley in between flies. Boyer and Staley were standing around shooting the breeze when the captain of the ship strolled past and uttered a single, sarcastic comment. "You can't go nine," Stanky said, and kept walking. He made a circuit of the outfield, walked by Boyer and Staley again, and said it again. "You can't go nine."

Stanky did this a few times and left Boyer and Staley staring at one another wondering about the manager's point and whom he was directing his comments at. "Finally, I said, 'Who are you talking to?'" Boyer said. "He said, 'I'm talking to you. You can't go nine innings.' I said, 'Well, I'd like to have the chance. Just give me the ball and see.' So he did. A couple of days later I started and I pitched a shutout."

The shutout was recorded against the Philadelphia Phillies on May 3. St. Louis won, 3–0, at Sportsman's Park, but it was a very sparse crowd. Attendance was just 5,676. Boyer worked fast. The game took only two hours and nine minutes. The Cardinals scored two runs in the fifth inning and one in the seventh, and the losing pitcher was Karl Drews. Boyer twirled a six-hitter.

That season, once again in limited action, Boyer got into 23 Cardinals games and finished with a 6–6 record and a 4.24 earned run average. He had long stretches of inactivity, though.

Gene Mauch, later a respected big-league manager and a hard-luck one, was a member of the Cardinals part of that season, and Boyer said he later learned that they were not allied forces. Stanky sent Mauch out to the bullpen when Boyer was warming up in order to serve as a dummy batter. His instructions from Stanky were to "Go down there and stand up as his hitter and see what he's got. See how he looks." Mauch did as he was told, returned to the dugout and informed Stanky, "He ain't got nothin'. He won't last long.'"

Boyer promptly pitched that shutout against the Phillies. Years later, when Mauch had his managerial troubles, including presiding over the worst pennant collapse in National League history in 1964, Boyer thought back to Mauch's actions that day. "That's how smart he was," Boyer said. "That's when I figured maybe he had outsmarted himself all of the time as a manager. I heard a few times that Mauch was the greatest mind in baseball, but I never thought that."

For the second time in Boyer's short major league career, he had arm trouble. He had overcome it the first time and hoped to overcome it again. Boyer's money pitch had always been his fastball, but in a June 29 game against the Pittsburgh Pirates, he ran up against an opponent on the mound who relied on completely different kind of stuff.

Southpaw Howie Pollet, who broke into the majors in 1941 and spent the best years of his career with the Cardinals (including a 21-win season), had drifted to the Pirates' rotation by this 1952 encounter. Boyer not only went head to head with Pollet on the mound, he had to face him in the batter's box, and the crafty, aging pitcher was not easily thrown out of rhythm.

I could always hit a fastball, no matter how hard a pitcher threw it. I could hit it. And Pollet just wouldn't throw a fastball. He had the best change-up that you could have. I kept thinking, "He's got to throw a fastball." He never did. He just kept throwing slow stuff and I was swinging and missing. He was smarter than I was.

Pollet got the win in that game, a rain-shortened, 2–1 decision at Forbes Field. There was a lesson in there that perhaps Boyer could adapt and still get batters out with slower pitches. But he wasn't thinking that way. He was thinking about a cure for his arm, a return to 90 mph speeds.

George "Catfish" Metkovich was a semi-regular first baseman for the Pirates that season, a solid .271 hitter. Boyer and Metkovich had a little tension between them because of an earlier encounter, when Boyer threw a ball as fast as he could and as inside as he could without actually nailing Metkovich.

"I knocked him down and he spun around so fast it left his cap sitting there," Boyer said. That confrontation had repercussions later; the Pirates wanted to make a statement and get a little revenge. Years later Boyer couldn't remember the pitcher who was chosen to buzz him, but he wasn't very surprised when he came to the plate for the first time in the game and was sent sprawling. It was what followed that had him blinking in shock.

You know, you expect it. I've knocked guys down if they knocked me down. I was a pitcher, but I wasn't a bad hitter, so I figured it was over with and that he wouldn't do it again. I dug in at the plate. He did it again. Two times in a row throwing inside. I mean, I went down, too. So you know he ain't doing it again for a third ball. But he did. He did it four times. You don't do that unless the manager tells you to. It wasn't as if I was Babe Ruth digging into the batter's box. The manager was Billy Meyer and the Pirates were terrible that year, 42–112, one of the worst teams ever. My manager was Stanky and he said, "God, I thought you were going to get hit with every pitch."

By that point Boyer was making a $6,000 salary in the majors. Between 1950 and 1952 he recorded 15 wins for the Cardinals against 18 losses. But the issue was his right arm and the pain he felt when he pitched. He was young, only 25, and on the way up. But when the 1952 season ended Boyer's future was clouded because of the nagging pain in his right arm, the second time he had gone into an off-season disturbed about the status of his livelihood. "I'm thinking, 'I hope it quits hurting by spring training,'" Boyer said. "I actually went down to Hot Springs to soak in those baths because people said it helped cure aches and pains, but it didn't." Boyer spent a week in Hot Springs soaking his arm until he thought it would catch fire, all to no avail, on his way to spring training in Florida with the Cardinals.

The season had ended by October 1 of 1952, and it was now entering March of 1953 and Boyer was still in pain, unable to throw hard. "I went down to spring training and I couldn't throw," Boyer said. "I couldn't do any pitching. It was bad. So they had to take me off the roster."

Boyer's major league career was hanging by a thread, just as his arm appeared to be. The Cardinals sent him back to the minors, back to Houston where he had performed so well. Farm director Joe Mathis wanted Boyer to get well and wanted him to be treated by a doctor in Houston.

Whether the heat and humidity of the Texas city agreed with him or it was something else, Boyer's arm got a second wind. Houston manager Al Hollingsworth, an old big-league pitcher, refrained from rushing him or overusing him.

> My arm started coming around. It was starting to feel good. Al Hollings-worth was taking care of me. I pitched the first game of a doubleheader, seven innings at Forth Worth, and we won 2–1. The very next day Hollings-worth got fired. Dixie Walker came in as manager and he used me in relief eight days in a row. My shoulder wasn't bad at the time, but it did seem like a bit much. I would have liked to have stayed in the rotation. If Hollingsworth was still there, I wouldn't have been in the bullpen. I don't think Dixie Walker knew much about pitching.

Boyer's shoulder was sketchy, but he didn't protest when he was whistled in from the bullpen for his next eight straight appearances. "I was pitching pretty good," Boyer said. "I did all right. If you get in there eight days in a row you've got to be getting them out."

Boyer had hoped for a few positive things to result from his sojourn in the minors with Houston. He went south wishing that his arm would bounce back, and it seemed to do so. He wanted to be a starting pitcher, and he did that until the change of administration. And he wanted to be recalled to the Cardinals. That did not happen. He spent the entire summer, the entire season, in Houston. A more accurate summation of the status of Boyer's shoulder was that it behaved so-so. It was erratic. Some days it was better than others, but compared to spring training it was terrific. But doubts remained. Could Boyer's right arm hold up for a whole season? Would he get another chance to make it with the Cardinals?

"I was wondering if I was going to be able to pitch in the big leagues again," Boyer said.

The first Boyer to reach the major leagues worried that he might be finished with the majors. As his younger brothers signed contracts to play professional baseball, Cloyd Boyer endured a worrisome 1953-1954 off-season. Winter never felt so cold. There is nothing like the major leagues. It is the dream of every ball player to make it to the top, and whenever a player does make it he wants to stay in the Show.

Boyer couldn't fool himself into believing that his right arm and right shoulder were 100 percent, but he did still have confidence that if he got a shot he could still pitch for the Cardinals. He wanted that one more chance.

9

SIGNING WITH THE CARDINALS
(Lynn)

Any time a scout happened to pass near Alba, Missouri, it was worth his while to turn off onto a backwoods road and look for a baseball diamond because there was bound to be a Boyer brother playing ball and excelling.

By the time Lewis Lynn Boyer graduated from high school, older brothers Cloyd, Wayne and Ken had signed professional contracts. Lewis Lynn, who was commonly known as Lynn in the family, was born in 1935 and finished high school in 1953.

Admiring his older brothers and hoping that he too could follow in their baseball footsteps into pro ball, he was itching to affix his signature to a contract before the ink was dry on his diploma. Although he wished it was a virtual tie, the 18-year-old had to wait a few months to secure a deal. He signed a contract in the fall with the St. Louis Cardinals organization—they were up to date on the family, for sure—and reported to play ball in the spring of 1954.

In 1951, when he was still a high school student, Lynn made a trip to St. Louis to watch Cloyd pitch in a game. That was something to see—your own brother in the big leagues. "It was great," Lynn said. "It absolutely was. Everybody around Alba was pretty proud of him. They had a metal manufacturing plant out in Alba and they put up an advertisement with Cloyd in it. His picture was in the paper and all that."

Lynn, who was 6 feet tall and was listed at 175 pounds as he was poised to make his debut, was a switch-hitter and a left-handed thrower. He was a first baseman who believed in his talent. Like his brothers, this

Boyer cared about getting a chance to prove himself more than anything else. Baseball was in his blood and he wanted to show his stuff.

Assigned to a team in the Mississippi–Ohio Valley League based in Hannibal, Missouri, mostly famed for being the hometown of that quirky gentleman of American letters, Mark Twain, Boyer became about as familiar with the Mississippi River as Huck Finn. While most of the teams in the league were based in Iowa, other teams were in Illinois and this one was in Missouri. What they had in common was being situated on the big river.

This was the first time Lynn had ever been away from home, although Hannibal was in the same state and not far away. Yet he was not only homesick, he constantly felt as if he was about to pass out from the heat and humidity. "First we were training in Georgia, and this was Class D, so we didn't stay in fancy hotels with air conditioning," Boyer said. "It was terrible. It was a terrible summer. I don't think we felt air conditioning all summer. Oh, man."

The Cardinals' minor-league camp was located in Albany, Georgia, at the time, and that is another place where one of the main exports is heat and humidity. This was one jam-packed training camp. The only minor leaguers who got better treatment were the players who were going to spend the season in AAA and were deemed the most ready for major league play if needed. Lynn Boyer was one of the novices, set to play in the lowest rung of the minors.

Organized baseball never did have a classification that went deeper into the alphabet than Class D, and in later years, when the minors contracted, the entire tier of Class B, C and D were discontinued. It was said, only partially facetiously, that baseball teams didn't want their young players to become demoralized when they were sent to Class D. After all, a D on a report card was not a very good thing. The lowest classification in use in the modern era is Class A.

> There must have been 400 or 500 guys in the camp. They had a lot of clubs, a lot of teams. And they didn't all make it, of course. Half the guys who showed up in spring training weren't going to have a place on a team. That was the heyday of the minors when it seemed as if any town of any size had a team.

Although Lynn Boyer was the fourth brother in line to be targeted and signed by the Cardinals, by 1954 only Cloyd had reached the majors. It could have given him extra confidence to know that the organization had proven its appreciation for the Boyer family by signing four of them, but he also knew that how his brothers fared had no bearing on his case.

He still had to prove his own worthiness and show off his skills when tested.

One thing did improve a little bit between the signing of Cloyd and the signing of Lynn, though. Cloyd's original cash came in the hundreds of dollars. Lynn signed for $2,000. Ken Boyer did get more— probably around $6,000—but the two grand sounded good to Lynn. Some of Lynn's money also went to the family. He gave a chunk of the check to his father Vern. "He needed it worse than I did," Lynn said. "We had a big family."

That was one thing about the Boyer brothers. They did not take the money and run. When they received payment for playing baseball they all contributed to the upkeep of the younger kids.

Lynn Boyer wearing a Cardinals uniform— he played in the St. Louis organization, but not for the major league club (courtesy Cloyd and Nadine Boyer).

When Lynn reported to Albany and checked out the competition on the field, he counted five other first basemen. All five could be in his way on the depth chart. He could have quietly watched them and just dug down for the determination to beat them all out. Instead he adopted another tactic, not one designed to make friends. "I told them the first day, 'You guys want to be playing somewhere else,'" Boyer said. "Three of them did go somewhere else to another team and one went to right field. I had a good spring training. It was a year that I hit the ball well. Everybody was worried about defense, though. They sent me to the Hannibal Cardinals."

Hannibal's first baseman that scorching summer was Lynn Boyer. After the concern about his defense, he played exemplary D, but didn't hit as well as he had shown in spring training or as well as he thought he should have hit. "Fair," is the way Boyer summed up his season. "I had several stolen bases and played a good first base, but I was about a .250 hitter. I never had any problems on defense. But you've got to hit better than .250."

Actually, Boyer's official average was .252, but that is the difference of only one hit over the course of the 68 games he appeared in. Batting .252 in Class D does not earn raves in the front office. It can put a player's career in jeopardy very quickly. Whether the Boyer name carried some magic or not, whether it was more a sign of the times when clubs had more minor-league teams and more roster space, Boyer did not get cut loose. The Cardinals were still interested in keeping tabs on his progress— but they did want to see progress.

For the 1955 season, Lynn Boyer was dispatched to Ardmore, Oklahoma, which had a team in the Sooner State League, another league now defunct. It was still Class D. Although Ardmore was hospitable to mosquitoes and flirted with the 100-degree mark on the thermometer, Boyer was faring much better in his second year in the pros. He had the experience of being away from home for a while under his belt, so he was more used to it, and he opened the season playing reasonably well. He was just more at ease. His average had started to dip, dropping to .219, when Boyer was injured. He broke his arm. "I got hit with a pitch and it broke my right arm," Boyer said. "In those days they didn't have much in the way of rehabilitation programs, so they sent me home to Missouri instead of hanging around with the team."

It also wasn't as if Boyer spent a long time in conditioning once the bone healed, either. One day he had the cast sawed off and the next day he reported to the Cardinals for duty. As fast as he could return he was playing again, only he was shipped to a different team, back to Albany, Georgia. "I showed up at the ball park after they took my cast off and I was in the line-up that day," Boyer said. "I don't know if I was really ready to play, but I was anxious to play again. It didn't hurt me, but after I came back I didn't hit as well as I had at the beginning of the season."

Boyer competed in 24 more games that season, but hit just .152 with a single home run for Albany. Albany was in the Georgia-Florida League, but was also Class D.

> I didn't produce offensively. In high school I had hit .320, .330. My senior year I hit .400. The pitching was just different. Everybody you faced was a good pitcher. A lot of them were very fast, but they were wild. You didn't know where the ball was going to go. They walked a lot of guys and struck out a lot of guys. That's how I got my arm broken. I had OK power—for my size, being about 175 pounds. I figured I would get stronger as I got older and hit harder, but I did not do it playing pro ball.

The 1955 season was not as much fun as it could have been. Boyer was injured for a good number of weeks and hit below his weight when he came back. He thought the arm injury would be a mitigating factor and buy him some more time with the Cardinals, but a wealth of young, up-and-coming talent in the team's farm system meant Lynn was expendable. Suddenly, Lynn Boyer was an unemployed baseball player. He was adrift, still believing he could play, but with no team to call home. Washing out in Class D—which from the Cardinals' standpoint is what happened— does not usually get a player another call. Although Boyer is glad that he played, he feels somewhat unfulfilled. He was barely over 20 years old when he was released and he still thinks he had potential that went untapped.

> I wish I knew then what I know now. I would have been a better player. I'd have worked more on my hitting. I didn't have anyone to work with me on my hitting, and I wish I could have found someone to help me. I think you can probably learn to hit better if you are a good enough athlete and spend enough time at it. I didn't work at it, spending extra time. I think back and I was playing in games, but I didn't work at it. There were no hitting coaches in Class D. We had a minor-league pitching coach who roamed through the system, but no hitting coach. I never had anybody in the time I was in the minors really teach me about baseball. It was a different era. Now, from Class A on up they've got them.

When Lynn was younger he was a superb basketball player, good enough to be on the watch list for various colleges. He thought he was a better basketball player than baseball player and was tempted to forgo professional baseball for a free college education. Probably influenced by the success of the other boys, father Vern actually talked Lynn into taking the money up-front and giving baseball a whirl.

"I had scholarship offers for baseball and basketball," Lynn said, "but dad talked me out of going to school and instead playing ball right away. He said, 'Why would you go to school when you can play ball?' One scout even suggested I go to school—there was a place in Texas interested—get my degree and then play ball."

Lynn had his fling in the minors, though it didn't last nearly as long as he thought it would, and by the time he completed his minor-league career he would have still been a senior in college. Once his baseball playing career ended, Lynn embarked on a college career. He spent two years at Joplin Junior College and then finished his degree at Pittsburg State University of Kansas. "But I had to pay for it," he said. "I had to work 40 hours a week and then at night go to school. They were long days. Almost every Friday I swore I'd never go back to school, but by Monday I forgot. I was exhausted. But when I finished college I taught and I coached in high school for 11 years."

After baseball Lynn Boyer became a high school basketball coach. This was taken during the 1965-1966 season (courtesy Cloyd and Nadine Boyer).

When Boyer wearied of doing that, he started working in construction and took a job in Kansas City through the International Electrical Workers. For five years, he also taught electricians at the Ford Motor Company. "I spent the rest of my career at Ford," he said.

Lynn Boyer had hoped to spend his working life at first base, but settled for Ford. Still, he advanced in baseball farther than 99 percent of high school baseball players. It was only a cup of coffee in the play-for-pay ranks, but those high school teammates of his back in Alba would have given years off their life to be able to say that the St. Louis Cardinals once scouted them and signed them to play ball.

10

INJURIES WRECK
THE PLANS
(Cloyd)

C loyd, essentially the lead singer in the Boyer band, was at a cross-roads. His injured wing meant that he could not fly as high as he had before. His right arm, representing his future in the game, was letting him down. He wondered if this was the end, if he was finished with big-league baseball and the St. Louis Cardinals prematurely because of injury.

Only 25 years old in the spring of 1953, Boyer did not seem to have a future in baseball. It seemed as if all of the promise had evaporated. "My shoulder was so-so, at best," Boyer said. "I was wondering if I was going to be able to pitch in the big leagues again. After spring training, the Cardinals began playing and they didn't take me with the team and they didn't assign me to another team. I was left behind for a couple of days so I got in the car and drove home."

Boyer very much felt forgotten and overlooked and was miserable at the state of his pitching arm and his tenuous connection to the team. Farm director Joe Mathis sought him out, finding him at home in Missouri when he telephoned.

The conversation went something like this: "Where are you?" "Home," Boyer replied. "Why?" "I'm going to send you to Houston," Mathis said. At that point Boyer informed Mathis that he was giving up baseball. "No, I don't want to go to Houston," he said. "I've decided I'm going to quit." That gave Mathis pause.

Mathis told Boyer that the Cardinals still liked him and if he couldn't pitch they would like him to coach in the minors for the team somewhere. "No, I've already made up my mind," Boyer said. "I'm going to pick up my wife and go to California. Her sister's out there and I can probably get a job out there somewhere."

At the time, brother Ken was in the service and his wife and child were staying with Cloyd's family. That arrangement stood up for two years. They were all going to pile into the car and motor to California. Mathis kept lobbying Boyer not to forsake the game and eventually he won him over with his arguments.

"Joe was a guy I really liked and respected a lot," Boyer said. "So, anyway, I finally said OK. I couldn't pitch at all. They took me off the roster. Dixie Walker was managing in Rochester and Harry Walker was managing Houston. I had played for Dixie the last half of 1953 and I knew him pretty well. I didn't know Harry very well."

This was at the Cardinals' major-league camp in St. Petersburg. Ken had emerged from the service and was assigned to the Louisville roster, but he was out of rhythm from his layoff and wasn't playing very well. He was at the minor-league camp in Daytona Beach. The Cardinals were going to send him to Omaha. In a sense Cloyd was offered the chance for an intervention, to try and determine what was bothering Ken before he was dropped to a lower classification in the organization.

Cloyd and Ken were neither teammates, nor affiliated with the same minor-league team at the moment, but they were both in Florida, so Cloyd invited Ken for dinner and probed for what might be the problem with perhaps the most talented of the Boyer brothers.

When they got together Cloyd initiated a baseball status conversation by informing Ken that Harry Walker told him he was "having a lot of trouble. He's thinking of maybe sending you to Omaha." Ken replied that there were plenty of problems with the way the minor-league camp was being run. "I'll tell you right off," Ken Boyer said, "we don't ever get any batting practice. We don't take infield. We go out and listen to those guys talk." Cloyd said he understood completely that the manager and coaches spent too much time chattering and not enough time working on fundamentals.

> I knew exactly what he was talking about. They'd start in on telling you what you ought to be doing in the clubhouse. Then they would tell you what you ought to be doing in the dugout. Then they would tell you what you ought to be doing in the on-deck circle. Then they'd go on to talking about being on the bases. Ken said, "We haven't had batting practice for a week." I said, "Don't say anything. I'll get some balls and we'll go take batting practice."

Cloyd called a scout he knew who was around, begged the use of bats and balls, and also said he wanted the session to be private at the park in

Daytona Beach, just him and Ken. "I don't want anybody in the park," Cloyd said. "We'll go out there at eight o'clock in the morning, or whatever we've got to do."

Spring games were being played so the Boyers had to work around that. The weather was cold that year, and in both of their minds there was too much talking going on and not enough live practicing, chill or not. Cloyd was going to have a little workout session with Ken, just between the two of them, to try and determine the root of Ken's problem.

"That's what I'm gonna do. Even if I have to go out and buy those balls." A promise was extracted that he would have the equipment he needed.

> The next morning we went out there and I had my bag of balls and I said I didn't want anybody around, and that included him (the scout), too. So Ken and I went out and we hit that bag of balls and then we'd go run them down and talk on the way back, just BS-ing. We did that for two or three days and gol' dang it you couldn't believe how he was doing. Ken just started wearing the ball out. He went to Houston and drove in 119 runs that year and he was in the big leagues the next year.

All Ken Boyer needed was the opportunity for hard work and a little bit of patience shown to him by a coach. The coach happened to be his brother, who recognized what the remedy for his slump was. It may be said that the rendezvous between Cloyd and Ken was fortuitous for both of them. Ken regained his stride and Cloyd learned that he might well have the intelligence and knowledge to become a coach. A few days of hitting in the Florida sunshine may have influenced two careers.

"They were just going to give up on Ken and send him back to Class A ball," Cloyd said. "They might have ruined him. They could have. Maybe they wouldn't have because Ken was too good of a competitor, but I thought about it for a long time what might have happened. Just give a guy a little bit of your time, you know what I mean?"

After that spring training interlude, the Cardinals sent Cloyd to Rochester although he couldn't pitch in 1954. Nadine went with him and suffered through the frustrations he had of being unable to compete.

> I couldn't even throw. They didn't even get me into any games. Finally, I could throw a little bit. As I went along I got better and I'd throw a little bit of batting practice on the side. A couple of times if we were getting beat 15–0 or something Harry Walker might stick me in a game for an inning or something like that. I could understand his point. I'd been injured. There didn't seem to be any way that I could help him.

By the middle of the season Boyer realized his arm and shoulder felt sound enough for him to pitch again, start games, and that he might well be able to work his way back to the majors. He wasn't going to get the chance to upgrade his situation in Rochester, though. Boyer's old friend Johnny Keane was managing the Columbus, Ohio, team in the American Association, so he talked it over with Nadine and made a call to Keane to see if he could give him an opportunity.

Keane said, "Well, give me two days and I'll have you over here." He worked a swap and Boyer and infielder Vern Benson departed Rochester for Columbus while someone else moved to Rochester. Benson was not happy. Boyer said that Benson told him, "I didn't give a crap if you left. I didn't want to go with you."

The move to Columbus worked. Boyer was employed by a manager who believed in him and suddenly he was healthy enough to pitch. Thrust into the rotation for a period of time, Boyer finished 2–3 with a team that made the playoffs. "I told Johnny, 'I can't throw as hard as I could, but I think I'm smarter now,'" Boyer said. "I can change speeds and my control is better. I think I can get hitters out." Keane gave him his shot and it rewarded both of them.

Columbus advanced into the post-season against Louisville. One of Columbus' key starters was Stu Miller, who later was an All-Star relief pitcher in the majors. Miller was a so-called junkball pitcher who mostly threw slow stuff up to the plate and never appeared to tax his arm. Miller pitched the opener of the series, pitched exceptionally well, but lost the game, 1–0. Boyer started the second game and took a 3–1 lead into the ninth when Miller entered from the bullpen and saved it.

> The seventh game was supposed to be my turn. Keane called me up into his hotel room and said, "I need to talk to you. You and I have been together for a while and you've done good for me ... this, that and the other ... and I appreciate it. I know it's your turn to pitch tonight, but I'm going to pitch Stu." I said, "You know Johnny, if I was the manager I'd do the same thing. He's pitching better than anybody else, even on two days' rest, and he throws that stuff up there." He had the slow ball. Slow and slower. He was a helluva pitcher. He went into the tenth inning tied 2–2 and he had pitched all of the way.

Alas, gutsy effort aside, Miller gave up a home run and the game was lost, 3–2. Miller had pitched fantastically well throughout the entire series and lost three times in pitchers' duels. Like Boyer, Miller had already spent some time in the majors with the Cardinals and was back down in the minors. He eventually spent 16 years in the big leagues for a variety of teams, most prominently the San Francisco Giants and the Baltimore Orioles.

Boyer shook his head, marveling over how Miller could fool hitters with slow pitches. "Hell, he was liable to strike out ten or 12 guys with that stuff," Boyer said. "One time Roy Campanella [a three-time National League Most Valuable Player for the Dodgers] was swinging at a Miller pitch and he flipped around and fell to his knees. He just looked out there at the mound at Miller and shook his head."

But Boyer, who watched first-hand as Miller baffled batters with his slow-motion tosses in the minors, never forgot an incident later in the majors that left him thunderstruck. "I think it was a 0–0 game and Miller came in for the ninth inning," Boyer said. "It became 1–0, but he had the bases loaded with two outs. This was against the Cubs. Typically, Miller is throwing that slow crap up to the plate and the count was 3-and-2 on the hitter. Then guess what he did? He threw a fastball right by him. Just paralyzed him. He probably shocked him." A fastball from Stu Miller in the clutch?

During one of Boyer's good outings for Columbus he faced the Kansas City Blues, managed by Harry Craft. During the off-season, the Philadelphia Athletics moved to Kansas City, abandoning their long-time home. They became the Kansas City Athletics in time for the 1955 season. Lou Boudreau, who led the Cleveland Indians to the American League pennant and a World Series championship in 1948, was the manager of the relocated team, and one of his coaches was Craft, who convinced the club that Boyer might be able to help.

With a 1954 record of 51–103 the Athletics needed all of the help they could find. They improved in 1955 and finished sixth in the AL, 33 games behind the pennant-winning New York Yankees.

> Harry Craft remembered my good game from the year before and he got me picked up by Kansas City. I went up there and boy, I got started off good. I was feeling pretty good. I didn't have my good fastball the way I did when I was younger, before I hurt my arm, but I had learned control and a nickel curve. I could change speeds and really pitch.

As an aside to the continuation of Cloyd Boyer's major league pitching career—a fresh start as a starter—that spring, of all teams the Athletics, and not the Cardinals, signed the fifth Boyer brother to come along to a pro contract. It was the New York Yankees who had their eye on Cletis Boyer, but under the rules in effect at the time they couldn't sign him for the bonus he was worth because they had signed two other then-called "bonus babies." In a rather strange twist, the Yankees lobbied the Athletics to sign Clete with the plan of eventually trading for him.

That season Clete came right out of high school in Missouri to the

Kansas City roster. He was just 18 years old, but played in 47 games while batting .241. Cloyd, who was 27, and Clete were actually major league teammates for the season. Although they did not consult a crystal ball, one brother was on the last legs of his big-league career and the other was just starting out on the road to stardom.

Cloyd Boyer got off to a swift start and was sitting on a pitching record of 5–1. He was doing so well that Boudreau went to the front office and got him a raise from $7,000 to $10,000. And as soon as the raise kicked in, Boyer

Cloyd Boyer pitching for the Kansas City Athletics in 1955. Cloyd is the oldest of the seven Boyer brothers who played professional baseball, and one of three who played in the majors (courtesy Cloyd and Nadine Boyer).

never won another game for the Athletics. His 5–1 start turned into a 5–5 finish with a horrendous 6.22 earned run average. The shift was abrupt and startling, and Boyer never could quite figure out what happened, what went wrong.

> I don't know. It got to the point where I didn't have anything on the ball at all. The hitters were blasting it 500 feet off of me. I never could throw hard again. One minute I was 5–1 and pitching pretty well and the next I had nothing left. All of a sudden. I always felt bad for what happened with Lou Boudreau. Boudreau got me that $3,000 raise and I couldn't get anybody out.

Whatever speed Boyer had retained deserted him. His command deserted him. Boyer pitched 98⅓ innings for the Athletics that season and issued 69 walks. He gave up 21 home runs. Enemy batsmen were teeing off on him. It was apparent to Boyer that he could no longer get the job done as a big-league pitcher, that his arm was never going to be as strong or as good as it was, and that he was at the end of the line as a major league pitcher.

The Kansas City Athletics had offered a second chance, and for a while things worked out, but in the end Boyer's arm and shoulder were not sturdy enough to hold up over an entire major league season of 154 games. The 1955 season in the American League was the last time that Cloyd Boyer pitched in the majors.

While discouraging, it turned out that while Boyer's baseball career as a major league pitcher was ending, he still had a long baseball career ahead of him.

11

1950S BONUS BABY
(Clete)

Cletis Boyer was a different cat than most of his brothers. The Boyer boys were basically conservative, low-key, stay-at-home types. Clete was by comparison the wild man of the family, an outgoing jokester who loved to drink and be the life of the party. Several of the others seemed to have farmers' blood in them, early to bed and early to rise. Clocks were only an inconvenience for Clete Boyer's late-night habits.

Yet he also had baseball on his mind—and baseball goals—as much as the others did. Cloyd, Wayne, Ken and Lynn were older brothers. Clete was fifth in line among the boys. He was born February 9, 1937. All of the Boyer brothers were good athletes and all seven were good enough to sign professional baseball contracts. But Clete was a better all-around athlete than any of them except Ken.

Clete Boyer was not as stocky, as firmly muscled, as Ken and he could not hit for power the way Ken could. But he was vastly talented and, of the three Boyer brothers who reached the majors, he made it faster, making his big-league debut at just 18 with the Kansas City Athletics in 1955, the same year he graduated high school in Alba.

Clete also received a $35,000 bonus to sign his pro contract, much higher than Cloyd nine years earlier, higher than Ken, and higher than the other brothers who were closer to his age. The New York Yankees wanted Clete, but were committed to other bonus babies. It was the same situation with the Cardinals, who had signed all of the older Boyer brothers, but were committed to two other bonus babies that year and couldn't keep all of them on the roster.

Clete may have been fun-loving and tended to stay out at night in bars (taking in the night life with Billy Martin later in life), but he had the same value system as the other Boyers and was a caring individual in the minds of family members. And not just because he made them all laugh with either his escapades or his jokes.

"Clete and I were always very close," said Lenny Boyer, who was nine years younger. "Of course, Clete had a heart as big as the state of Texas. He would give you the shirt off his back. He was just that type of person. I got to do a lot of fishing with Clete. Clete was a really smart baseball man. I don't think a lot of people ever appreciated the fact of how good a baseball mind Clete had."

The two most prominent big leaguers in the family, Ken and Clete, ended up playing the same position in the majors as third basemen. Ken Boyer was viewed more as a salt-of-the-earth kind of guy while Clete was seen as someone who really wanted to enjoy his time on the road away from the ball park.

"Clete was a little more flamboyant, I'd say," Lenny Boyer said. "To put it kind of mildly, he was more flamboyant than Kenny. Kenny was more reserved. I think Clete could have managed in the big leagues had he really wanted to do that—if he had a mind to do that. I don't think he wanted to do it badly enough."

As a high school athlete, Clete Boyer was All-State in baseball and basketball. Brother Ron, who was seven years younger, couldn't get over the talent that the 6-foot-tall Clete displayed on the basketball court. "I always wondered why he didn't hit .400 in baseball the way he could hit a basket with a basketball," Ron Boyer said. "He was 'Dead Eye Dick.' He hardly ever missed a free throw, though I don't know if his field-goal percentage was that high because he liked to gun it. I don't know whether he was a shooter or a gunner because he knew how to shoot."

One thing all of those athletic Boyer brothers had in common was the ability to field. They all wielded good gloves, but both Ken and Clete were exceptional infielders in the majors. Practice and hard work were involved, but the basic skills were present, too. "Some things you don't have to be taught as much as other things," Ron Boyer said. "Some things maybe you learn by watching. As far as the fundamentals go, I think we all knew them. Clete, me, Lenny, and of course Kenton, we were all good at fielding."

Clete hit the big leagues at a young age, but when he got married and had his first children, he still maintained a home in Alba. It made him more accessible to the public, and his high school feats took longer to fade. Ron remembers his nieces Valerie and Stephanie as darling girls. "They were always my favorites," he said, "the first two he had. They lived in Alba over near the Methodist Church right near Main Street."

When Clete and Ken came home it was a big deal to the younger brothers. Clete and Ken would go out to the local baseball field they used to play on with a bunch of baseballs and practice hitting. Ron and Lenny chased down the swats in the outfield, gathering up the balls. They also went hunting together. That was a big off-season activity when the weather wasn't too severe. According to Ron,

They'd have three or four dozen baseballs. Guess who got to take batting practice and guess who got to shag balls? Me and Lenny did a lot of ball shagging when they took a couple of hours of batting practice until most of the balls went over the fence. We did a lot of squirrel hunting, too, and rabbit hunting. We'd take a dog. Cloyd and Clete were also big quail hunters. There was a lot of quail around. Cloyd and Len used to do a lot of quail hunting together. Clete, when he was home, would go out and shoot squirrels and rabbits to have a good time, but also put a little meat in the pot. There's nothing better than a good rabbit with biscuits and gravy for breakfast.

The price of signing talented ball players had gone up by the time Clete graduated from high school in 1955, and there were some off-beat rules in place affecting bonus babies. The worst rule was that if a player signed for a certain amount he had to be kept on the major league team's roster for two years. That harmed the development of numerous players before the rule was dispatched. However, Clete Boyer fell into that category when he received his $35,000 bonus from Kansas City. That put him on the Athletics roster.

The 1955 season was Cloyd Boyer's last in the big leagues, his career cut short by injury, but he was able to spend it as a teammate of his brother, Clete. The age difference, from 27 to 18, was significant enough that Cloyd barely spent much time with Clete at their home in Missouri when they were growing up. Clete was a third-grader when Cloyd graduated from high school. Then Cloyd spent a considerable amount of his year playing baseball in another city.

So it was a gift from the baseball gods when Cloyd and Clete overlapped in Kansas City and spent a season together. According to Cloyd,

Clete and I were together in Kansas City. They had to keep him for two years so we roomed together. He was just a kid. He was young, but I thought he could play. I thought he was going to be good. I think he was one of the best-fielding third basemen there ever was. He had such good instincts. He was so quick, it was unbelievable. Nobody will ever be able to convince me that he wasn't the best fielding third baseman of all time. Brooks Robinson even said that. Brooks Robinson said Clete was the best defensive player.

Once he matured and settled in at third base in his big-league career, Clete was called "The Vacuum Cleaner" by some for his uncanny talent in scooping up ground balls or any other type of hit that came near him. Clete Boyer was so skilled that he made impossible plays appear almost routine. He dove for the ball and threw runners out at first base while lying down or on his knees, exhibitions of fielding that left close watchers goggle-eyed, even when they were with the same team and saw him play every day.

"He was able to do that because he had tremendous arm power," said long-time Yankees coach Frank Crosetti, who himself was a former left-side infielder for that team, sometimes at shortstop and sometimes third base. Crosetti had seen all Yankees third basemen for more than 30 years and considered Boyer to be the best at that position.

> He not only threw hard when he was down, but he threw strikes. I've never seen a man field that way. His glove seemed to be a separate living thing. There would have been times that I would have bet anything that the ball was going to be at least a double, and I was wondering if even the outfielders could get to it. Then he'd have it in his glove. I swear he used magic. What can't he do?[1]

Whether the glove was a living thing as Crosetti said, or simply an extension of his hand as others imagined, Boyer excelled in knocking down and spoiling base hits.

Compared to Ken and Cloyd, Clete was more slightly built. He was listed at 165 pounds during his playing days. He was agile and light on his feet and initially he was baby-faced since he was so young compared to many of his Kansas City teammates. Clete finished high school, signed a contract, and reported to Kansas City. Although it was fun for Cloyd to be a fellow Athletic with his younger brother, Clete's arrival did not come at a particularly good time for the older Boyer.

Cloyd had begun the season 5–1 and then went into a tailspin as his arm failed him. Clete did not report to the Athletics until his brother had banked all of his wins for the year. Cloyd's slow demise began just when Clete showed up. "I had started off doing so well and then I was so bad after that," Cloyd said. "I couldn't get anybody out and it was embarrassing for me, and for me to have Clete watch me. My five wins were over. I know I had to embarrass him for how much I struggled the rest of the year."

The two Boyers led different lifestyles, as well. Cloyd was married with children and Clete went out at night with his teammates. "I didn't run around with him," Cloyd said. "He was excited to be there. He was still like a high school kid."

By nature Cloyd was a fairly calm man who could step back and view a situation and assess it. He didn't get rattled by much. Clete was more excitable as an individual, but in his own way Clete could also avoid getting rattled by a tense, pressurized situation on the field. Maybe it ran in the family, at least where baseball was concerned. Clete was confident, if not cocky. Cloyd was around to dispense brotherly advice, if necessary, but Clete didn't always approach game days with his ear turned to big brother. According to Cloyd,

> The only thing I ever said to my brothers was, "Play as hard as you can and don't worry about the outcome." My attitude about everything in life was that as long as you gave it everything you've got, that's all you could do. If I cut wood, I'd go as hard as I could until I ran out of gas. In sports, I played hard. I got in shape. I ran. I did a lot of whatever I had to do. When I was playing, I played as hard as I could play.

The Athletics were going nowhere that season. They were a weak team. If Kansas City had been better, had been in the thick of the pennant race, Clete Boyer might never have gotten off the bench. Because the team was mired in mediocrity, he got periodic chances to play. Still, he appeared in only 47 games during the 1955 season and accumulated just 83 plate appearances. Boyer's .241 average included zero home runs and just six runs batted in. Yet just being on the same club was a bit of a treat for Cloyd. Being so much older than Clete, he had rarely seen him play any baseball.

"I got a thrill just watching him play because he'd make some of the damnedest plays," Cloyd said. "Of course, he didn't hit much. Once in a while he'd get a hit or two, and later he got to the point where he was a pretty good hitter, but his first year or two right out of high school, he didn't hit."

It was apparent immediately, though, that Clete had big-league fielding capability. Cloyd never stopped raving about Clete's instincts in the field, the way he positioned himself, the way he played hard bounders, yet always seemed ready for the line shot. "He got such a quick jump on balls," Cloyd said. "He had the best instincts. He'd dive and catch balls clear over on the third-base line, get up and throw out the runner. He was real quick and he had a great arm. And it was accurate."

The way Cloyd described that season with Kansas City, sharing a team with Clete, he comes off sounding more like a dad than a brother. Those protective instincts were probably there, too, because of the age gap. Cloyd didn't let on to Clete all of the time just what a thrill it was for him to watch a little brother make it into the majors, and be up close and present when he took the field, too. "It was a thrill for me," Cloyd said. "But every time he went onto the field to play I'd get a little nervous. You don't want to say anything, but I didn't want to see him make an error, make a mistake, or cost anybody the game."

The summer of 1955 was unique for the Boyers because it was the only year that all three brothers who reached the majors played in the majors. Ken broke in with St. Louis that year after spending four years in the minors. Clete broke in with Kansas City that year, fresh from high school. And Cloyd was making his last major league stand with the Athletics.

12

TRYING IT
ON THE MOUND
(Ken)

K enton Boyer, superb high school football player and star high school basketball player, competed in those sports for fun. He played baseball because he loved it and wanted to make a career out of it. He was the most powerfully built and athletic of the seven brothers.

What he never imagined was that the St. Louis Cardinals would try to make a pitcher out of him based on his strong infield arm. At first he didn't mind because he was looking to make the majors any way he could. But after a few trials and tribulations in the minors, both he and the organization recognized after all that he was better suited to being an infielder, where he had started. According to brother Lenny Boyer,

> Kenny was strong. His arm was so strong they started him out pitching. I think they got that idea because Cloyd was a pitcher. Nobody really lifted weights in those days, but Kenny was naturally strong. A lot of guys he went to school with used to talk about it. He was built strong. That's why he also played football and basketball so well. Eventually, the Cardinals saw that he was going to make it as a hitter.

There were mixed feelings about Ken Boyer within the hierarchy of the Cardinals. The fact that Cloyd was a pitcher swayed some feelings when scouts studied Ken's arm. But he was a good hitter when given the chance. George Kissell, who spent 69 years in the Cardinals' organization, most of it in the minors but with some coaching in the majors, thought Joe Mathis, the farm director, was the one who started to ease Ken into a role as a third baseman as early as 1950 when he was pitching in Hamilton, New York. Hamilton was in the PONY League, or the Pennsylvania-Ohio-New York League.

Boyer made some erratic starts as a pitcher, going 11–9 in 33 starts in the 1949-50 season, but when the team cut a third baseman he was assigned to cover that territory temporarily until a new player could arrive to handle the spot. The Cardinals seemed torn about where his future lay, and he wasn't too sure about it either. Boyer had shown some serious power as a pinch-hitter in between his stints as a pitcher, and in the spring of 1951, when Ken was being assigned to Omaha, Mathis instructed Kissell to work with Boyer and make that guy a third baseman.

"You mean Boyer?" Kissell asked. "One thing about Boyer, Joe, he's got the four pluses. He can run, he can field, and he can throw. I have only seen him hit in spring training, but the third baseman I have is hitting .320." But Mathis insisted that Boyer go with Kissell to Omaha and emerge as a third baseman.[1]

Kissell managed the Omaha club in the Class A Western League in 1951. Intriguingly, Kissell's second baseman that season was Earl Weaver. Weaver never advanced very far as a player, but he did become a Hall of Fame manager with the Baltimore Orioles. And before too long Ken Boyer, who batted .306 that year, was an excellent prospect as a third baseman. Boyer and Weaver were voted the fans' most popular players that summer. "The first month he hit everything to right field," Kissell said. "The second month he hit it to right-center. The third month he hit to left-center. And the fourth month he hit it in the bleachers. That was the start of the career of Ken Boyer."[2]

From 1951 through 1954, Ken Boyer fought his way through the minors in the Cardinals chain. Soon enough the idea of him becoming a pitcher was forgotten and he remained a third baseman. According to Lenny Boyer,

> He may have made it as a pitcher. He had a good arm, but he could play every day as a hitter, as an outfielder, as a third baseman, which he obviously became. He played some outfield, but third base was his strong suit. He had great reflexes, a great ability to make judgments in game situations, something you don't see too often in the majors now. I'm amazed at some of the basic, fundamental mistakes guys make that I don't think any of my brothers would have made. I don't think they ever did. They all had such a basic, fundamental knowledge of the game and how to play it and how to approach it. I don't remember Cloyd, Kenny or Clete making dumb mistakes. I guess growing up in baseball and playing it your whole life it's just ingrained into you.

Ken had a stopover with the Rochester Red Wings in 1949 when Cloyd was pitching for them and Johnny Keane was managing. He was assigned to Rochester, but the Red Wings were fighting for the International League pennant and didn't make much use of him. He was impatient to get on the field, but the line-up was set, the team was trying to win, and even Cloyd told him he was probably going to have to wait his turn. "They'll find a spot for you," Cloyd said. "We're in the middle of the season. As soon as there is a spot on some roster, they'll send you out."[3] In other words, don't count on hanging around in AAA right away.

But Ken did hang around for a while. He was getting bored with inactivity and one day Keane, sensing that, decided to put him to a test. He told Ken to get his glove, get out in the field, and handle some grounders that he hit him. "Can't have you getting fat sitting on the bench all day," Keane said.[4]

Ken took batting practice with the subs and sat on the bench during games, studying Keane's strategy. Like his brother Cloyd, he developed a fondness for the manager. Finally, after some time had passed, Keane summoned Ken into his office to give him his orders. He was being sent to the Lebanon, Missouri, team. "You're being sent to the Lebanon club tonight, where you'll have a chance to play," Keane told him. "By the way, I told the front office that you're a terrific prospect. I told them you can do anything. Don't make a liar out of me."[5]

In Boyer's first outing on the mound, he was so wild it felt as if he walked everyone he faced. His new manager, Hal Contini, put him in center field between starts. He ended up being eased out of the pitching racket. He showed well running the bases and fielding, and began hitting. It took a while, but the Cardinals came to see Boyer as a full-time position player. However, that season at Lebanon it was almost like high school all over again. He finished 5–1 pitching and batted .455.

Actually, the only reason that Ken Boyer did not make faster progress through the minors for the Cardinals was because he served in the United States Army and missed the 1952 and 1953 seasons. He spent some time assigned to Fort Bliss in Texas, and while in the Army he also met a young woman who became his wife, Kathleen Oliver. After serving in Germany, Boyer was sent back to the States and discharged. By then he was also the father of a baby girl, Susie.

Ken got out of the Army in October 1953, and in January he went to the Cardinals' minor-league complex in Florida. That's where Cloyd worked with him to regain his hitting touch.

The two years of missed time in the Army were costly to Boyer. It not only held him back in the minors, it meant he had to unlearn bad habits and make up for the lost time. When he was still in the Texas League with Houston in 1954, Boyer actually heard some low-key taunts from a catcher or two encouraging a pitcher. He was being set up as an easy mark, as someone who pulled everything, took big swings and missed balls that were out of the strike zone. He had to train himself to hold back, pick his spots, and hit the ball where it was pitched.

"You've got to learn to lay off that bad outside pitch," Houston manager Dixie Walker told Boyer. "Until you do, the pitchers will keep taking advantage of you. They tease you by throwing pitches on the outside— just far enough outside to keep away from your power. Then, when they know they have you leaning into the plate, they jam you with a tight, inside pitch."[6]

Dixie Walker did know hitting. He was a .306 lifetime batter during his major league career. Once Boyer learned not to repeat the mistake, once he adapted, he was on his way. Another thing that sped along Boyer's improvement after his two-year hiatus was being sent to Cuba to play winter ball. This was the heyday of baseball in Havana, before Fidel Castro's revolution turned the country upside-down and halted the regular flow of top Cuban talent to the majors.

Winter ball was for good players who wanted to make an extra buck, Latino players who wanted to show off their skills in front of the home folks, and young players like Ken Boyer who could benefit from additional experience. The Cardinals and Ken wanted to fill the hole in his resume resulting from his military stint. Boyer was reluctant to leave his young family behind in the United States for the two-month season, especially after his long separation during Army service, but he knew reporting to Havana was the best move for his career.

It could have been and it should have been, but Boyer had the misfortune to be struck in the head by a pitched ball in Cuba. It was a frightening experience. A high, inside fastball struck him behind the left ear. He dropped to the ground in a heap and lay still in the batter's box as emergency help was summoned.

This was not a brush-it-off hit-by pitch by any means. Boyer was rushed to the hospital where he lay unconscious and didn't come around for five days. The concussive hit was violent and knocked Boyer cold. Even when he awoke he suffered dizzy spells sitting up in bed. Once he stood up from his bed and passed out, falling over. Even ten days after his release from medical treatment, when Boyer resumed light workouts he suffered a blackout after looking up at the sky to field a pop-up. Boyer's career could well have been wrecked.

The winter season that could have been instead turned into an uneasy off-season of recovery. Instead of gaining much-needed playing time, Boyer suffered an injury setback that could have prevented him from ascending to the major-league club at all. From the moment he appeared at spring training in 1955, manager Eddie Stanky took him aside and assured him he was going north with the big club and that he was going to be his full-time third baseman that season. Stanky proclaimed the rookie his starter at the hot corner, installed him at third, and left him there. Boyer rewarded his faith.

Stanky's thoughtful approach—one which he did not have to make—put Boyer at ease, helped him make the transition, and above all, was proven correct when the player spent a healthy year at third and made his mark as a rookie on the rise. Boyer had a fine year. It was not quite good enough to earn National League "rookie of the year" honors—that award went to his friend and Cardinals teammate, outfielder Bill Virdon. But his performance heralded the start of a long and illustrious career in the big leagues.

That season Ken Boyer turned 24 and played in 147 games. His batting average was an okay .264, but he hit 18 home runs, drove in 62 runs, stole 22 bases and once installed there claimed possession of the third baseman's job for more than a decade. Eventually he became the Cardinals' captain on a team that featured Future Hall of Famers Stan Musial, Red Schoendienst and Bob Gibson.

"Kenny was a leader," Lenny Boyer said. "I think he was a leader from the time he was born. It was just in his soul to be a leader and that's the kind of person he was. I always looked up to him tremendously. He never had a bad word to say. He was just a class act. When he said something, you listened to him."

It was no surprise to any of the other Boyer brothers that Ken was chosen as the captain of the Cardinals. If they sailed ships, he would have been a captain of them. If it was another endeavor in life, he would have been the group leader. That's how they felt about Ken. According to Lenny Boyer,

> If somebody came up from the minors, a rookie, and needed advice, or needed a little money, needed help with anything, they always went to Kenny. Mike Shannon (a Ken Boyer teammate) talks about it a lot. That's the type of person Kenny was. I wasn't around him growing up because I was younger, but for the people that I know that knew him growing up, he was the go-to guy. Everybody looked up to him. He was really discreet about his personal life. He wasn't really flamboyant. He may have had some issues in his personal life, but he kept them quiet. He addressed them himself. I talked to people in the organization about him who played ball with him. Everybody described him the same way, as someone who was a class guy with a lot of charisma. I think that's why he became captain.

As evidenced by Ken's conversation with Cloyd when they took off for their own private hitting sessions, Ken Boyer did not lack a work ethic. He brought a mature approach to his baseball, wanted to keep improving, was willing to put the time and effort necessary into it to make it to the majors, and became an All-Star once he reached the majors.

13

GIVING IT A SHOT
(Ron)

During the years Clete spent playing for Kansas City, 1955–1957, he made frequent trips home to Missouri to spend time with the family. "When he was in town we always had a big family gathering," Lynn Boyer said. "One time Clete left 50-some tickets for a game. We had a big family gathering at our house and then went to the ball park. He expected me to go to downtown Kansas City and get him and bring him to the house and eat dinner. Then I took him to the ball park and after the game brought him back to the hotel. It was a hotel when he was playing for the Yankees later. That was always the ritual when he came to the house."

With 14 children in the family there was a large age spread between kids. Cloyd's major league playing days ended before some of his brothers were out of elementary school. Ron was born in 1944 and Lenny was born in 1946. They really were just kids by the time Cloyd's days as a big-league pitcher ended. They were from a whole other generation.

Ron was 5-foot-10 and weighed 175 pounds. He was much younger than the big-league Boyers, but he was anxious to follow in their footsteps on a path to the majors. He was only 17 when he graduated from high school and made the journey from Alba, Missouri, to Harlan, Kentucky, to play in the Class D Appalachian League in 1962.

In 37 games, Ron batted just .151. He was in over his head at such a young age, his batting stroke not quite ready for pro ball. Unlike most of his older brothers, Ron was not scooped up by the Cardinals, but was property of the New York Yankees. Ron may have been considerably younger than the oldest boys in the clan, but their success at baseball, their high-profile careers in baseball, made him want to do the exact same thing when he was growing up.

They influenced me quite a bit. Baseball was kind of my life growing up. Sports, baseball and basketball, was kind of what I lived for, basically. Cloyd was always my hero, the one I looked up to and all. Then Kenton came along, and the thing of it is that in our family we're kind of spread out age-wise and chronologically, and I don't remember seeing Cloyd, Wayne and Kenton playing. Even Cletis is only seven years older than me, but that's quite a bit when he's like a senior in high school and I'm in the fifth grade or so. So you didn't really see these guys playing. Kenton is 13 years older than me. When he got out of high school I was like five years old.

Much later, when Ron was trying to fight his way into the big leagues, Cloyd was coaching, and Clete was holding down third base for the Yankees, so they were all working for New York at once and posed for a picture together in Yankees duds in spring training.

Ron Boyer was just a little kid, playing with his toys, just getting interested in the sport of baseball by the time the three oldest Boyers were pursuing careers. They visited and he knew them, but didn't play baseball with them and he didn't see them perform for the high school team, the Alba Aces, or their minor-league teams. But as he grew and baseball also captured his fancy, Ron became more impressed with their accomplishments, and all of the older brothers' achievements in baseball made him wonder if he had the same kind of talent in him.

They were making names for themselves in the sports world and they were pretty darned good. You've got three brothers playing at the major league level so you know there's something there. When you talk about thoroughbred horses and blood lines, maybe that's why a major league team took a chance on me. I was a Boyer, so maybe something was there. At least they knew my name because of my brothers. You get a little bitty town like Alba and all these brothers sign pro baseball contracts, so you've got to think a team would take a chance on another brother. There might be something there.

There was enough there in Ron Boyer's baseball performances to intrigue scouts. His childhood, though separated by so many years from Cloyd's, was almost identical. There was a ball field nearby and Ron and his friends used it. In the summer when it was hot, they could go swimming.

We lived across the street from the baseball diamond. So we spent part of our summer days there, the neighborhood kids and the kids from out in the country. We'd be over there playing ball and we played for three or four hours. Then we went down to the cave, an old strip mining pit, and spent a few hours there swimming. There wasn't much else to do in Alba. The baseball diamond was surrounded by corn fields. When I was a kid and the older boys were playing they would give you a nickel if you went and got back a foul ball. I remember chasing foul balls out there.

Unlike the era when Cloyd and the older brothers grew up, organized baseball for young people was proliferating during Ron's youth. Not only was there Little League, but the Ban Johnson League allowed slightly older boys to keep competing on organized teams. Ban Johnson was the founder of the American League in 1901 and his name was affixed to the organization for boys.

> That was a pretty good brand of baseball. I remember going over and watching those guys play. You had guys coming from all around. I remember some players became local legends. It was a pretty good field for a small town. It even had lights. We chased foul balls at night, under the lights, too. The ground was bare in between the corn, and it's black, so you could see the white balls. They were pretty easy to find.

In high school Ron almost always played third base, but dabbled a little at shortstop. "I never did get into pitching, which most of my older brothers tried," Ron said. "Even Kenton was a pitcher when he signed. He was such a great athlete. He could do it all. But I always played third base. I played a little bit of short and a couple of games at second base in the minors, but basically I was always a third baseman."

There was enough Boyer history in pro ball that major league teams were duty-bound to check out the next brother in line. Once that had been a St. Louis Cardinals monopoly, but no longer. Ron was just ahead of the imposition of a big-league draft, and scouts still roamed the hinterlands on the lookout for talent. It was the Yankees who were interested, perhaps by then because Clete Boyer anchored third base for them.

If a scout was sketching out some notes on a pad of paper, Ron figured that he was most likely to compare him to Clete among the other brothers, that if he had a distinct strength it was in the fielding game.

> I think I was more on the lines of Cletis. My game was more defensive than offensive. Of course, in high school I had some pretty good stats, but when you get into pro ball and you face good pitchers every day, it's not the same. Tom Greenwade, the same scout that signed Mickey Mantle, spotted me. And Cloyd was working in the Yankee organization by then. When they signed me he was actually at the house.

Some other teams were showing interest, but Ron did not entertain offers from other teams. Once the Yankees came after him, with Cloyd in tow, and Clete manning third base, he made his allegiance clear. "I signed real quick with the Yankees. Cletis was playing third base for the Yankees and I don't know if that helped me sign with them. Detroit was interested in me. Philadelphia was, too. The main team for me was the Cardinals.

They were looking at me. Runt Marr, who signed the older boys, was scouting for Kansas City at the time and he was interested."

Marr, the same scout that had signed Cloyd years earlier and who Cloyd said was practically a member of the Boyer family, came to Alba to woo Ron. He also provided a memorable road trip. "He took me to Kansas City," Ron said. "He drove me in his big Cadillac. I sat in the front seat and his wife sat in the back. I think Runt had to sit on a pillow to see over the steering wheel, he was so short. The Cadillac ride was pretty cool."

Ron was supposed to work out for the Yankees around the same time, but the session was rained out. The Yankees signed him anyway, coming up with a $25,000 bonus. That was decent money at the time and a barrelful more money than Cloyd got to sign in the 1940s. The bonus was actually spread out over three years, but Ron was happy with his payday.

> Clete got more and I think Lenny got more, but I was satisfied with that. I thought that was pretty good for me. I always wondered if I could have got more money if I had talked more to some of those teams before I signed. Some of them seemed surprised that I had already signed when they got back to me. I wanted to sign with either the Yankees or the Cardinals. The Cardinals were always our team in Southwest Missouri. But you know, the Yankees were the Yankees. The New York Yankees. They were winning all of the time. So that's what I did.

The Appalachian League, Ron Boyer's first stop, was a rookie league, and the Yankees shared the team with the Chicago White Sox. That meant both teams sent fledgling prospects to Kentucky. "The White Sox sent Denny McLain there, so I batted against him in some intra-squad games," Ron said. "I don't think he was even there by the time the season started. They sent him to Iowa or someplace."

Ron Boyer's memory let him down on that score. McLain, who in 1968 became the only major league pitcher to record 30 (31–6) wins since 1934, was 18 years old that summer, fresh out of Mount Carmel High School in the Chicago area. In his first start for the Harlan Smokies he pitched a no-hitter, striking out 16 batters. In his next start for Harlan, McLain gave up just two unearned runs (and lost) and struck out 16 men again. Then he departed the Appalachian League for the Midwest League. Even before McLain made his mark quickly with those outings, Ron Boyer knew that McLain could become a special pitcher. "He made my hand sting a little bit if I was lucky enough to make contact," Boyer said.

Boyer's eyes stung a little bit, too, in Harlan, playing for the Smokies.

> It was smoky, too. It was right in the middle of coal country and there was a lot of coal dust blowing around. It was a terrible year for me. It was a combi-

nation of everything. I didn't hit. I didn't play that much. Because there were two teams, the Yankees and White Sox, combining their players, you got to play about every other game. That's how I ended up playing a little second base, just to get into games.

Ron Boyer didn't mind when that season ended, but he was refreshed and hoping for a better situation and a better performance when he reported to Class A Shelby in the Western Carolinas League for the 1963 season. However, at 18 he was still adjusting to the way things were done in the pros. Although Boyer appeared in 94 games, he batted just .181. "That was another tough year," Boyer said. "There was a lot of traveling."

The reality was that at his young age with minimal experience, Ron Boyer wasn't ready for the pros quite yet. It took until 1964, a second season at Shelby, for him to begin to blossom. He batted .251 in 127 games, stole 21 bases, hit seven home runs and drove in 56 runs. He was a whole new ball player.

"I progressed," Ron said. "I batted leadoff quite a bit and I had a few stolen bases. Overall, I just made more progress offensively and defensively, learning the game a little bit more."

The second season in Shelby was critical for Boyer's development. If he hadn't shown signs of improvement, his pro career may have ended right there. Instead, he earned a promotion within the Yankees' system. The simple move to Greensboro, within the same state of North Carolina, was a big one, even if the Carolina League was still Class A. It was a better league. A maturing Boyer, 20 in 1965, hit .255 in 140 games. He was a full-time player.

> That was a ball. That was pretty cool really. I played with some guys like Fritz Peterson and Bobby Murcer, guys with a lot of talent who went on to play for the Yankees. Thinking things over, back then they only had a manager with a minor league team and now minor league players have a bigger advantage. All of the teams have two or three coaches in addition to the manager. As far as working with you, that's a lot better and it helps you.

Greensboro saw the organization's roving minor-league pitching coach once in a while—it happened to be Cloyd Boyer that year—and the roving minor-league hitting coach—Wally Moses—about every month and a half.

> Nowadays you have the coaches who are there every day and work with the players every day. It's a huge advantage. Now there are a lot more college kids coming out with more experience. In my day it was a lot of high school kids, though I still think there are high school kids who get drafted high. But the teams realize they have a lot invested in these players and they work with

them more. I remember much later, when the Yankees drafted Drew
Henson, the athlete who was both a football and baseball player, and sent
him to Columbus. They hired Clete as a coach just to go there and work
with him.

Cloyd Boyer was on the same kind of schedule rotation as Wally
Moses was, only for pitchers. That meant Cloyd came to Greensboro for
two to ten days every five or six weeks and worked with the young pitchers.
He never worked with Ron, but they did spend time together away from
the park that season in North Carolina.

> Mainly just going out and having supper together after the game or some-
> thing like that. There wasn't a whole lot of business discussed when we were
> together like that. But I do think Cloyd had some influence with the front
> office and he might have saved my job a year or two when I wasn't hitting.
> The Yankees had some money invested in me with that $25,000 bonus. I was
> very young, so I didn't think they were going to cut me loose when I was 18
> or 19. But I had to improve or they would cut me.

After his solid year at Greensboro, Ron Boyer was elevated one notch
higher on the ladder by being assigned to Class AA ball in Columbus,
Georgia, in 1966 to play for the Columbus Confederate Yankees, an oxy-
moron if there ever was one.

"That was the year I thought I was making progress," Boyer said. "I
got to AA and I kind of hit a stone wall. The Vietnam War was going on
and I knew I was going to get drafted. I was 100 percent sure that I would
be drafted. So I went and joined the National Guard."

That entailed an obligation of drills on Mondays, some weekend
drills, and a two-week summer camp in the middle of the baseball season.
Boyer's hitting rhythm, his groove in the sport, was constantly interrupted.
He was still able to play ball instead of fighting in a war in Southeast Asia,
but the schedule played havoc with his game.

> I think it impeded my progress. That was a six-year deal. I think it had a big
> impact on me, missing two weeks of play every summer. Maybe that's an
> excuse. I don't know, but that was going on the rest of my career, playing ball,
> going home, going with the National Guard. I wondered if I should have
> taken my chances about getting drafted. I knew guys who were drafted, spent
> two years in the Army, came back to baseball, and were successful. But I
> didn't want to go to Vietnam. I was 20 years old and the military issue came
> up at the exact time I was starting to improve on the field.

Due to military obligations, the 1967 season was almost a write-off
for Boyer. "I went to spring training and I got the call for my basic training,"
he said. "I went in and actually missed most of the 1967 season. I was

activated for 16 or 17 weeks and when I got out there were maybe three weeks left in the season."

Boyer played two games for Binghamton in the Class AA Eastern League and went zero-for-two at the plate. That's it. He also was given a boost by being sent to Syracuse, a AAA team in the International League, for 23 games. He batted only .161 in that sort-of tryout for 1968.

They needed somebody up there to play third base, to finish that season, so I finished out the last few weeks of the season in Syracuse. That was my big AAA claim to fame. Cletis was also playing at Syracuse and we played a game against Jacksonville. Tug McGraw, who later was famous as a relief pitcher with the Mets and the Phillies, pitched for Jacksonville and he pitched a one-hitter. He was a starter in the minors. I got the only hit off of him. It was a base hit up the middle. Years later he and Cletis ran into each other and they talked about that game. Tug said he pitched a one-hitter and I was the one who got the hit. He always remembered that hit. Tug probably said if I hadn't got the hit to spoil his no-hitter he would have been in the big leagues earlier.

While Ron collected a few baseball memories from his brief stay with Syracuse, overall 1967 was a frustrating year for him. No matter where he suited up, he had difficulty hitting. Perhaps if he had hit better at the tail end of 1967, he would have been assigned to Syracuse for the entire 1968 season instead of being returned to Binghamton. The two upstate New York cities were only 73 miles apart, but much farther apart on the organizational chart. A player in Binghamton was still fighting his way through the minors. A player at Syracuse was only a short hop from the majors.

The one redeeming feature of Ron Boyer's 1968 season in Binghamton was that his manager was Cloyd Boyer, his older brother, who was moving up the coaching and managing ranks to earn his own return to the big leagues by traveling a different road than he had as a player.

During that stretch the Binghamton team faced the Cleveland Indians' farm club from Waterbury, Connecticut, in an exhibition prior to a Yankees-Indians game. Cloyd was coaching third base when Ron came to bat and smashed a ball hard down the left-field line. It was soaring high enough to leave Yankee Stadium. The only question was whether it would stay fair. Cloyd leaned and leaned, as if he could will the ball fair through body English. In the end the shot was ruled foul. "If that home run went out the Yankees would have brought Ronnie right up," Cloyd said. "Ronnie missed a home run by that much, by inches."

That day Steve Kline, also on his way to the majors, pitched. Luis Tiant pitched for the Indians in the main event. Forevermore when Ron Boyer told baseball stories he told the one about the time he hit one out of Yankee Stadium foul. A friend eventually told him, "Don't tell them it was foul. Just tell them you hit one out of Yankee Stadium."

It wasn't a bad idea at all. Still, at that point in his baseball life, Ron Boyer was hoping he would yet get the call to play for the Yankees and he would have another opportunity to hit a fair ball out of Yankee Stadium. But that wasn't meant to be. That season Boyer knocked the ball out of minor league parks only twice, and he finished his 72-game stay with Binghamton with a .183 average. The handwriting was on the wall foretelling the end of Boyer's career. He had just never hit for a significant average with any of his minor-league clubs.

One of the notable aspects of the season was teaming with up-and-coming catcher Thurman Munson, the Yankees' No. 1 draft pick and the fourth overall pick in the 1968 amateur draft.

"Thurman rode into town in his orange Corvette," Ron said, evidence of where he had spent some of his bonus money. "I roomed with him and a guy named Dennis Cook who was a catcher. Thurman was an inspiration. I'll tell you what, he was a competitor. A couple of weeks after Thurman got to Binghamton and he was hitting over .400, the Yankees' front office asked Cloyd where he thought Thurman should be playing. Cloyd said, 'Well, do you want the truth?' And they said they did. 'Well, Yankee Stadium is where he should be playing.' There wasn't any doubt about it. I think they actually took him up there at the end of that year."

Cloyd Boyer said the Yankees were reluctant to bring young players to the majors during that period. Munson, at 22, made a 26-game cameo for the Yankees at the end of the 1969 season and he became the American League's "Rookie of the Year" in 1970. Before Munson died tragically at 32 in a plane crash, he became a seven-time All-Star for the Yankees and won a Most Valuable Player Award. He was very possibly on his way to the Hall of Fame.

So Ron Boyer spent most of the 1968 season playing for his brother Cloyd. Although he did not play as well as he wanted to, he remembered it being a unique experience. "Was it an extra challenge, or not?" Ron said. "I don't know. Maybe. I wouldn't say it was any more pressure. It was kind of a fun deal. One of his sons, Jimmy, my nephew, was our bat boy. Maybe it was just a bad team. We had ups and downs, but overall I got my chance and the opportunity to play and do what I wanted to do, play professional baseball."

Ron Boyer's last chance came in 1969. He was sent to the Manchester (New Hampshire) Yankees in the Eastern League, again in AA. The manager was Jerry Walker, the one-time Baltimore Orioles pitcher. "It was still the Yankees' organization," Boyer said. "I never did go to any other organization. Nobody else wanted me. By then they'd seen enough of my act."

If that sounds cynical, it was a fact that Boyer had not hit well in most of his stops and was running out of opportunities. "Word was out on him," Cloyd Boyer said.

As the season progressed, Ron Boyer appeared in 26 games with 94 plate appearances, and he was again batting under .200, stuck on .192. The day came when Walker summoned Boyer and informed him that the Yankees were letting him go.

> He had to give me the news that I was released. The circumstances were that I wasn't playing every day and I wasn't hitting and I wasn't doing anything. I had been around for eight years and I wasn't progressing. I was still in AA. There's always somebody looking over your shoulder. I played with some guys that made it to the bigs and had real illustrious careers.

Thurman Munson was one of those guys. Ron Blomberg, the first designated hitter, was another. Pitchers Fritz Peterson, Steve Kline and George Culver were one-time teammates. Another teammate, from back in Shelby, was Mike Ferraro. Ferraro wasn't a big-time hitter, either, but he possessed a very good glove and did make it to the Show, playing parts of four years. However, he had a long coaching career and even briefly managed the Indians and the Kansas City Royals in the 1980s.

> In Shelby, in 1963, he was our shortstop and I was the third baseman. He was about as slow as molasses in the middle of the wintertime. They switched him. He converted to third base. There's a guy, he got a chance. He played a little bit. The Yankees brought him up when Cletis was still playing. Cletis told a story about him. One day Cletis had the day off and Ferraro was playing third. John Buzhardt was pitching for the White Sox and he buzzed old Ferraro with an inside pitch. I guess Ferraro turned pale as a ghost, but the pitch didn't hit him. It might have grazed his helmet. Cletis had to go in and play the rest of the game.

Ron Boyer was released in mid-season, but was unwilling to give up on his baseball career. He wrote letters to other teams seeking a job. He knew he had not shown the type of progress that teams wanted to see, but he also had his moments when he thought he was about to experience a breakthrough and take his game to the next level successfully.

Once, after a game in Greensboro when he hit a home run and a double, one of the Yankees' scouts, who had seen the effort, told Boyer he was looking good. "Every once in a while I showed a little spark," Ron said, "that I might be a prospect rather than a suspect. There were times. I never really gave up on the dream, but I never really did get over the hump."

Boyer played in 627 minor-league games and batted .215, with 28 career home runs and 127 runs batted in. He was not shocked when the Yankees dropped him, but he was bummed out.

> You can kind of see it coming if you're not playing every day. After you've played a few years and you're still in AA, you're just kind of waiting for it to happen although you're not looking forward to it. But it wasn't a surprise. That was my life's dream, to make it to the majors, and I always appreciated the opportunity that I did get to play professional ball. But after I got out of baseball I drifted for a while.

Ron Boyer took his rejection from the Yankees hard, and he took his rejection from baseball harder when no one responded positively to his job appeal in his letters.

Boyer went to work for a Coca-Cola distributor in nearby Joplin, Missouri, and drove a delivery truck. However, he had a serious accident and gave up that work, moving on to become an automobile salesman. He sold cars for 12 years. He worked as an insurance salesman and then spent more than ten years working at a dynamite plant in Missouri. When the plant closed, about 200 people lost their jobs. He spent the last nearly-dozen years of his working life employed by a roofing company and then retired.

If anything, during his years working near home in Missouri, Ron Boyer became an even bigger St. Louis Cardinals fan than he had been after becoming property of the Yankees. They were the team of his youth, and brothers Cloyd and Ken played for the Cards. Ron Boyer remains a huge baseball fan, and he watches every Cardinals game he can see.

14

FIGHTING TO HANG ON
(Cloyd)

When the 1955 season ended, Cloyd Boyer did not know that he had seen the last of the majors as a pitcher. He reported to the Kansas City Athletics' spring training in early 1956, focusing on making the big-league roster again. Only he had a lousy spring. "I didn't get anybody out, so they sent me to Sacramento," he said.

The Sacramento Solons were members of the Pacific Coast League, a AAA club one step below the majors. Sacramento finished 84–84 that season and Boyer did not have a bad year at all. His win-loss record was 10–9 and his earned run average was 3.95. Not fantastic, but for a guy who was supposed to be washed up, it was a hopeful year.

The day of Boyer's first start, manager Tommy Heath got sick enough that he could not attend the game. Boyer hardly knew him, but he started and he led the Solons to a 2–0 victory. After the game he visited the incapacitated Heath in his hotel room as a gesture of respect. "I said, 'I won that one for you,'" Boyer said. "We got to be pretty good friends. We had a bunch of guys on that club that were rounders and drinkers and rowdies. I was actually rooming with one."

That was pitcher Gene Bearden, who went 15–14. In 1948, Bearden came out of nowhere to win 20 games, sparking the Cleveland Indians to an American League pennant and a World Series championship. But after that 20–7 season, Bearden was never a big winner again and bounced around to a few other teams. In 1956 he was much like Boyer, trying to regain a spot in the big leagues. "The strange thing was that he and I pinch-hit a lot for that team," Boyer said. "One time I pinch-hit for Bearden and hit a grand slam to win the game, 4–3."

Boyer and Bearden were roommates on the road, but they did not keep the same hours. Boyer turned in early and Bearden went out on the town. The Solons did bed checks, with the coaches stopping by to knock on the door and make sure the players were in their rooms for curfew. One night a coach showed up asking for the other pitcher of the room.

"He said, 'Is Bearden in?'" Boyer said. Since it was obvious that Bearden was not there and no one thought he was hiding under the bed, Boyer said, "'No, he ain't in.' The coach said, 'Well, we're looking for him.' I thought, "Uh, oh, here we go.' He had been in trouble before. Later on that night Bearden came in. I guess they had found him. He got into a fight and was drinking. Him and Ferris Fain were big drinkers. Bearden had to pay a fine. Fain was another one who when he got a couple of beers in him he liked to fight."

Fain was a left-handed first baseman who won two batting titles for the Philadelphia Athletics and was selected to five All-Star teams in a nine-year career. But in 1956 he was out of the majors, scrapping to earn a promotion back to the bigs. Apparently the fight that cost Bearden his fine was not a one-on-one bout. Fain had also been involved, and when Boyer talked to Heath he learned that while Bearden was in his hotel bed perhaps nursing a hangover, Fain had other accommodations. "Fain got in trouble and he's in jail," Heath told Boyer. "He can't get out tonight. How about meeting me down in the lobby at 10 a.m. and we'll go get him out." Boyer joined the manager in retrieving Fain.

When they returned from the jail, Heath, Boyer and Fain were sitting around the hotel lobby and all of a sudden Fain stood up and bolted out of the building. A bit agog, Heath asked Boyer to follow Fain and see what he was up to.

> I said I didn't really want to, but I guess I can. Of course I found him in a bar down the street. At that time of day there was no one else there except some gal waiting tables. I went in and sat down in a corner where he couldn't see me, but I could hear him. He was ripping baseball up one side and down the other, just going on and on. Pretty soon he was sitting on a stool at the bar and some guy came in and sat down. Right away Fain wanted to fight him. He jumped up and doubled up his fists.
>
> I went over and got between them and said, "Ferris, if you've just got to hit somebody, go ahead and hit me and get your ass back to the hotel room." Well, he didn't do it and went back to the hotel and went back to bed. But then the manager told him, "Don't show up at the park tonight." He didn't come at first, but then he showed up in the eighth or ninth inning. Anyway, that was the kind of club we had that year.

For much of the season, although he was only playing on a .500 club, Boyer led the Pacific Coast League in earned run average. But the last two weeks of the season his arm went haywire again, he lost all his stuff and he got battered by the batters. It was discouraging.

> I kinda got racked pretty good there for three or four games. That's the way things went with me. It just seemed like I'd lose after I hurt my arm. I pitched several years with a sore arm. I kept thinking my arm was going to come back and I was going to get back to the big leagues. After that season in Sacramento we were so bad that they got rid of just about everybody that was making a pretty good salary. I was making $10,000, the same as I was making in Kansas City.

To the disgruntled independent owners, the ten grand salary made Boyer expendable, especially when he started the next campaign 1–4. Cloyd was still not ready to pack it in, so he accepted it when he was sold to the Indianapolis Indians in 1957. That began a four-and-a-half-year stay in Indianapolis with the American Association club. He didn't fare badly, especially in the beginning. That season he went 6–4 with a 3.70 earned run average, pitching mostly in relief, although he pitched with pain. Boyer shared main relief duties with George Spencer, who went 8–3 out of the pen. "I was owned outright by Indianapolis, but they were affiliated with the White Sox and Reds," Boyer said. "They were the Indians, but they didn't belong to the Indians."

The Indians were on their way to a 74–80 finish, not really going anywhere. At the end of the season the schedule was cluttered with doubleheaders, some of them make-up games. At one point Indianapolis was looking at five doubleheaders in six days, three at home and then two on the road in Wichita. Boyer pitched in both games of the first doubleheader, throwing seven innings in the second game. Then he pitched in a third game in a row, always on call from the bullpen.

A day off loomed in the schedule, and manager Andy Cohen called Boyer to tell him to rest not only that day, but the rest of the season. "'Why don't you go home and stay home?' Cohen said. 'We ain't going anywhere. You've had enough. I've pitched you to death. I won't pitch you over there (Wichita).' But I said, 'Well, I'll be there.'"

Unlike Indianapolis, Wichita was fighting for the pennant. Contrary to his intentions, Cohen called upon Boyer for the last inning of the seven-inning game of the doubleheader. But the game was tied and went on and on, and so did Boyer, into the 13th inning.

Boyer gave up a home run in the 13th and Wichita won the pennant.

"I figured, 'Well, now I'm done,'" he said. "The second game I'm sitting in the bullpen and it's the next to last inning and I'm back in the game. We had two more doubleheaders out there and I got in all four games.

After he said for me to go home and not pitch, I pitched in six games in three days. My arm didn't hurt me. It wasn't hurting."

The stamina test wasn't an altogether bad thing heading into the off-season. If Boyer's arm and shoulder could withstand that much use, maybe he was on the trail back to the majors.

So in 1958 Boyer was back with the Indians and back in the starting rotation of a AAA team and while Indianapolis' record was nothing special, manager Walker Cooper gave Boyer a regular turn on the mound. Cooper, then 43 and into his second baseball career, periodically played behind the plate and sometimes caught Boyer. A rejuvenated Boyer looked as good as new. Remarkably, his record was 13–8 and his earned run average was 2.97.

> I had a pretty good year and my arm didn't hurt, but I was never able to throw hard again. I didn't have any arm trouble. It had been a long time since I had pitched without being sore. It helped me sleep better. I thought I'd go back to the big leagues. Cooper thought so, too. But we had a terrible club (72–82). There were five of us older guys and we got the ball over the plate. Hell, we pitched some games that were over in an hour and 25 minutes. They were 1–0, 2–1 games. We couldn't score.

There actually was a great deal of talent on that Indianapolis team, but it was young talent, players still finding themselves, on the cusp of becoming major league players but not quite ready. Included on that roster were such future notables as Johnny Callison, Norm Cash, Harmon Killebrew and Johnny Romano. They just weren't ready yet for higher competition.

Cooper liked what he saw in Boyer, who was a shade over 30, not too old to rebound if his arm held up and he got another chance from a major league team. Cooper enjoyed being a battery-mate of Boyer's and thought he could still make it back to the top. When the season ended Cooper said, "I'm going to get you a job in winter ball if you want to go." Boyer wanted to know where and Cooper told him he had connections in Havana, Cuba. "That sounded good to me," Boyer said. "The salary wasn't very big, but it seemed like it was going to be good. My wife would come down with me and we'd go to the beach. Nadine likes the beach."

Before the Boyers could head to Cuba, Cloyd got a phone call halting the arrangement. The Indians general manager told him he couldn't go. The reason? The Indianapolis Indians were trying to sell Boyer's contract to a big-league team, the Cleveland Indians. If the deal was consummated, Boyer stood to gain 25 percent of the sale price.

> He said, "I think I've got you sold for $25,000. You'd get $6,250." I said, "That's all right. That'll work." So he didn't want me to go to Cuba. I said, "I

can still go down there and you sell me and I'll come home. I don't have to stay." He said, "We don't have to let you go. We can keep you from going." I said, "Well, that's kind of chickenshit." I'd been in Indianapolis for a couple of years and fans liked me. They had me on the front page of the yearbook or scorecard one year. But he said, "No, you can't go. That's it." I said, "Well, I've got to go look for a job now." And they never got me sold. I couldn't go to Havana. They wouldn't let me go.

As spring training was about to begin, Indianapolis officials called Boyer and told him he could go to the Cleveland Indians' spring training on a trial basis in Arizona. No money was involved in any deal at that point.

The damnedest thing happened. The day before I was going to go, the kids got sick. I had two kids in the hospital with pneumonia really bad. Frank Lane was the general manager of Cleveland, the guy they called "Trader Lane" because he would swap his grandmother for a player if he thought it was a good deal. I called him and said, "Frank, I need two or three days," and I told him why. He said, "Either be here by the opening day of camp or don't come." I said, "I can't go off and leave my kids in the hospital. They're really sick." He must have thought I was trying to fool him or something. He just said I had to show up on the opening day of training camp.

So it was no dice with Cleveland, and Boyer was back with the minor-league Indians. During the summer of 1959 Boyer went 10–14 with a 3.30 earned run average. It was a hard-luck season. With that ERA the win-loss mark could have been better, but worse, Boyer's arm aches were back, though not debilitating. There was less and less hope that Boyer would be a prospect again, that a big-league team would find his phone number.

In 1960, Boyer remained a key member of the pitching staff in Indianapolis. His record was 12–8 with a 3.88 ERA, and he pitched 209 innings. That was quite a work load for a guy who was supposed to have a dead arm. Boyer accomplished that with pain excruciating enough to keep him awake nights. Ice was not seen as a remedy for such a problem at that time, so mostly Boyer just put up with the pain when he pitched. "Just suffered with it," he said.

In 1961, with Cot Deal the manager, Indianapolis finished 84–64. This time Boyer was not a major contributor on the mound. His record was 3–5 and his ERA was a ghastly 6.79. There were a number of talented young pitchers on that team, which was affiliated with the Cincinnati Reds that season, including Claude Osteen, Sammy Ellis, and Mike Cuellar. Partway through the season, Deal approached Boyer and told him he wanted to make him a player-coach. He wangled a $100 month raise for him.

Cloyd was doing both jobs, pitching some and at age 33 teaching pitching to the next generation. It was not difficult to pinpoint the moment when Boyer morphed more into the coaching side than the throwing side. Near the end of the season Boyer joined some of the players for a BS session at a bar and drank beers with them.

"I didn't think anything of it. We were a little ways from the hotel," Boyer said. "He (Deal) went out checking up on us and found us. Later, he called me up to his room and said, 'If you're going to go down there and have a few beers with those guys, why didn't you tell me?' I said, "I didn't know I had to.' He really didn't like it."

At that moment Boyer realized he had become management, but it had happened so subtly he barely noticed the transition.

15

FINDING HIS POSITION
(Ken)

Perhaps if the Cardinals hadn't had Ken Boyer fooling around on the pitching mound for a couple of years in the minors, he would have made it to St. Louis before 1955, when he was 24. Although Boyer didn't mind, since all he wanted to do was become a big-leaguer, it probably wasted a couple of years of his career.

The problem was that Ken kept the organization guessing. His arm, if not his know-how, was enough to keep the Cardinals guessing while he was in the minors—he pitched well enough to go 7–1 one season. Boyer was victimized a little bit by his reputation as a guy who could do everything, and the Cardinals grasped for the right way to make use of his talents.

"He was always the best athlete in the family," said brother Lynn. "I don't know what it was, hand-eye coordination or better eyes. He was probably the best athlete that ever went to Alba High."

Not only wasn't Ken Boyer a boastful person, getting information out of him required a crowbar. That included even filling in his family about what was going on in his life. According to brother Lynn,

> He was private. You had to ask him things. He never volunteered anything. Ken didn't talk about things. It was as if everything was a big secret. One time, I can't remember whether it was Thanksgiving or Christmas, we drove to Lenny's house and played cards, me, Clete, Ken, and Cloyd, and that whole trip down there he never said a word. With Kenny, you never knew what he was thinking.

It turned out that even if Ken was no blabbermouth, he was the best hitter in the family and his versatility appealed to the Cardinals. But he had never even been a pitcher in high school. "Hell, Kenny was always good at everything, hitting, but he hadn't pitched," Cloyd said, "Not that I know of. They told him he had a good arm. He stayed with Nadine and I and worked out for two weeks. His first year he pitched he was 7–1 in Lebanon, Pennsylvania, in the New York-Penn League."

In Hamilton, Ontario, Ken went 8–6 the next year. According to Cloyd, who was still playing at the time,

> I followed him all of the time that I could. He pitched for about a year and a half. When the third baseman got hurt, Kenny played third and he never pitched again. That was the best thing. That was an act of the Lord, I think. He was in the right position, where he should have been all along. I was having good years when he was still in high school and I kept telling everyone in the Cardinals' organization that I saw how good he was. I'm sure they would have focused on him anyway. One or two people in the organization asked if I thought he was as good as I was. I said, "He's a hell of a lot better than I am. You're going to find that out someday."

Because Cloyd was the oldest, went off to play ball first, and made it to the majors, many observers always felt that he paved the way for his brothers. He doesn't see it that way. "I think they admired me when I was going good," he said. "I think a lot of it rubbed off. I think that helped them some. Maybe it gave them a little more confidence because I made it to the big leagues. A lot of people say, 'You're the one that paved the way.' But I don't know. I guess."

When the Boyers were streaming out of Missouri into pro ball, Buzzie Bavasi, a prominent major league executive for decades starting in the 1940s, once made a crack about the Boyers that eventually got back to Cloyd. "'Hell,' Boyer said he heard of Bavasi saying, "'instead of signing all of those boys, let's go sign their dad and hire him out for a stud fee.' Somebody told me that story later."

Ken Boyer had his one adjustment year in the majors in 1955, but he was already the St. Louis Cardinals' regular third baseman. He was hyped quite a bit as a potential star right from the get-go. In spring training that season a headline in the *St. Louis Post-Dispatch* announced his arrival. It read, "Cards, Luke-Warm at Hot Sack, Boom Boyer As Best Ever." Right from the opening line of the newspaper story Boyer was awarded high marks. The article began, "If looks didn't deceive, the Cardinals would have their greatest third baseman ever in Kenton Lloyd Boyer." No pressure.[1]

The reporter did explain that the Cardinals, while enjoying great overall success through the decades, had almost never fielded a star at Boyer's position. When he joined the big-league club, observers also took note of a facial resemblance to older brother Cloyd.

Bill Virdon, who played with Boyer in the minors, is the one who beat his friend out for the "Rookie of the Year" Award in 1955 when he broke into the Cardinals' outfield the same season that Boyer took over third.

"That's probably the only year I had a better year than he did," said Virdon, who later managed the New York Yankees, Pittsburgh Pirates, and two other teams. "The first time I came across him was at Rochester and he was a pitcher. He was a decent pitcher. Overall, I think he really knew the game. He knew what he was doing on the field, but that was his personality, too."

Also before meeting up again with the Cardinals, Virdon and Boyer spent some time together in winter ball in Havana, Cuba. "It was one of the best experiences we had," Virdon said of the winter after the 1954 season. "It was ideal playing conditions. You played every other day. Once, we got locked in a plane and they wouldn't let us out. They said they were looking out for us. Fidel Castro was in the hills, they said."

Ironically, Boyer admitted that at first he didn't even enjoy settling down at his infield position. "I didn't like third base at first," he said, "and I was terrible, too. In fact, I didn't really begin to improve until two years ago, after I realized I had spent so much time hitting that I had neglected my defense."[2]

A year later, in 1956, Ken Boyer was an All-Star. He played 150 games, hit 26 home runs, knocked in 98 runs and batted .306. He made his first National League All-Star team. And sportswriters were scrutinizing his potential. "If anybody is handing out 'sophomore of the year' awards, they'd better take a long look at the large young man from Berkeley, Missouri," a wire service reporter noted just after the All-Star Game. Discussion was floating around that Boyer could be "another Pie Traynor," the Hall of Fame third baseman of the Pittsburgh Pirates.[3]

The NL won that All-Star Game on July 10 by a 7–3 margin over the American League. Boyer deserved his encomiums after smacking three hits, driving in the winning run, and playing superbly in the field. Boyer had been touted as a potential "Rookie of the Year" in 1955, but his place in the running for that award faded at the end of the season. He admitted his education was still underway and by comparison he was pursuing a college degree at the plate in 1956. "Now I've learned a little bit about the pitchers, too," Boyer said.[4]

For Ken Boyer it was a magical time. He was playing for the team he rooted for growing up, the one team he followed closely. Among his teammates were some of the most famous Cardinals of all time, whom he had cheered for over the years. Boyer was in a lineup with Stan "The Man"

In 1959 Ken Boyer (left) was awarded one of his several Rawlings Gold Glove Awards for his work at third base (National Baseball Hall of Fame Library, Cooperstown, N.Y.).

Musial, the most esteemed and accomplished Cardinal of them all, and Red Schoendienst was still around at second base.

Musial, the left-handed slugger from Donora, Pennsylvania, played 22 seasons with St. Louis, batted .331, and won seven batting titles and three National League Most Valuable Player awards. Revering him as one of the game's great gentlemen, the Cardinals built a statue of Musial that stands outside their ball park. Musial passed away at 92 in 2013.

Musial was very down-to-earth. He was not a snooty superstar. Still, during his first days with the Cardinals, Boyer was too shy to communicate much with Musial. He was still a bit scared of the player he had admired from afar. He once told a roommate, "Musial was like a god to me then."[5]

Although Schoendienst did not play his entire career with St. Louis, he is an icon of the franchise, and when they played together he and Musial were best friends. He later coached and managed the Cardinals for many years and as he turned 91 in early 2014, he was still active with the team, doing some scouting and attending home games. Another Hall of Famer, Schoendienst was a ten-time All-Star and as a player, coach and manager won five World Series rings, four with the Cardinals.

Just getting to know those players and associating with them helped make Boyer a hero in his hometown, though he quickly became an equal as a teammate and All-Star himself.

However, despite Boyer's All-Star selection, not everything was hunky-dory. For some reason, at the same time he was being hailed as a special commodity at third base for the 1957 season, Boyer began the season playing almost in a trance, making way too many mistakes in the field. That was very uncharacteristic of him. New manager Fred Hutchinson played a hunch. He took Boyer aside in late May and suggested a position change.

"How would you like to try playing center field?" Hutchinson asked his young prospect. "Hutch, I think it will save my life," Boyer replied. "I've got to get off third base for my own sake, as well as for the team's."[6]

Hutchinson, who had been a successful pitcher for the Detroit Tigers, was a popular manager in clubhouses. He could be firm, but he was no dictator. He had insight into what made players tick. "Fred was the kind of manager who was a friend of the players," Schoendienst said. "But he also knew he was the manager and drew the line at becoming real buddy-buddy with them."[7]

Boyer spent the rest of the 1957 season as St. Louis' center fielder, which for some is a forgotten chapter in his career. Certainly the position switch liberated Boyer from worry and stress handling ground balls, and he did a good job roaming the outfield. His hitting, however, reverted to the level of 1955. His average dropped 41 points to .265 and his home runs (19) and RBI (62), were almost identical to his rookie stats. With an 87–67 record, the Cardinals played well. Eddie Kasko handled the third-base duties and batted .273.

The next season Hutchinson informed Boyer early that he would remain in center field. It seemed he had found his comfort zone. Then, just as spring training concluded, St. Louis coach Stan Hack informed Boyer that he was going back to third base. Hack had been an excellent third baseman for the Chicago Cubs and was there to help. But once he shifted back to third, Boyer's jitters evaporated and he felt at home again. Except for some short vacations at other spots on the field, Boyer remained a third baseman for the rest of his career starting in 1958.

Musial called Boyer "an excellent third baseman," though he did note Boyer, much like the rest of the team, hit a fielding slump early that season.[8] A turning point for Boyer occurred in a crucial game against the Cubs, with future Hall of Famer Ernie Banks at the plate. Banks smashed a hard shot down the third-base line, but Boyer made a game-saving play. The success helped restore his confidence. He told himself, "I can do it. I can play third base."[9]

From then on Boyer was a more valuable member of the team in the field. However, the Cardinals had a dismal season, ending up 72–82 and in fifth place in the NL standings. Hutchinson was fired, and Hack managed ten games. Boyer thrived at third base and grew into one of the best at that position in the league during his era.

One teammate who was a fan was Schoendienst. He liked Boyer's style. According to Schoendienst,

> Kenny was a real fine ball player. When he played third he came out and played hard. No fancy stuff with him. He was just a good player. He was a tough out. He was a good third baseman and for a big man he ran real well. He knew how to play the game, when to take the extra base. He knew what inning it was and what to do at all times. He was a good baseball man from a good baseball family. He was an outstanding guy.[10]

Teammates did like and respect Boyer. He was not a showy guy in the newspapers, either, making outrageous statements. He let his glove and bat draw attention to him, and as his brothers were aware, he didn't speak out of turn or make waves with conversation. He was the same quiet guy with the Cardinals as he was with family. "Ken was a good person," Virdon said. "He was one of the better players in baseball at that time."

Basically, the rocky days of Ken Boyer's stay with the Cardinals ended with the end of the 1958 season. From then on he became a perpetual All-Star.

16

RIGHT TO THE TOP
(Clete)

C lete Boyer made it to the majors more rapidly and at a younger age than either of his older brothers, Cloyd and Ken.

Of course, in the mid–1950s the sarcastic joke uttered often was that the Kansas City Athletics weren't really in the majors, but were just a farm club of the New York Yankees. At the time it seemed that any time Kansas City obtained or developed a good player, the Yankees swooped in and traded for him. What the perennial World Champion Yankees wanted, the Yankees got, it seemed.

So 18-year-old Clete Boyer played his 47 games with a .241 batting average for Kansas City, sharing the roster with Cloyd in his rookie season of 1955. He got into 67 games and batted .217 the next year when he was on his own in Kansas City. Bonus baby signing rules had kept Boyer in the majors for two years, mostly on the bench, when what he really needed was the time to develop in the minors.

In 1957, Boyer played just ten games for the Athletics before being swapped to the Yankees as part of an 11-player trade. New York immediately sent him to the minors for the seasoning he had missed out on, and he did not resurface in the big leagues until 1959. Boyer was more bench-warmer than regular that year, playing in just 47 games for New York that summer (he hit .215). It was not until 1960, at age 23, that Boyer became the regular third baseman for the Yankees.

Essentially, Clete Boyer's major league career did not get under way until that year. Light hitting for much of his time in the majors (to the consternation and surprise of his brothers), Clete played the hot corner for 124 games and hit .242. That season the Yankees won the American League pennant, though they were defeated in one of the most dramatic

World Series of all time. The Pittsburgh Pirates won the crown on Bill Mazeroski's ninth-inning home run in Game 7. That was the first of five World Series in a row that Boyer played in.

Although his hitting did not earn the rave reviews reserved for popular Broadway show openings, from the start Clete distinguished himself with his glove. He poured his athleticism into making diving stops and jumping grabs, stealing base-hits from batters who slammed line drives down the third-base line. He also played to deny the bunt.

"I always felt a third baseman should play up close and be able to make the plays on line drives anyway," Clete said. "I enjoy fielding from up close like that. You know, the ball comes at you so fast you don't have the time to think about it, and when you begin to play instinctively, you're better. Besides, you're so much closer to those slow rollers down the line."[1]

Boyer was fortunate he never took one of those line drives in the teeth, but the style worked for him. Although fans and fellow players loved his fielding, Boyer never won a Gold Glove Award in the American League because the Baltimore Orioles' future Hall of Famer, Brooks Robinson, won the league's Gold Glove Award at third base every year.

"Clete was different," brother Lynn Boyer said. "I've seen him make catches Willie Mays couldn't even make. He'd dive and catch balls. And the gloves are so much better and bigger now. I've seen Clete's old gloves. They looked like a work glove. That's why defense is so much better now, because of the gloves.

Clete was right up there with Ken as one of the best all-around athletes in the family. He excelled in baseball and basketball, but like everyone else he was the product of the same hard-working family in Alba, Missouri. "That part of the country was all baseball," Clete said when reminiscing long after his retirement. "I played against Mickey Mantle's twin brothers and against Ralph Terry. Each little town in the area built its own park. In my town of 300 people, we had a park with lights."[2]

Also long into retirement, when Boyer was riding the circuit signing autographs at memorabilia shows, he lamented not being a more avid baseball card collector when he was a kid.

> We wanted the bubble gum that was in the cards. I don't think many collected the cards. I remember putting them on bicycles. I wish I had saved them. I wish I had saved the stuff from all the great teams I played for. Back then you never thought about souvenirs. We used to keep pictures more than a glove or a bat. I think I have an Atlanta Braves and Oakland A's uniform where I coached. I also have a jersey from when I played with the Kansas City A's. I carry a uniform with me for old-timers' games, but I don't have the uniform I played with.[3]

Clete Boyer was so attached to one of his favorite gloves that he used it for five seasons. It is more common for a player to blow through one glove a season. What he did save were many autographed baseballs and photographs. At one time he had perhaps two dozen Mickey Mantle autographed balls, but he used them as auction material to help raise money for charities. "If I had saved all my stuff, it would be worth $400,000 to $500,000," Boyer said.[4]

Boyer grew up a Cardinals fan like everyone else in the family, and it was his goal to join the Cardinals organization, just as several of his brothers did. But it came down to money. Boyer could make a lot more money being signed for a bonus—the $35,000—by Kansas City because St. Louis was already committed to two other bonus babies. The trade from the Athletics to the Yankees changed his life, although the competition for playing time was much tougher, resulting in his demotion to the minors for a couple of years.

"I knew when you got to the Yankee organization it would be tough," he said. "But I knew when I was 18 I was going to play in the big leagues. I didn't know what I would do offensively. I knew I could out-run most of the guys and knew my arm was as good or better than most of them. But it really was a big thrill for me when the Yankees traded for me."[5]

Andy Carey and Gil McDougald had been solid third basemen for the Yankees, but after Clete had worked this way through stops in Binghamton and Richmond, Carey was traded. McDougald was still around, but spent much of his time at shortstop before retiring young. Those fighting to claim the New York third base job besides Boyer were Hector Lopez, Joe DeMaestri, and Jim Finigan. They all played in the majors, but Finigan never suited up for the Yankees.

The Yankees of that era were a powerhouse. They had All-Stars at almost every position and were loaded with power at the plate. With Mickey Mantle, Yogi Berra, Roger Maris, Bill Skowron and others at the ready, New York could afford someone in the lineup who was mostly there for fielding rather than hitting. While it originated in the 1930s, the early 1960s Yankees revived common usage of the nickname, "The Bronx Bombers." In 1961, the Yankees set a then-record of 240 homers for one team in a single season, a mark that has since been broken.

"They brought me up because I was a pretty good infielder," Clete Boyer said. "Truthfully, I was lucky to be there."[6]

Once in a while, when it came to hitting, Clete got that reminder in jarring fashion. When he rose to the big leagues the Yankees were managed by the colorful and creative Casey Stengel. Stengel won ten pennants in

Clete Boyer during his Yankees days with his young family (National Baseball Hall of Fame Library, Cooperstown, N.Y.).

his 12 seasons as field boss of the Yankees, but he could be unorthodox in his handling of players and sometimes made off-beat strategy maneuvers.

In 1960, when the Yankees faced the Pirates in the World Series, Boyer started at third, but Stengel pinch-hit Dale Long for him in the second inning of the first game. Stengel seemed to be the least likely manager to pull a stunt like that because long ago he had been treated the same way and felt humiliated. In 1922, when Stengel was playing for the New York Giants, another legendary manager, John McGraw, yanked him for a pinch-runner in the second inning of the second game of the Series. "I was so damn mad when McGraw done that I couldn't see straight," Stengel said.[7]

He was lucky Boyer didn't clock him. Stengel was beloved by the press because he was so entertaining and many baseball experts considered him to be a genius on the bench. But he was not always the most sensitive of managers. Players became angered at him because he did make changes on a whim occasionally, and he didn't have to explain himself to them. "He once cut shortstop Fritz Brickell by asking him if he could run," Boyer said, "and when Fritz said he could, Casey said, 'Then run down to the station and catch the five o'clock train to Richmond.'"[8]

Decades later, when Clete gave an interview to a New York newspaper, the conversation turned to the time when Stengel embarrassed Clete with that early pinch-hitting move. Boyer never got over it, and it turned him against Stengel for good. At the time it occurred, Boyer said, "How am I going to live among all my people when they start riding me about this?"[9]

He did manage to survive and have a good career anyway, but Boyer never mellowed about the incident. "I hate him," Boyer said 38 years later of Stengel. "That is still inside me. It was so embarrassing. Mickey (Mantle) always said one of the biggest things (he was thankful for) was that he was never a goat in a World Series."[10]

There was considerable shock around the baseball world when the Yankees pulled the trigger and fired Stengel after the 1960 World Series, following the seventh-game loss to the Pirates on Mazeroski's miracle blast. There wasn't much more any manager could have done, and it was taken as a sign the Yankees were really spoiled, that no manager was safe unless he won it all. Ralph Houk succeeded Stengel, and Clete said the replacement was a breath of fresh air in the clubhouse. "I think a lot of it had to do with how Ralph took to the young players and Casey didn't. One day I was on third, (Tony) Kubek was on short and (Bobby) Richardson was on second. We all made errors in the same game. Stengel called us an air-conditioned infield. The next year Houk called us his Million-Dollar infield."[11]

That next season, when Houk took over and the Yankees bashed all of those home runs, was probably the most fun Boyer had during one season in the majors, not necessarily because of his own hitting, though. New York finished 109–53 and Boyer played 148 games. He hit 11 home runs with 55 runs batted in, though his average was a puny .224.

It was the year of the great home run chase, Roger Maris and Mantle chasing Babe Ruth's record of 60 homers in a season that had stood since 1927. Maris set the mark with 61 and Mantle finished second in the league with 54 homers.

"I think most of the older guys on that team were rooting for Mickey to win the race, but we wanted both of them to break the record," Clete said. "All the fans were rooting for Mickey, too, but I don't think it got bad for Roger until September. For us (the other players) it was something just to be on the same field with them and watch it all happen."[12]

Boyer roomed with Maris on the road, sharing hotels with him for five years, but not in 1961. He was one step away in the locker room instead of in the room, to watch one of the most exciting chapters in baseball power hitting history. "It was incredible," Boyer said. "Roger went through one stretch where he had something like 55 or 56 hits and 26 of them were home runs. I didn't care (whether Maris or Mantle prevailed). I ran around with Roger and I named one of my kids after Mickey. But I always will remember 1961. It was almost like a fairy-tale story watching those two guys."[13]

It was during the 1961 season, too, that Boyer began to get his props as a terrific fielder. His glove got him promoted to the majors and kept him in the Yankees lineup. Veteran outfielder Bob Cerv was one of the first Yankees to go public with his belief that Boyer was a special player at third. "He is the best I have seen in this league," Cerv said. "Did you ever see anybody play third base so close in as Boyer does at times? He dares 'em to hit it by him and they can't. It must be great to be a pitcher with a man like that behind you snapping up two-base hits."[14]

In 1961 the Yankees met the Cincinnati Reds in the World Series and, still smarting from the loss to Pittsburgh in 1960, were determined to live up to their billing as one of the best teams in history. New York polished off Cincinnati in five games and Clete Boyer became the first member of his family to earn a World Series ring.

As he had all season, Boyer showed well in the field against the Reds and made a believer out of Cincinnati manager Fred Hutchinson. Hutchinson had managed brother Ken with the Cardinals, so he was not particularly surprised what an infielder named Boyer could achieve. Hutchinson said the scouting report on Clete before the Series informed him that he could even out-shine Ken in the field. But Hutchinson said he would have to see it to believe it.

"Now I have seen," he said. "I am convinced Cletis is something special. But Ken makes the good plays, too." Hutchinson was a Ken Boyer fan when they shared a Cardinals dugout. "Ken is the kind of player you wish you had 12 of so that you could play nine and have three on the bench. He's kind of the guy you dream about—terrific speed, great arm, brute strength."[15]

The only thing Clete lacked in comparison to Ken was that brute strength. Not that New York manager Houk had any complaints after witnessing Clete's 1961 production. A sportswriter asked if Clete had any flaws. "If you are asking me that question, you won't get far," Houk said. "In fact, I'm stopped right now. What doesn't Boyer do?"[16]

One thing Clete did a lot of was win. In 1961 the Yankees were only two seasons in to their streak of five straight World Series appearances. He was getting the opportunity to add significantly to his jewelry collection.

17

ANOTHER BROTHER'S
TURN COMES
(Lenny)

I t was quite the achievement for every boy in the family to be signed to play professional baseball. Cloyd, Ken, and Clete reached the major leagues. Others came close. The youngest brother was Lenny, born in 1946. Baseball was on his mind as a youngster as a way to make a living as he watched some of his older siblings leave home and get a chance to play ball for money. No one provided a better incentive than those who made it to the big leagues.

Cloyd, for one, was a believer in Lenny's talents. He thought for sure he could make it to the Show. According to Cloyd,

> I thought that my last brother, Lenny, should have done it. I don't know what happened to him. I never did get to see him play. I was coaching when he was playing. Everybody talked about the ability he had. I worried that he wasn't taking it seriously enough. I got on him heavy one night about it. I said, "you need to concentrate on baseball." I actually had him crying. I gave it to him good.

Lenny was born on March 12, 1946, and he graduated high school in 1964 when Cloyd was coaching professionally and both Ken and Clete were at the height of their careers. Lenny signed with the St. Louis Cardinals and spent the next six years in the minors trying to make it to the top.

Lenny was the seventh brother and he made it unanimous that every one of them would sign a pro contract and take a shot at playing the National Pastime. It was a remarkable thing for the Boyer brothers to flood the market like that. Few families ever sent three or more brothers to the

Lenny Boyer (left) at about age 14, father Vern (middle) and Ron Boyer (right) at about age 16 (courtesy Cloyd and Nadine Boyer).

majors, and none other has ever sent seven brothers into at least the minor-league level. According to Cloyd,

> First of all, the Lord gave us the ability. I think we just worked hard. You've got to have some ability, but our work ethic was good. Once when I was coaching with the Yankees I went to early camp and there was Clete. God, I never saw anyone work so hard on taking ground balls. I always thought he was the best and then I knew why. He just took a bunch of grounders, and then he took a towel and wiped the sweat off and went back for more. He just worked like the devil at it. I couldn't believe it. I think working hard was the biggest thing for us. Of course our mother and dad were both hard workers and honest people, and I think it just carried over.

Lenny Boyer was a good enough basketball player at Alba High that as a senior he was named to a Little All-American basketball team of the top 100 players in the country. Naturally, though, his heart belonged to baseball, and when the Cardinals returned to the Boyer nest he was prepared to put his autograph on a contract.

> I got started playing baseball because of my brothers. Of course, we didn't have a lot to do where we lived other than play baseball. We grew up across

the road from that ball field. I was just like my older brothers, either playing baseball or swimming in the summer. Having Cloyd and Ken and Clete in the same family was inspirational. Very much so. You always had a hero right there in your family. They came from such a meager background, a small town like ours, and they had done pretty well for themselves. I always looked up to them. I was always a fan of the big Cardinals stars like Stan Musial, but having my brothers play big-league baseball was quite a deal.

When it came to baseball and basketball, Lenny Boyer didn't have to search far for role models. He could just look at photographs on the wall of the family home and watch his brothers play baseball on television.

It was pretty special for me. I don't know if it was in our genes because I don't know that my dad was athletic at all. Of course he was raising 14 kids, so he had to work hard all the time. But he did encourage us to play and he spent a lot of time preparing the field. He and a lot of the older men around town spent a lot of time with us kids, giving us the opportunity to go out there and play our games. I think the main reason we got so good was that we played all of the time.

This was an era when kids entertained themselves outdoors. They ate breakfast and essentially mom turned them loose to go play on weekends and in the summer. If they even had a TV set, they were not allowed to sit around all day watching it. There were no other electronic games or the like to use for amusement.

In the off-season, when school was in session and basketball was the most popular sport, the boys put the same effort into improving their games and invested massive amounts of time playing hoops. "In basketball season, when the school would close, we'd just stay up there for an hour or two and play basketball into the evening, and then we'd show up early in the morning and play some more," Lenny said.

The Boyers didn't take family vacations to resort areas. They couldn't afford it. They didn't, as Lenny put it, "have video machines." The kids had each other to play with, and the consensus was that in the winter they should play basketball any time they had free time, while in the summer they should play baseball with their free time. If it got so hot and uncomfortable they felt they were going to melt in the summer sun, they retreated to the swimming hole. Not a city pool, not a lake. "We didn't do any of that stuff," Lenny said.

It was a big family and money was tight. They couldn't afford to do "any of that stuff." So the kids did what they enjoyed the most and they got the most out of it. Those who were the best were rewarded for all of the time they put in. Lenny's Cardinals bonus was $30,000, better than most though not all of his brothers'. St. Louis was paying for potential and for a name brand, too. Lenny was an infielder and with Ken and Clete playing at supreme levels, the Cardinals figured here came another Boyer who could scoop up those grounders and blaze a trail to the bigs.

"I was actually a shortstop, but I was taller and looked like I was going to get a little bigger," Lenny Boyer said of his 6-foot-1, 185-pound frame. "So I moved to third base right away. I played third base all of the way through."

Step one for Boyer was the Western Carolinas League, where he played for the Rock Hill, South Carolina, team as a 19-year-old in 1965. It was Class A ball and Boyer got into 98 games, but he didn't hit well, running into the same fate as the non-major league brothers. His batting average was .149.

Boyer's manager was George Anderson, better known as "Sparky." Anderson was starting his second career in baseball at age 30 in the low minors, too. Anderson, who later won championships with the Cincinnati Reds and Detroit Tigers and was elected to the Hall of Fame in 2000 after winning 2,194 big-league ballgames, guided Rock Hill to a pennant. The next year he took over St. Petersburg, also in Class A, and led that club to a pennant. Lenny Boyer followed him there. In 1967, they both spent time with Modesto in the California League, and won the crown there, too.

"Sparky Anderson was my manager the first three years I played," Lenny Boyer said. "As a matter of fact, I babysat for Sparky's kids. He was like a father figure to me for three years, and when he and his wife wanted to go out I was the babysitter. The majority of what I know about baseball I got from Sparky."

During the 1966 season in the Florida State League, Lenny played in 96 games and batted .244. That season St. Petersburg lost a 4–3 game to Miami in a contest that lasted 29 innings. The game was played in one day, with no time out overnight.

In Modesto in 1967, Lenny hit nine home runs, knocked in 55 runs, stole 10 bases and batted .249. It was probably his best all-around pro season. Once again the team was a winner. Anderson had a passion for the game and a knack for giving good advice to young players. Lenny was like a sponge, soaking up any detail.

> I had played baseball all of the time and I basically knew how to play the game, what to do here and there. But Sparky taught me a lot about baseball that I didn't know. You couldn't carry on a conversation with him for more than five minutes before the topic changed to baseball. If you talked for three

hours, baseball was all you talked about with Sparky. He taught me a lot of fundamentals and how to approach the game mentally.

Each year Lenny was playing at some version of Class A, but as he went along those leagues became a little bit tougher and he ran into more experienced players. Lenny and Anderson split up in 1968, and Lenny went to Little Rock to compete in Class AA ball for the Arkansas Travelers of the Texas League. He got into 109 games and batted .250. The plan for 1969 was for Lenny to attend spring training and then be assigned to AAA ball, another promotion.

The problem that arose, however, was something faced by another sibling. Lenny Boyer was certain he was about to be drafted into the Army and sent to Vietnam. That would ruin his momentum in baseball just when he thought he was on the way up. Scrambling for the best solution, Lenny joined the Army Reserve, missed spring training in 1969 altogether, and was sent back to Little Rock and AA. It was a disappointing turn of events and it quelled his momentum in the Cardinals' organization.

That season Lenny was 23. He appeared in 70 games and batted .240. In his fifth season with the franchise and in the minors, he was under scrutiny. His future was in the balance.

> I was doing well in the field and doing everything else well, but my hitting was not coming around like they wanted it to, or I wanted it to either. There was no really good reason, but maybe I wasn't as dedicated to it as I should have been. I worked really hard on my fielding. I worked really hard on my fundamentals. But I probably didn't work as hard on things that I wasn't doing with the bat as I should have. That's probably my fault. Cloyd did take me aside and talk to me. I don't remember the details, but I had people tell me that I was probably my own worst enemy because I was doing a lot of running around and things like that that I shouldn't have been doing. I was having a good time away from the field and not applying myself and working as hard as I should have. Looking back at it, I regret it. I was pretty hardheaded.

Failure to make a dent in the pitching at AA was costly to Lenny. Rather than move up to AAA he spent a portion of the 1970 season back in Modesto. He was demoted back to A ball. In 73 games back in California, he batted .233. The Cardinals moved him back to AA Little Rock for another try, and in 24 games in Arkansas he hit .230. The 1970 season was his last season in pro ball. The Cardinals released him after that summer.

For whatever reason, Lenny Boyer's bat never got untracked. He never hit the way he believed he could. His finest average in the minors was .250. That was not good enough to move up. The timing was all wrong for him when he had his shot at AAA, and the second chance never came around because of the weakness he showed at the plate.

Years later Lenny second-guessed himself for not working harder at the plate to lift his average. He believed he could have given more time and effort to improving his hitting. But he always thought he would succeed in baseball. He had the love of the game and the lifetime commitment to it. But he couldn't get promoted past a certain point in the organization.

> I never really had any doubt about my ability. I never did. I always thought from the time I was about 12 years old that I would play in the big leagues. I feel that if I applied myself more I would have. I don't think I was cocky about it, but I had confidence in what I could do. I felt I knew the game. I could play the game. I had the talent and ability, but I didn't push myself hard enough. The Cardinals released me after six years in the organization.
>
> I didn't help myself in 1969 when I was sent to AA instead of AAA. I had a falling out with the manager, Ray Hathaway, and once you get labeled with a bad attitude that sticks with you. They send reports to the front office and they believe the manager. It was probably true. I probably did have a bad attitude that year.

Being told he wasn't good enough to progress to the majors—and performing the self-analysis that he was at least partially at fault—left Lenny Boyer depressed for a while. Baseball was the only thing he wanted to do in life and now he had to find a new life. He drifted from job to job, said he wished he had gotten into coaching, but didn't.

> I knocked around. When I got released I felt as if I had let myself down. It was hard to explain the feelings. I came home to Missouri, didn't do much. Then I started college at the University of Arkansas. I met my wife Gail in Arkansas. Had I not met my wife then, there's no telling where I would have ended up. I may have ended up on the street, but she got me straightened out.

Boyer got a job working for Arkansas Power and Light Company, then spent another 32 years working for an energy company in Missouri. Overall, he worked as a lineman for nearly 40 years while raising two sons, and indulging his passion for the outdoors, hunting and fishing. He continued to root for the Cardinals until his death in 2013.

18

THE SEVEN SISTERS
(The Boyer Girls)

The seven sisters did not play professional baseball. Growing up in the United States in the 1920s, 1930s, 1940s, and 1950s, the Boyer girls may have been sports fans, but America wasn't ready for them to be athletes. It was not until the federal legislation Title IX was approved in 1972 that the athletic world began to change and open up for American women. Congress' passage of the act led to vastly increased participation and funding opportunities for women in sports.

For the most part the Boyer sisters were decades ahead of the curve, their youth long gone before the expanded chances to compete in high school and college sports became law.

Juanita was born in 1923 and still lives in Alba. She is the matriarch of the family, the eldest child, older by four years than Cloyd, the oldest boy. LeLa Thelma, born in 1925, died as a child. Juanita was followed by Delores in 1933, Pansy in 1939, Shirley in 1941, Bobby Jo in 1948, and Marcella in 1952. Juanita is nearly 30 years older than the youngest of the 14 Boyer children.

In the early days the girls helped their mother Mabel with the chores, which were considerable since there were so many kids in the family. It was thought to be unseemly and not ladylike for girls to sweat, and certainly if they were going to sweat it was because it was hot in the house in the summer, not because they were competing in sports. For decades, whatever girls sports were offered in the schools were extremely limited. Some of the younger girls did get the chance to join some teams, but the true opening up of opportunities across the country came after all of them were finished with high school. The youngest, Marcella, turned 20 the year Title IX passed.

"Of course, we didn't have girls' sports at our high school," Pansy Boyer Schell said. "Just the guys. And when I was in school (she completed public school in the late 1950s), they didn't even have football. We just had a gym and played amongst ourselves at school."

The closest thing to organized athletic opportunity the girls at Alba High School had going for them for years was trying out for the cheerleading squad. "The girls were cheerleaders for the boys," Pansy said. "They played basketball and all of us girls were cheerleaders during the years the boys played. I don't think Juanita was, but all the rest of us girls were cheerleaders for the boys playing basketball."

Given the age disparity—Pansy was born 12 years after Cloyd—she had no recollection of watching him compete in sports before he went off to join the Cardinals. That was true of older brothers Wayne and Ken, too.

Then Pansy got married, her husband worked in construction, and for a while they lived in California. Although she is a baseball fan, Pansy saw little of her brothers playing in the majors because for a large percentage of their careers there were either no big-league teams in California or none near where Pansy lived.

> I finally got to see Ken play out there when St. Louis came to play the Dodgers. My husband was working on a job there, so we got to go and see a game. It was amazing to get to see him play, and there were large crowds. They came to see Stan Musial. Of course, we were there to see Kenny. That was exciting. Those were exciting times to see him in the major leagues. I'm not sure we appreciated how special that was until we got older, though.

The boys were immersed in baseball, and one after the other signed a professional baseball contract, several of them with the beloved Cardinals, but all of them marching off to the minors, as if they were going to fulfill an obligation to their country just like being in the military. "We grew up with all of the boys playing ball and it was just matter of fact," Pansy said. "You just didn't realize the importance, the place they had in the game by reaching the majors. When we got older we all used to get letters about Cloyd and Kenny and Clete."

They came from small-town Missouri, where the kids knew everyone in the community of what was 350 people at the time. The adults rooted for the boys when they went away to play, and everyone around always asked how they were doing and how they were progressing. "Everybody followed the boys," Pansy said. "They kept up with all of it and they were just excited for them. They all had just so much support from home, from the family and the town. Everybody knew everybody back then. Now people move in and move out."

The fact that Ken Boyer played for the Cardinals was an extra blessing for the family. It wasn't just that he was in the big leagues, but he was associated with everyone's favorite team. There was no higher sports ambition than to become part of the St. Louis Cardinals if you were from Missouri. While the Boyers didn't have the wherewithal to buy a television set right away, they were glued to that radio when the Cardinals were on and Cloyd or Ken was playing.

"We never missed listening to the game," Pansy said. "Harry Caray always brought so much excitement into the game when he was announcing. My mother never missed listening to the Cardinals, even before the boys were playing with them. We loved listening to Harry Caray."

The Boyers lived on the opposite side of the state from St. Louis, a distance easily covered by automobile now in around five hours. But they also didn't have a lot of money to spend, and regular employment was essential to keeping the household rolling. For those reasons, an outing to attend a game was a special occasion and was not undertaken very often.

It was a treat to drive to St. Louis and watch Cloyd pitch a game during his few seasons with the Cardinals, or to watch Ken hold down third base and swing away in the batter's box. There was a lot of pride connected to those visits to Sportsman's Park up through 1953 and then to Busch Stadium through 1966. "I recall all of those games we went to," Pansy said. "We'd go up to St. Louis and the folks would load as many of us as they could into the car. We went once a year. Clete came to Kansas City, but I never got to watch Clete play."

As siblings aged, married, and some settled down in other towns, there were few occasions when it was possible for everyone in the family to get together. Over time the big gathering date for reunions and sharing a holiday became Thanksgiving. That was bigger than Christmas for the Boyers. "We always got together at Thanksgiving," Pansy said.

Juanita Woodmansee explained that the get-together was over the Thanksgiving holiday weekend, not on Thanksgiving Day itself.

> The kids all came home because they had a four-day weekend. They'd usually spend Thanksgiving with their own immediate family and then all drive down Friday. We'd have our big get-together on Saturday and then they could drive home on Sunday. That was always the way we did it. When everyone got together they usually stayed up all night playing cards and talking baseball. There were always card games going on. I think they played casino and pitch. My dad liked to play cards. He would play cards 24 hours a day if he had somebody to play with. The boys sat there and played cards all night. They'd have separate tables and then whoever won from that table, the

winners would get together and play, and the losers would play. They just kept going."

Sometimes Juanita played cards, too, hearts. She remembers a show-down with Kenny. She thought he was playing recklessly and she had him beat, but he shot the moon and won. "Sure enough he did," Juanita said. "That was the last time we played."

One thing that always surprised the sisters, something that they underestimated until they either saw Ken or Clete in their element, in the ball park, or later in life, was just how well-known they were.

"We always just enjoyed watching them play ball games," Juanita said. "All these years later we appreciate the excitement they caused and we enjoy getting together and talking about them. It doesn't seem that it was that long ago."

When Clete was in the early stages of his pro career he had his first child, and Juanita visited and spent time with him helping out as a babysitter. That was the best chance she had to watch Clete play regularly in the pros.

I was very excited to watch him. We were excited when they were playing around here in Alba. They were all from this little town. I don't remember when Cloyd played, but when Ken played and he hit a home run the fans would pass the hat, take up a collection. It might not be a lot of money, but every time he hit a home run they would do it and get up a little bit for him. He did hit a lot of home runs. The people around here were excited when they played in the big leagues.

Although girls were not known much for baseball card collecting, and Juanita said nobody really took good care of their cards, attaching them to the spokes on the wheels of their bicycles so they would make a cool noise, she does own baseball cards of her brothers. Whether they are actually worth much or not to collectors doesn't interest her. She has them for sentimental value and obtained them as an adult. "I didn't collect them until I was a little bit older," Juanita said. "I've had several given to me because people knew they were of my brothers. I wouldn't even think about the expense of them."

As casual a baseball fan as Juanita is, she did realize that having seven brothers all sign professional baseball contracts was pretty unusual, and she admired Cloyd's, Ken's and Clete's achievements making it to the top rung of the game. "We were all real proud of them and we still are," Juanita said.

Way back when she was just a kid, Juanita said, the brothers needed an extra body on the field sometimes and she joined in the baseball games. "But after there got to be several of them, they didn't need me," she said.

Age makes a difference in what each sister remembers about their brothers playing pro baseball and how the family followed them from afar. One key difference amongst the younger girls was the addition of a television set. But a constant was support for the Cardinals. Cloyd and Ken played for the Cardinals, and several of the others signed with the Cardinals. However, the Cardinals were the home team anyway. Maybe the rooting wouldn't have been as fervent—that's not a given—if the Boyer brothers had not been employed by the St. Louis organization, but it just provided more reasons, more motivation to cheer for the Cards.

"My mom and dad always had the Cardinals' baseball games on the radio," said Shirley Lockhart, who was a child during the 1940s and into the 1950s. "And then any time they were playing on television, it was on."

Shirley does recall making trips to Kansas City with her husband to catch up with brother Clete, who was four years older, when he played for the Athletics and later when he was on road trips representing the Yankees. One way Shirley fondly remembers Clete was the way he always wanted to have a good time in life and make sure that everyone with him also did. "He took us to Kansas City a time or two. Clete was a fun-loving guy and he wanted everyone else to have fun, too. Whether he was playing baseball or making a big pot of chili it had to be fun. He was quite proud of making his chili. I wouldn't say he was the chef of the house, though. Lynn wanted to catch fish and then have a fish fry."

Although some of her sisters said they never dwelled on the matter and just watched some of the boys advancing to the majors, and all going on to play professionally despite the odds against seven siblings in the same family doing so, Shirley occasionally did pause on the fact. Not that she could figure out exactly how or why it happened. "I wondered how it came about," she said, "how we were so blessed by it. But I don't have any explanation for it. It must have been the water."

She knows that is a cliché and she was making a joke, but the magical properties of Alba water are as good an explanation as any for how seven boys in the same family developed the skill to play professional baseball. All these years later, long after all of her brothers retired, Shirley said she remains a baseball fan sort of—she roots for St. Louis Cardinals success. "I am a baseball fan to the extent that I watch the Cardinals all the time," she said.

Her brothers and parents would approve.

Delores Boyer Webb, who was born in 1933, when girls were not expected to go near athletic equipment except to pick it up off the floor if their brothers sloppily left it somewhere, said she is not a baseball fan.

"I was not really a baseball fan," she said. "We girls did the work. That's how the boys had so much time to play baseball. I guess I was a baseball fan for a time."

The truth was, what she really was getting at, is that Delores was not a baseball fan, but she was a Boyer fan. She followed the teams they played for and hoped for their success, though when she was in high school she was on Alba's cheerleading team and naturally cheered for her brothers.

All the years Kenny was in high school I went to a lot of ball games. I was proud of him and went to see him play ball. Everyone in the family talked about how amazing it was that all of them got to play baseball professionally. I followed the Cardinals (for Cloyd and Ken) and the Yankees (for Clete). Later, my sons kind of kept me up on how their uncles were doing. They were big baseball fans. I could tell people about my brothers.

Delores was not above a little bragging about her brothers playing in the major leagues, and that was consistent with how other family members felt about them, too. There was widespread pride in the family about what the trio of big leaguers did and were doing, and how the other brothers were also playing for pay in the minors. These were pretty glamorous jobs, not the average come-out-of-school and go to work in construction or being a police or fireman, even teacher, doctor or lawyer. Professional baseball player was one of the most sought-after jobs in America. It probably carried almost as much cache as being governor or president.

While Ken Boyer in the National League and Clete Boyer in the American League were always praised as being amongst the very best third basemen in their leagues and they played the same position, they were very different people for brothers who grew up in the same town in the same family.

"Clete fun-loving? That's an understatement," Delores said. "He did always have a good time. I don't think anybody could match him. He was a show by himself. Kenny was a little more reserved, a little more serious."

Although the occasion occurred after Cloyd was done playing and Ken and Clete were well into their major league careers with their signature teams, the moment that capped everything for the Boyers in Missouri was the 1964 World Series. That season the championship of major league baseball pitted Kenny's St. Louis Cardinals against Clete's New York Yankees. Taking sides was pretty much forbidden amongst the siblings and the parents, but everyone in Alba—as well as the nation—was riveted to the doings going on in those two big cities.

"We got a new television set for the World Series," Delores said.

19

NEXT STOP
(Cloyd)

N ot wanting to believe that his active pitching career was at a stand-
still, a dead end, Cloyd Boyer kept signing on with minor-league
clubs, hoping to regain some of his best pitching stuff. He prayed that his
arm and shoulder got healthy again. He wanted to be a starter, but accepted
work in a bullpen. When Cot Deal made him a player-coach, he didn't
balk. It kept him with a team.

By the time he had his last fling with the Indianapolis Indians in 1961,
a dispassionate look at his situation would have told him it was all over.
But he refused to accept that sentence and was willing to try anything that
would keep him on the mound and give him one last shot at the big
leagues.

As is often the case with pitchers who throw their energy into learning
the knuckleball, Cloyd Boyer was at the end of his rope, otherwise out of
ideas. The baffling knuckleball, which at its best is a tremendous tool for
pitchers in terms of fooling batters, is famous for being difficult to control
and master. It is often the pitch of last resort for pitchers who still cling
to the possibility of resurrecting their careers. Boyer gave it a try.

"I finally went to the knuckleball the last couple of years," Boyer said.
"I was still under contract to Indianapolis. I didn't know if I could still
pitch, but I was going to try. A couple of guys suggested trying the knuckleball. I just had to come up with something to get some hitters out."

Catcher Ken Retzer—who played parts of four seasons in the majors
with the old Washington Senators—was Boyer's guinea pig. Cloyd had
trepidation about committing his all to the knuckler. In his prime he got
people out with the fastball. It was a big step to trust the knuckler. "I told
Ken Retzer, 'I've been messing around with the knuckleball down in the

pen and I'm going to start throwing it.' Once in a while I would shake him off to throw the knuckler, but he wouldn't let me. Finally, he said, 'If you're going to be a knuckleball pitcher, you're going to have to throw it all of the time.' That helped me. He made me throw it."

The new manager of the Indianapolis Indians for 1961 was a veteran coach, John Hutchings, a one-time big-league pitcher for the Cincinnati Reds who was a member of that team's 1940 World Series champions. At spring training in Hollywood, Florida, Cloyd was giving it a last fling trying to stick around and become a regular pitcher again. As a former pitcher himself whose major league career spanned just six seasons, Hutchings was sympathetic to Boyer. But he also related to him because he was one of the older players.

Boyer said Hutchings was diagnosed with cancer. Distraught over the situation, Hutchings remained on the scene, but he kept badgering Boyer to stay up late and play gin rummy with him.

Hell, he wouldn't let me go to bed. He made me sit up and play gin with him. I kept telling him, "You know, I'm used to getting my rest." He didn't want me to leave. What he was afraid of was if he went to sleep, he wouldn't get up. He latched onto me because I had been there with him in Indianapolis for a while when he was coaching. I always had a tendency to get along with people pretty easily. The season started and we didn't get off to a good start. I got off to a bad start. We went on a road trip to Denver, flying in this little old DC-6 airplane. As soon as we landed he said, 'Come up to my room. Gotta play some gin.' I said, "John, damn, I've got to get some rest, you know."

Cloyd informed Hutchings that he was pitching so poorly that every day when he woke up he worried he was going to get released. Hutchings told him that as long as he was there, Cloyd had nothing to worry about on that score. "I didn't want to say it, but I was thinking, because of his health, 'You may not be here much longer,'" Boyer said. "I felt sorry for him because his health was getting worse, and around the Fourth of July they let him go."

Hutchings was only 47 when he died on April 27, 1963. The official cause of death was uremia. Hutchings was out and was replaced by Ted Beard as manager and Dick Littlefield as pitching coach. Soon after, Cloyd was called into the manager's office and asked if he could pitch every third day. His arm didn't hurt, though he had little of his old zip, but he said he could. "I was throwing that knuckleball," he said. "That's about all I was throwing at the time." Indianapolis won 17 of the 21 games that he started.

Cloyd probably threw his knuckler at a velocity of 70 mph. As every pitcher swiftly learns, mastering the knuckler is a relative term. He may think he is in charge, but often the pitch is. Cloyd said his knuckler was not very good. Once in a while he was so wild the catcher couldn't catch it. That is far from unique to him, however.

"You know, I wasn't really a knuckleball pitcher," Cloyd said. "I would never claim to be. I was just doing it to hang on. I found out that the more speed I got on it, which is only common sense, the quicker it would break. I found out that would help me throw it better. I talked to Phil Niekro about it."

Niekro, a member of the Baseball Hall of Fame, won 318 games, mostly counting on a knuckleball.

"My knuckler didn't break that much," Cloyd said. "Sometimes the hitters would miss it pretty good, but really that kept my arm alive for a couple of years. It helped me feed my family, was the way I looked at it."

The end was in sight, though Cloyd never quite officially retired. In 1962, brother Clete used his influence with the Yankees to get Cloyd a job coaching New York's minor league affiliate in Richmond, Virginia, for $6,000 a year. He was technically on Indianapolis' playing roster in spring training, but had no faith he would be kept on. "I don't know if I would have made it through spring training with Indianapolis," Cloyd said. "I might have and I might not. I wanted to stay in baseball. That's all I knew."

Richmond was a pretty good place to be. The team was in the International League and belonged to the Yankees, so there were some pretty talented players. The manager was Sheriff Robinson, who later was a coach and scout for the New York Mets. Cloyd often coached third base, trying to coax runners home. In mid-year, however, the organization fired the manager in Shelby, North Carolina, of the Western Carolinas League and asked Cloyd to take over.

The Yankees signed young pitchers and sent them to Cloyd to work with and teach. He might only work with a young guy for a week at a time, and then the Yanks reassigned the fuzzy-cheeked hurler somewhere else. "I worked pretty hard," Cloyd said, one of the hazards of the low minors being that the team insignia baseball cap is not the only hat that must be worn to earn a salary. "I had to manage. I had to coach. I was the groundskeeper, trainer and bus driver."

Of all the tasks, driving the team around was the most challenging. When offering him the job the Yankees informed Cloyd that was going to be part of his job description. "Hell, I've never driven a bus," he responded. "I don't have a chauffeur's license. I have never driven a bus and I don't like to drive big trucks. They said, 'Well, that's part of the job.'"

When Cloyd reported to the team and informed the local leadership group that he did not have the proper license to drive the bus, the man said, "'You don't need to worry, I'm the judge in this county.' So I drove the bus, somehow getting it up and down those country hills."

Cloyd's days as a pitcher for pay were over. It was not a premeditated decision. He had not thought about retirement over the winter. Going into the spring of 1962, he fully intended to play. Rather abruptly, he was a coach, no longer a hurler.

"It just came up suddenly like that," Boyer said. "I knew I wasn't going to go anywhere as a pitcher again. I was done. I was just hanging on. It was my time. I knew I was about finished. If the job hadn't come up, I would have kept trying to pitch. If I could have still brought the knuckleball to the plate, I might have made the Indianapolis roster."

One of Cloyd Boyer's friends in the game was Stan Lopata, a catcher for both the Philadelphia Phillies and Milwaukee Braves who retired in the early 1960s. He watched Boyer's struggles to stay on and marveled at his adjustment to the knuckleball. He teased Boyer about it. "Old Stan Lopata told me one time, 'Cloyd, dang, you're getting slower every year.' 'I'm going to have to move the plate up for you.' He was kidding me. Maybe he was just jealous of my knuckleball."

In a way, retirement loomed over Cloyd Boyer's shoulder like the Grim Reaper. He knew he was going to face the issue soon. He didn't want to, but if he had to it was important to have a landing spot where he could continue his livelihood in professional baseball. That made the coaching offer to head to Richmond, and then manage in Shelby, particularly timely.

"I wanted to stay in baseball so I was grateful I was able to stay in by becoming a coach," Cloyd said. "It was gonna happen (retirement). I was hoping a coaching opportunity was gonna happen, too. I worked hard at sticking with baseball. I stayed in it and that was one thing I was very proud of. I got a pension out of my years in the game."

That was the beginning of a much longer scouting, coaching and managing career in baseball than Cloyd Boyer ever spent throwing. A year later the Yankees rewarded him with a more intriguing job. He became the roving pitching instructor for the entire minor league organization rather than sticking with just one team for the summer. That's how Cloyd absorbed the coaching role through the mid–1960s—on the go, watching and studying just about every pitcher in the organization from the lowest rungs of the minors to the big club.

I generally stayed in town long enough to see the pitching rotation twice, which would be about ten days. I kept that up and everything was going along all right. I was doing my traveling chores in 1968 and the manager in

AAA Syracuse quit. The Yankees wanted me to go manage in Syracuse. But the guy who ran the team there didn't want me. He wanted Frank Verdi, who was managing in Binghamton. He got his wish. Frank went there and I went to AA Binghamton. My brother Ronnie was playing there.

That was when the Yankees signed their top draft pick, Thurman Munson, and sent him to Cloyd Boyer for evaluation. Farm director Johnny Johnson wanted Cloyd to watch Munson and then tell him what level he was capable of playing at right then. Cloyd made a quick assessment that Munson was ready for the majors right away, and that's what he told the hierarchy. When asked where he thought Munson should be playing, Cloyd was blunt. "Yankee Stadium," he said.

Johnson thanked him for his frankness, but said he didn't think manager Ralph Houk would go for it. Houk had a reputation for not wanting to take on young players if they were shy on pro experience.

He was out of college. He went to Kent State and he played for me for a week. You didn't have to be Einstein to pick him out. Thurman really appreciated the things I said about him. That was putting a feather in his hat. But I was just giving my opinion. We had a bad club and he was catching shutouts for us and batting .400. For better than a month I'd say, he was hitting over .400. He was a straightaway hitter, hitting line drives all over the park. Then he started thinking, "Well, I can hit the ball out of the park." He'd go two or three at-bats and make outs and you could tell what he was trying to do.

In Boyer's mind, Munson was tampering with a good thing. If he stayed calm and just did what came naturally he would hit. But he was starting to force things, as if he had to go for home runs. So Boyer took the young player aside and asked what the heck he was up to.

I said, "Thurman, what are you trying to do?" He said, "What do you mean?" I said, "Are you trying to hit a home run?" He'd go, "Well..." I said, "We talked about this. We went through this. I don't want you to go for it all. You're going to get your home runs. But you're not really a home-run hitter. You probably never will be, especially at Yankee Stadium being a right-hand hitter."

Besides Munson, one of Cloyd's other charges was brother Ron Boyer. When fathers and sons end up together in such situations, they muddle through them. Cloyd could have said he was extra hard on Ron compared to other players, or that he was going to treat him exactly the same, but years after they teamed up he admitted that he gave Ron every chance to succeed in Binghamton.

"I knew I was going to play him even if it cost me my job," Cloyd said. "But I didn't think Ronnie was a prospect. I never did tell him that, not to this day. But I was going to play him every day because he was my brother. It wasn't right. I knew that. But that was just the way it was going to be."

The Binghamton Triplets had another third baseman that may have deserved more playing time, Cloyd said. But he was not particularly enamored of his skills. The player was a good power hitter, but didn't drive in runners in the clutch. He also struck out a lot.

"I didn't think he was a prospect, either, so I wasn't going to play him over my brother," Cloyd said. Practically no one was hitting well on the club besides Munson, but a few times the other player challenged Cloyd, saying he might not have been hitting for average more than Ron Boyer, but he had more power. "Finally, I said, 'You might as well know it right now. Ronnie is going to play. As long as I'm here, he's going to play.'"

Cloyd and Ronnie went out to dinner together, spent more time together than they had before because Cloyd was so much older and was out of the house when Ronnie was playing in Alba. "It was a bonus experience for me," Cloyd said. "I was proud of him even though he wasn't doing as well as I hoped he would."

The arrangement didn't end up lasting all season, however. Cloyd thought Munson would be gone quickly, promoted, but Munson stayed in Binghamton and Cloyd did not. Before the season ended the Yankees called upon him to make another move. The American League was expanding by two teams in 1969, adding the Kansas City Royals and the Seattle Pilots, who quickly morphed into the Milwaukee Brewers. The Yankees were going to have to make judgment calls on many players throughout the organization. They needed to understand who in the minors had the capability of moving up and whom they should protect from the expansion draft on the major league roster.

They didn't want to give away young players with the potential for long careers and they didn't want to hang onto veteran players who might soon be on the downside of their careers. Cloyd and a scout were asked to tour the country, checking out the teams in the Yankees organization before the end of the season in order to help the front office make its decisions prior to the draft.

"My job was to send a report on all of the players," Cloyd said. "When I finished the season wasn't over yet, and they asked me to go to Rochester to evaluate a player at first base that they might make a trade for with the Orioles. I didn't think the kid was a prospect and they didn't make the trade."

Meanwhile, once Cloyd Boyer departed from Binghamton, Munson, whom he had a special rapport with, did not get along well with the successor manager—the third of the season there. Boyer and Munson were very tight.

> He told me he thought more of me than his dad. I don't know what happened after I left, but he didn't hit as well. In the end they had to keep him out of the lineup for a couple of days to let him finish at .301. They wanted him to hit .300. The next year in spring training Thurman told me, "I just couldn't get along with the guy." I said, "Well, that's your fault. I'm gonna blame you for that because I know the guy and he's a good guy. He isn't going to do anything to hurt you. And you didn't really need anybody to tell you what to do because the Lord gave you the ability to play."

When the team did make the trek to play Waterbury in New York City at Yankee Stadium, Cloyd made sure Ron was in the lineup, and he so badly wanted that long foul ball that Ron slugged to travel fair out of the building.

> He would have had something to talk about all his life, that he had hit fair ball out of Yankee Stadium. It just went foul. He played hard. I was really proud to coach him as my brother. Ronnie gave you all that he had. And that's all you can do. You can't do more than that. He was a good fielder, but I didn't think he was ever going to hit enough (.183 that year). I can't compare him with Clete or Kenny, but I thought he could have played in the big leagues in the field. He wasn't a speed demon like Kenny. He ran average. But he didn't hit and you feel even worse when the player is your brother. You don't want to see him look bad. He just didn't hit. The reason he did not make the majors was not that he didn't work hard enough for it.

During the time period when Cloyd Boyer was fighting the battle to stay in the majors as a pitcher and his early days coaching, he and Nadine had five children. There were three boys—Kenton, named after Cloyd's brother, Mike and Jim—and two girls. One girl, Theresa Ann, died when she was only three days old. The other was Cheryl.

In 1968, when Cloyd was managing in Binghamton, Jim was the batboy and he became quite close to Thurman Munson. He remained his biggest fan. That summer there was a picture of Munson and batboy Jim on one of the team scorecards.

When the season ended, ten-year-old Jim went back to school, Munson was poised to become a big-leaguer, and Cloyd was ready for his next assignment for the Yankees.

20

PLAYING WITH THE BEST
(Clete)

B y the time Clete Boyer became the New York Yankees' full-time third baseman in 1960 after his apprenticeship with the Kansas City Athletics as a bonus baby, time served in the minors, and playing part-time in New York, he was 23.

But walking into the starting lineup for the New York Yankees during that era was no small thing. Once the lineup was set, the regulars stuck around for years. Also, with the team located in the largest media market, in the nation's biggest city, players became better known than if they were regulars on teams like the A's.

One major reason for that is that the Yankees were winners. They were the biggest winners of all time in baseball, and their history of success dated back roughly 40 years to the acquisition of Babe Ruth. Arguably, the Yankees put together three distinct, dynastic eras from Ruth's heyday on, and this was one of them. Boyer was part of it and that meant he had a high profile in the game and among fans everywhere of the game.

Casey Stengel was out as manager following the seventh-game loss to the Pirates in 1960, ending his twelve-year run in the Yankees' dugout with a fantastic ten pennants. But that didn't mean the Yankees were about to start losing.

Between 1960 and 1964, with Boyer a stalwart at third, the Yankees won five straight American League pennants. New York faced five different opponents in the World Series: the Pirates, the Cincinnati Reds, the San Francisco Giants, the Los Angeles Dodgers, and the St. Louis Cardinals. The Yankees won twice, giving Boyer two World Series championship rings.

While Clete never hit for a high average in the majors—and his stats more resembled those of a typical light-hitting shortstop—he came up with his share of timely hits. In 1960, he hit 14 home runs and drove in 46 runs. In 1961, he hit 11 home runs and knocked in 55. The next season, 1962, was his finest at the plate with the Yankees. He smacked 18 home runs, batted in 68 runs, and hit .272. In 1963, Boyer's numbers were 12 homers and 64 RBI, and in 1964, he clouted eight home runs and drove in 52 runs.

To a large extent those were journeymen statistics at the plate. But if Clete Boyer was only an average hitter, he earned his Yankees pinstripes in the field. He was a magician with a glove and he stole runs from opponents the way he handled himself at third. On a weaker team Boyer might have been deemed a luxury item since third base is usually seen as a power position in the batting order. But the Yankees had more than their share of big boppers. Boyer added another dimension, contributing in a different way to team success.

"I always took as much pride with my glove as most guys take with their bats," Clete Boyer said. "I worked hard to become as good as I could. I broke in as a shortstop and always played third base like a shortstop. I covered as much ground as I could and took away a lot of hits by being quick."[1]

Clete's self-evaluation pretty much tracked Cloyd's observation of his work habits. Big brother always said Clete put his all into the game. It was appreciated by New York manager Ralph Houk, too, Stengel's successor on the bench. "Defense wins baseball games," Houk said. "That's why Clete was so important to us."[2]

The biggest power hitters, Mickey Mantle and Roger Maris, roamed the outfield, but the Yankees had a very solid all-around infield with Boyer at third, Tony Kubek at shortstop, Bobby Richardson at second base and Bill "Moose" Skowron at first base. Skowron also hit for power, but the quartet made for sound protection for the pitchers and worked together smoothly to pull off a high number of double plays. This may have been a home run-hitting team, but New York still had to get the other guys out, so high-caliber fielding was also critical.

Boyer also thought he would have hit better in the majors if he had played most of his career in a hitter-friendly park or a smaller one. Before it was remodeled in the 1970s, the original Yankee Stadium, opened in 1923, had voluminous dimensions in left and center fields, especially center field, where the Monument Park homage to Yankees greats was later constructed.

"I think I could have had some big numbers if I had played at a small stadium like the one in Atlanta instead of Yankee Stadium," Boyer said. But late in life he also said, "I still get a thrill when I get back to Yankee Stadium. I cried the first time I went out to Monument Park and saw those monuments and plaques for Babe Ruth and Lou Gehrig. I still cry when I walk out there."[3]

Since both Clete and Ken played third base, many comparisons were made between them. Ken was the better hitter. Cloyd said they were very different people. According to Cloyd,

> The thing about Clete was that he was pretty cocky. Ken was going out with this girl and trying to get her to marry him, and she didn't even know he played ball. He wasn't flamboyant and he didn't talk about playing very much. There were some headlines from newspapers when Ken was playing that called him a "mystery man." That's because he was reserved and kept to himself. Clete was more outgoing and liked New York. Some may have said he was suited for New York. Maybe Ken was better suited for St. Louis, but Ken would have been a success anywhere he played in the big leagues. He just liked to win.

Clete tended to talk more about what he could do than let his actions just speak on their own. When Clete played basketball he wanted the ball in his hands, and when Cloyd and Clete were together in spring training with the Yankees he boasted about his hoops ability and wanted Cloyd to back him up, provide verification. According to Cloyd,

> A bunch of us might be sitting around a table and Clete would say, "Cloyd, tell all these guys how I could hit that bucket." When he was a traveling coach with the Yankees he'd go around and talk to the coaches and minor league managers and tell them, "Next time you see my brother Cloyd, just ask him how I could hit that bucket." And of course I said, "Yeah, he could score, but he didn't tell you how he couldn't play defense or rebound any."

Cloyd said Clete always had a scorer's mentality, or perhaps a shooter's mentality, on the basketball floor. He wanted to be the high scorer and took shots even when they were misguided. "He was wanting to score 40 points a night," Cloyd said. "He could score a lot in high school, but a lot of times he had two or three guys guarding him and he would still shoot. He was kind of like some of those guys in college and the pros now. You know they're going to shoot even if they have guys all over them. But Clete could put it in the hole."

It made perfect sense to the other brothers that Clete would brag about his basketball prowess. That's because he probably talked more than all of the other Boyers combined. He was pretty young when he lost any hint of shyness, if he ever had any at all.

"Clete would sit down and tell you anything and everything," Lynn Boyer said. "He was a pretty good talker. Clete and I spent a lot of time fishing together, too, mostly for catfish. We'd go to Truman Lake, which is about 54,000 acres, a big one. Truman's a headwater for the Ozarks."

Clete Boyer was in his element playing with the New York Yankees. There was more attention on the Yankees than any other team. They won more than any other team. Five years in a row they captured AL pennants and appeared in the World Series.

In the 1960s, when Clete was holding down third base for the Yankees, Cloyd was coaching in the organization, and Ronnie was trying to work his way through the minors, Clete got into the spirit of the trio being decked out in the same uniforms in spring training. "Like old home week," Clete said. "Everywhere you step, you're tripping over a Boyer."[4]

Ron Boyer was pressed into a corner and asked who was better at third base, not a terribly fair question given that both Clete and Ken were his brothers. "They are both good," he said. "Maybe Clete's a little better fielder, but Ken carries that big stick."[5]

When he looked back from the vantage point of about 30 years later, Clete said the best Yankees team he played on was the 1961 squad, the one that many people rate as among the best ever in the sport. Not only was that a dominant club in American League play, it followed through and won the World Series, which some of the other Yankees squads were unable to do against the best of the National League.

"Health wise and everything, there's no comparison to the 1961 team. Everyone was healthy in '61. We had guys on the bench like Hector Lopez and guys that could play. We had three great catchers in Elston Howard, Johnny Blanchard, and Yogi Berra. They (the whole roster) could do most of the four things it takes, plus everybody had good instincts." Boyer also had perhaps his best World Series against the Cincinnati Reds. "I had a good year in the field, but didn't hit that well. All of a sudden in the World Series I made three or four great plays and got a couple of clutch hits. That was really a good Series."[6]

Boyer viewed the 1962 World Series against the Giants as a dangerous matchup, since the Giants had won 103 regular-season games. He felt the Yankees were just about as strong as they had been in 1961, and wasn't surprised the series went the distance.

"I thought we had a great team in '62 when we played the Giants in the World Series," he said. "I thought that was an even match because I thought the Giants had a great ball club."[7]

Ironically, one of Clete's memories of playing with such a powerhouse team that included home run sluggers like Mickey Mantle and Roger Maris was not a pleasant one. When those guys blasted the ball out of the park, Boyer felt pitchers, seeking revenge during an era when enforcement of throwing inside was not so common, took it out on him. "I got knocked down a lot batting behind Maris, Mantle and those other guys," Boyer said. "Somebody had to go. They're not going to knock the pitcher down. I went down a lot. I got used to it."[8]

Much later, when *Sports Illustrated* was reviewing Clete Boyer's career, it noted rather plaintively that his timing was all wrong because he was viewed as a great fielder, but not as great as Brooks Robinson, so Robinson won all of the Gold Glove Awards at third base. The article made the comparison that Boyer was to Robinson as Salieri was to Mozart.

Clete, true his nature, did talk about loving the spotlight in the field. "I had the same concentration in the field that Ted Williams had at bat," he said, meaning laser focused. "Even when we took infield, I knew people were watching me. Guys from the other team. The fans. I was alive. I was on stage. I loved it. With my glove, I felt I could handle anything. With my bat, I wasn't so sure."[9]

No question Clete's Yankees teammates admired what he did with the glove. Shortstop Tony Kubek held down the spot in the infield next to Boyer and saw him make plays close-up more than anyone except perhaps the third base umpire. "How can there be anybody better than the greatest?" Kubek said of Boyer.[10]

Second baseman Bobby Richardson, a very religious man who didn't drink, unlike Clete, who enjoyed hanging out in bars, said that the difference in their habits never made any difference in their mutual admiration, and they liked one another's company in other settings. According to Richardson,

> It was always a given that I wouldn't go out drinking after a game. We would all joke around and cut up in the locker room after a game and then we would go out in our separate groups. There was a group that went out drinking and a group that didn't drink—usually including Tony Kubek, Bob Turley and me. But there were no tensions or conflicts between the two groups. I never felt that the ones in my social group were my friends and the guys in the other group were just my teammates. It was more as if I had two types of friends on the team, and my rapport with both groups was great.
>
> In the off-season, even after I retired, I never lacked for teammates who came to visit me in Sumter (South Carolina) to go hunting, and that included guys from the "drinking" group. Clete Boyer is a good example. We were very close friends when we were Yankees and remained that way long after our playing days.[11]

Richardson played in the same infield as Boyer for eight years. He had the same viewpoint of his skills as the majority, and as New York sportswriters espoused in their papers. "I consider him to be one of the best third basemen of his time," Richardson said. "Clete was an excellent player who has never seemed to receive the recognition he deserved. Even though Clete and I were friends, we lived opposite lifestyles. He was known for his hard living and constant battle with alcohol. I prayed many nights for my good friend."[12]

One of Clete's good friends on the Yankees was Roger Maris, and he had an up-close-and-personal view of the home run chase of 1961 when Maris and Mantle were pursuing Babe Ruth's record of 60 home runs in a season. The worst thing that happened, adding pressure to an already pressurized Maris, Clete thought, was when Commissioner Ford Frick ruled that the record had to be broken within 154 games, the same as Ruth played, not in 162 games as the schedule now read.

"There was a strange feeling in the ball park all day," Clete said of the occasion when Maris set the mark by ripping his 61st homer off of the Red Sox's Tracy Stallard. "There was surprising quiet until Roger hit it and even more quiet afterward. Roger was never one to show his emotions, and even though he was obviously happy and smiling a lot when he hit it, there was an edge of sadness to the entire day. There was so much pressure that day, so much tension I could hardly breathe. Roger wanted that one badly."[13]

Actually, it is little remembered that Maris did hit 60 home runs within 154 games. His original number 36 homer against the Baltimore Orioles came in a game that was rained out, and he lost it from his total. Clete, who officially hit 11 homers on the season, also blasted a homer in that same game and later joked, "What about me? If it hadn't rained, I would have had 12."[14]

Later, Boyer said he was closer to Maris than any other teammate and in some ways closer to him than he was to his brother Ken, who was playing in the majors at the same time, but who was in the other league with the Cardinals. Their paths rarely crossed. "I was probably closer to Roger than I was to my own brother. We spent more time together. My brother was always playing someplace else. You had to get to know Roger. Sometimes he wouldn't let you. But if he liked you, he would really open up. He was pictured as a quiet, introverted, reclusive guy. He wasn't that way at all. He loved to laugh."[15]

Maybe some of that was being around Clete, who always tried to leave 'em laughing. He was always trying to have a good time and took it personally if anyone around him failed to enjoy the night, or his company. "We would go out and have a few drinks," Clete said. "I would have ten double Scotches, and he would quit at five, really have a blast. There wasn't anything mean about Roger. He liked to be alone with his friends."[16]

When Maris died of cancer on December 14, 1985, Clete was one of the pall bearers and he spoke at the funeral.

The dugout leader of the 1961 team was Ralph Houk, in his first season as successor to the legendary Casey Stengel. It didn't take long before he became a Clete Boyer fan and also was lured into making comparisons between Boyer and Brooks Robinson. According to Houk,

> After Clete played there a while there were arguments over who was the best third baseman—Brooks Robinson of the Orioles or Boyer. To me, Boyer was as good a fielding third baseman as I've ever seen. He could go to his left or his right, he could play deep, he could play in close. He'd stay in front of hard-hit balls. He had great hands. He had that outstanding arm. I think he had a better arm than Brooks, although he didn't get rid of the ball as well. But he wasn't that good a hitter. Clete was one player I might have helped a little. I think I gave him confidence. Casey would pinch-hit for him all the time, and that can get a player down.[17]

Clete Boyer was close pals with Mickey Mantle—they drank together at times—and Mantle said Boyer was part of the best infield he ever played with. He also echoed Houk in suggesting what Stengel did with Boyer at bat got into his head. Most notably there was that occasion when Stengel pinch-hit for Boyer early in the 1960 World Series. "Clete's family was there to see him play," Mantle said, "including his brother Ken, a great third baseman for the Cardinals. I'm not sure Clete ever got over being lifted before his first time at bat in the World Series."[18]

Clete made up for that the next season, even if he did hold a grudge against Stengel. He couldn't get over his good fortune being part of such an overpowering team in 1961 and being an eyewitness to the history being made by Maris and Mantle with seemingly every swing of their bat for six months.

> The year belonged to Roger and Mickey. Those guys were just such great players. I remember a doubleheader in Chicago where I hit two home runs. That was pretty good, considering the White Sox pitching. What the hell, you hit a couple of homers and you expect to see your name in the paper. But Roger hit four that day. His name was in the headlines and mine was only in the box score. But no one was jealous of Roger and Mickey getting all the publicity because they deserved it.[19]

Clete Boyer made an indelible mark in the 1961 World Series when the Yankees steamrolled Cincinnati. Boyer said it was his finest Series. He had Reds manager Fred Hutchinson raving about him. His teammates also recalled how superb he was during those five games that the Yankees dominated. "Clete always made great plays," said Yankees Hall of Fame pitcher Whitey Ford, "but no third baseman ever played better than Clete did in the 1961 Series."[20]

The plays that stood out above all others occurred during the opener, a two-hit shutout by Ford. In the second inning, diving towards the third-base line, Clete handled a one-hopper off the bat of Gene Freese and from foul territory, on his knees, he nailed Freese at first. In the eighth inning, Dick Gernert smashed a hard

Clete Boyer is considered one of the best fielding third basemen of all time (National Baseball Hall of Fame Library, Cooperstown, N.Y.).

grounder to the hole between third and short. Clete dove to his left and threw Gernert out, again from his knees.

Gernert called Clete "a switch diver." Clete said even he was surprised he managed the play. "I had a game where it seemed like I could reach everything hit to me. When I think about Gernert's ball, I still don't know how I got it. I mean, I don't know how I got a glove on it, and I don't know how I got the throw over to first base. All I know is that if it were a movie, there might have to be a hundred takes and I still couldn't do it again.[21]

The little miracles would have been replayed 1,000 times on highlight shows during this modern era, but they basically remain unseen.

Boyer, as he made clear, was not sorry to see Stengel depart. "Everybody hated him," Boyer said. "When he came out of his mother, the doctor slapped her."[22]

That feeling may not have been unanimous, especially among sportswriters and fans who loved Stengel, but Clete was happy to have Houk take over for the 1961 season. Houk was an organization man whom many of the younger players had encountered on his way up, and he seemed the right man to take over a phenomenal team.

Ralph had to wait a long time to get the job. It's like going into a bakery, taking a number, and then sitting there until you're called. When you do get called, it's almost an honor. I think Ralph was honored to manage the 1961 team. He took over a great team. He didn't have to scream, and he didn't have to tell us what to do, because we already knew how to play. While he had a great team, it was to his credit that he didn't mess it up.[23]

Mantle, Ford, and Billy Martin were drinking partners in the 1950s. Later, Clete and Maris were the same. They liked to go out on the town when they were on the road especially, and that meant hanging out in bars. Sometimes that led to problems. At the end of spring training in 1965, Clete and Maris were charged after a civilian in a bar claimed they assaulted him. Clete had to post $200 bail.

Sometimes, admittedly, players showed up for the next day's game at less than full speed. Once in a while Mantle was one of them, and he got the call to play when he was not feeling up to it. Clete recalled a game when Mantle was out of sorts, but still smashed a line-drive home-run into the left-field seats against the Baltimore Orioles.

"He could play with a hangover," Clete said.[24] During the last days of his life, when he was very sick, Mantle dried out, stopped drinking and repented some of his old ways, indicating that possibly he had squandered some of his great talent. This did not relate at all to his knee problems, which ensured that he played in pain for years. Just maybe, he said, he would have improved on his Hall of Fame career and legendary accomplishments on the field if he took better care of his body and didn't play so hard.

Clete didn't see it that way. "I hate it when people say how much he wasted," he said. "How much better could he have been?"[25]

Clete Boyer played for the Yankees from 1959 to 1966, though the heyday was the 1960 to 1964 stretch when New York won the AL pennant each year and Boyer was an integral member of the club. One by one, each of the stalwarts of that great team got older or was traded, as the Yankees sought to rebuild. Boyer was just 29, about to turn 30, when he was shipped to the Atlanta Braves.

He was not particularly happy to vacate New York, and as a career-long American League player, was not especially knowledgeable about Atlanta, but his stay in the so-called capital city of the South proved to be rewarding and added another very worthwhile chapter to his baseball career.

21

THE FACE
OF THE CARDINALS
(Ken)

Ken Boyer, the one-time high school basketball star in Missouri, and
the former pitcher in the St. Louis Cardinals' chain, found his niche
at third base once the Cardinals realized he did have a strong arm, but it
was better put to use throwing out runners at first base than trying to
strike out batters at home plate.

Boyer was an All-Star by his second season as a regular, became a
seven-time All-Star and won the 1964 National League Most Valuable
Player Award, the reward for his finest season.

A five-time .300 hitter, Boyer usually drove in more than 90 runs in
a season and generally hit 25 or so homers each year. He also captured
five Gold Glove Awards for his excellence protecting third base.

In 1959, Boyer put together a 29-game hitting streak on his way to
a .309 average, his best to date, and a second All-Star appearance. Playing
with Stan Musial, his boyhood idol, Boyer evolved into one of the faces
of the Cardinals of that era. That season Boyer was named captain of the
Cardinals, the team he had rooted for since he was a youngster. This was
not an everyday thing in St. Louis. Red Schoendienst, another Cardinal
Boyer had admired for years, was the previous captain, and no one had
fulfilled the role for some years.

"The ball players look to Ken to lead the club," said manager Solly
Hemus. "The job gives him authority to beef on certain plays. The young
kids look to Boyer for advice and authority."[1]

Being named captain of a baseball team is more of an honorific than
anything else, but in 1959 it also carried with it a bonus of $500. And

$500 meant a bit more to players then. Boyer had also become a leader in the community, and one of his off-field activities was leading the Multiple Sclerosis Fund drive.

It was a big deal in St. Louis (obviously an example of a much different era in major league baseball) when the Cardinals agreed to a two-year contract with Boyer in 1961. That was the era of one-year contracts, and even a two-year pact was practically unheard-of around baseball at that time. Boyer's deal was for $100,000 and was St. Louis' first multi-year contract with a player in 12 years, since 1949 when Stan Musial signed for two years.

"We recognize this is an unusual procedure," said St. Louis general manager Bing Devine, "but Ken, like Musial, is an unusual ball player. It's certainly not a break in policy. Each case is to be decided individually." One of the chief arguments against multi-year contracts in the majors was that players would let their motivation flag. "I know this won't happen. As the Cardinal captain he's too much of a leader to let that happen."[2]

The one thing that Hemus and Boyer talked about before he officially was named captain was whether or not the other players would respond poorly to the addition of any captain to the ranks. "Not if they knew I was really there to help them," Boyer said. "I think they know by now that that's what I would want to do."[3]

The Cardinals had last won the pennant in 1946, and in 1963, with the announcement that Musial was going to retire following the season, players definitely wanted to win one for him as a going-away present. The Cardinals won 93 games, but it was the Dodgers' year. St. Louis finished second, six games back. "We made a great run for it," Boyer said. "We just lost momentum."[4]

Boyer turned in one of his best years, with 24 homers, 111 RBI, a .285 average, and a Gold Glove Award performance in the field.

At the end of the season, during a retirement ceremony for Musial, Boyer presented "Stan the Man" with a ring from the players that had his No. 6 uniform number formed in diamonds.

First named captain, and in the early 1960s a perpetual All-Star, Ken Boyer emerged as the on-field and off-field leader of the Cardinals, the most recognizable face in the lineup, partially due to longevity and partially due to performance.

"Kenny had some big hits in big games," said Red Schoendienst, who was traded to Milwaukee in the 1950s, but rejoined St. Louis for the last few years of his career in the early 1960s. "That should have gotten him more recognition. He had good instincts. He definitely knew how to play third base."

Ken Boyer was outstanding year after year. Like Clete he was a phenomenal fielder, but his hitting helped carry the Cardinals' batting order. He was the key guy. While Schoendienst was heading towards retirement, and Musial was on a farewell tour in 1963, the Cardinals beefed up the roster any way they could.

One critical addition was Dick Groat. In 1960, as the shortstop for the World Series champion Pittsburgh Pirates, Groat batted .325 to win the National League batting title, and he was also named MVP of the league. But in an ill-fated trade following the 1962 season, the Pirates parted with Groat and Diomedes Olivo for Don Cardwell and Julio Gotay. Score one big plus for the Cardinals.

Groat stepped in at short, led the NL in doubles with 43, batted .319 and made the All-Star team. He had gone from a pennant winner, playing next to a future Hall of Famer at second base in Bill Mazeroski, to a pennant contender, playing next to an All-Star third baseman. "I always said I was the luckiest guy in baseball," Groat said. "I always had great help in the field. Kenny was just magnificent. We palled around together. We drove to and from the ball park together. We were all business. Period. We both worked at the game. We talked about who was pitching that night."

Groat set a personal high for RBI with 73 in 1963, too. For someone who is very fondly remembered in Pittsburgh, particularly in connection with the World Series title, and who makes his home in that area, it seems surprising to hear Groat say that "I had the greatest year I ever had in my career in 1963. I was hitting behind Stan Musial and fielding next to Ken Boyer."

Tim McCarver, the long-time broadcaster following his long career on the field until his retirement from the booth following the 2013 World Series, was a younger player on the Cardinals when Boyer emerged as an All-Star and was anointed captain of the team.

McCarver, who was from Memphis, Tennessee, was just 17 years old when he made his major league debut with the Cardinals in September of 1959. He remained with the Cardinals through 1969 and played 21 years in the big leagues, retiring in 1980. He didn't see much major league action his first few seasons, but caught 127 games in 1963, his first year as a regular.

"Ken Boyer continued to be called captain for many years," McCarver said. "It's not a word that always comes with a lot of weight in baseball, but in his case it did. He was the captain in the truest sense. It was respect. That's what it was." While that is a testimonial to Boyer's leadership,

McCarver thought very highly of Boyer's on-field skills, too. "His range to the left was extraordinary," McCarver said of Boyer's patrolling of the turf around third base. "He was a magnificent base runner. He ran the bases with a long stride."

McCarver said that not only did he at one time date Boyer's sister-in-law, he grew very close to the team leader by socializing away from the diamond. "Every Sunday Kenny would invite us to a cookout at his house," McCarver said. "We became very close friends."

That might not have happened if one-time St. Louis general manager Frank Lane had his way. Lane was nicknamed "Trader Lane" because of his propensity to swap ball players around as if they were not human beings but merely the cardboard cutouts of themselves issued as baseball cards.

It didn't matter to Lane if a player was an icon, an All-Star, or a budding superstar, there was no such thing as untouchable. Lane would never be accused of being timid, of standing pat, or failure to explore all avenues to improve his team. He was a one-man circus of activity and if for some reason he didn't think a player was going to work out for him, he was quick to trade him again. More than once in the 1950s, Lane was willing to include Ken Boyer in a deal. Once, team owner Gussie Busch stepped in and put the kibosh on a trade with the Pirates.

Later, the Phillies approached St. Louis with another offer. Lane was gone, and Bing Devine was in, but he said no. While the trade is "a fair enough deal," Devine predicted, "I'll stake what little baseball reputation I've got that Boyer will become a great player."[5]

Devine was right. Boyer remained with the Cardinals and blossomed into a star.

Boyer was a very consistent player and at a high level. He hit between 23 and 28 home runs seven times in nine years in St. Louis. The other two seasons he hit 19 and 32. He drove in 90 to 98 runs five years in a row and then upped his production to 111 and 119, a figure that led the National League in 1964. Overall, Boyer smacked 282 home runs in his career.

"If Kenton had played in Chicago," said brother Ron Boyer, referring to Wrigley Field, "he probably would have hit 400 home runs. It's just a matter of where you play a lot of the time. Kenton didn't have injuries. Kenton was big and strong. He could hit a ball 500 feet, but a lot of his hits were line drives. As far as strength alone, he could hit a ball as far as anybody. I've heard people who lived locally (near Alba) who used to work in the mines in Pennsylvania and they used to go to Cardinals games in Philadelphia to see Kenton hit balls out over the roof in that Philadelphia Park (Connie Mack Stadium)."

During his days as a perennial National League All-Star with the St. Louis Cardinals, Ken Boyer proved to be the best hitter in the Boyer clan (National Baseball Hall of Fame Library, Cooperstown, N.Y.).

Alba, Missouri, kept close tabs on the progress of all the Boyer brothers, but because Ken played for the Cardinals and the residents could see his games on TV or listen to them on the radio, combined with his success, he retained a big following his home area. According to Ron Boyer,

> You talk to people that grew up with him and he was a legendary figure. When they had Ken Boyer Appreciation Day in St. Louis, they chartered a bus and drove all of these people to St. Louis. The people of Alba went in together and bought him a shotgun. Kenton was a big hunter. There were pictures of him with Stan Musial and Red Schoendienst hunting pheasant or quail. Ken really enjoyed hunting.

However, based on his stats, it's possible that Ken enjoyed hitting more than he did hunting. Ron remembers Ken rising to the occasion against the best pitchers of the time, from Don Drysdale to Juan Marichal. Ken Boyer said, referring to Warren Spahn,

> I've learned you can't pull some pitchers. I've found a right-handed hitter can't pull his screwball, fading low and away, and the only fastball he shows you is up and too tight. Hitting to right field, switching to a heavier bat a few years ago so I wouldn't commit myself on a pitch too soon, and choking my grip just a bit have given me a better control of the bat and made me a better hitter.[6]

The fact that Ken learned on the job and improved at the plate didn't surprise Ron Boyer at all.

> He was just an awesome overall hitter. He wasn't just a clutch hitter. It would be nice if you could just figure out how to explain things sometimes. Maybe you're seeing the ball better against this guy, the way he delivers the ball. You concentrate more against some guys. He just had a natural-born talent for athletics. I always thought Kenton could have been a football player, or a basketball player. Anything.

As good as Ken was on the field, Ron admired his brother for the way he handled himself off the field, as well. It didn't surprise him at all that Ken was appointed captain of the Cardinals. He had that demeanor and natural leadership qualities, too. According to Ron,

> One thing about Kenton is that he was the consummate pro. The way he carried himself, the way he acted, he was just so professional. He had character. Nowadays you see a lot of athletes in baseball, basketball and football, all sports and they score a touchdown and celebrate, or they hit a home run and stand at home plate and admire it. You can't do that. Years ago you'd be picking yourself up off the deck the next time you came to the plate. Some of these guys hit a ball and stand at the plate and the ball doesn't even go out of the park. That's the one thing that really gets me. If you hit the ball 600 feet, well yeah, but if you hit the ball and you're out at the warning track....

Periodically, old-time baseball stars are asked to make comparisons between stars of their generation and stars of the present. In 1964, someone approached the flamboyant hurler Dizzy Dean with that question about Ken Boyer. How did he match up against the greats of history in Dean's mind?

"Him and (Pie) Traynor," said Dean of the Pirates great who is in the Hall of Fame. "Boyer can out-run, out-throw, and out-field (Freddie) Lindstrom (another Hall of Famer) and hit with him, too."[7]

Dean, who won 30 games for the Cardinals in 1934 when they won the World Series, was aware that at that time Traynor was considered the greatest third baseman of all time. Dean talked a lot, but he knew what he was saying.

During Ken Boyer's best years in the majors, he represented St. Louis. At the time, St. Louis remained the southernmost city in big-league baseball, and the Cardinals had fans for a radius of hundreds of miles. This time period also overlapped with the Civil Rights movement, marches in Alabama and Mississippi, bloodshed in the battle for dignity and rights long denied.

St. Louis was considered the worst town to visit for many African American players, but in the midst of the maelstrom and controversies, as Americans began to catch up in reality to the image of the land of opportunity and fairness, stood the Cardinals. The team was a mix of white and black players, and it included white and black stars. Stan Musial, Red Schoendienst, Ken Boyer, Dick Groat and Tim McCarver were white. Bob Gibson, Bill White and Curt Flood were black. Julian Javier was Hispanic. Yet the team was harmonious, even if its city was not.

"The Cardinals were different," said Gibson, a Hall of Fame pitcher in the making at the time. "A group of us would go out to eat after a game on the road and there'd be a dozen guys or so, black and white. Some of the white players—Stan Musial and Ken Boyer, to start with—were as adamant against segregation as the black players were."[8]

Players do not have to love one another to succeed, even to win pennants and World Series, though most would admit that it helps. In 1964, when Ken Boyer had his finest year and was the true leader of the team during that first season after Musial retired, the Cardinals collaborated for a memorable run.

22

NATIONAL LEAGUE MVP
(Ken)

What a year it was for Ken Boyer. The 1964 campaign was his dream season, the best year of his career. In his prime, everything came together for Boyer at the plate and in the field. Boyer was a star by then, but in 1964 he elevated his game even more.

The season after the legendary Stan Musial retired (it was a shame he didn't hang on for one more year to reach another World Series), Boyer emerged as the heart and soul of the Cardinals. He was the leader in the clubhouse and he played superbly.

For the only time in his 15-year playing career, Boyer appeared in all 162 games. He batted .295, smacked 24 home runs, scored 100 runs, and led the National League with 119 RBI. He was the NL All-Star third baseman and, after his efforts led St. Louis to the pennant, he was voted Most Valuable Player.

Boyer had been in the majors since 1955. By the end of the 1964 season he was a seven-time All-Star and five-time Gold Glove Award winner. But in that era there was only one path to the World Series. There was no National League Championship Series. There was no Divisional Series. If your team didn't win the pennant, you went home for the winter. Boyer craved the opportunity to play on the October stage, to compete for a world championship.

"I've had just about everything there is in baseball," Boyer said. "But there's one thing I've missed. I think it would leave anyone like me with an empty feeling to have played 12 to 15 years without getting into a World Series."[1]

Ken Boyer filled that hole in his heart in 1964. He had plenty of help lifting the Cardinals to a 93–69 record and first place in the ten-team league. It was one of the most riveting pennant races in National League history. The Cardinals won the crown by one game over the second-place (tied) Philadelphia Phillies and Cincinnati Reds. Fourth-place San Francisco also won 90 games and was just three games back.

The man in the dugout for St. Louis was Johnny Keane, the old friend of the Boyer family. General manager Bing Devine built the team, but ownership ran out of patience and fired him in August before the team reversed itself and made its charge.

Still, by late September this was the Phillies' pennant to lose—and they did, enduring one of the worst collapses in history. Philadelphia played awful ball down the stretch and gave the pennant away. Going into the last days of the race, it was so crowded around first place that it was like a bunch of mosquitoes buzzing around a discarded piece of fruit.

St. Louis seized the opportunity, though the club's late surge came as a surprise to many. As late as August 23, the Cardinals were 11 games out of first. Between September 24 and September 30, the Cardinals won eight straight games, including a three-game sweep of Philadelphia. Then, alarmingly, the Cards lost two straight games to the lowly New York Mets to jeopardize their chances. It took a Bob Gibson gut-it-out win in relief over New York on October 4, the last day of the regular season, for St. Louis to prevail.

The bats really did it that day, however. Boyer walked three times, doubled in the tying run, and scored three runs. Tim McCarver had three hits and three RBI. Dick Groat had two hits. So did Lou Brock, Bill White, and Dal Maxvill. The 14-hit attack was the difference maker.

St. Louis needed them all to pull away. Before the Cardinals really loosened up the Mets built a 3–2 lead. Although Gibson was not at his best, he did claim his 19th win of the season.

Gibson was the staff ace, and when everything was on the line Keane wanted Gibson on the mound. He figured a weary Gibson still might be better than anyone else. Gibson was not anxious to get into the last game, but when the call came he put fatigue out of his mind. "Adrenaline has a way of making an athlete forget about his problems," Gibson said much later. "There's really no way to explain the velocity I had that day without bringing in extracurricular influences. I'd say the pressure helped. I loved pitching with pressure."[2]

In the locker room after the game, Boyer tried to analyze his emotions. "No matter what happens after today," Boyer said, "this winning the pennant has got to be the biggest thrill of all."[3]

From the vantage point of a half-century later, the Cardinals were an excellent team. Lou Brock became a Hall of Famer. So did Gibson. Boyer has been a borderline candidate. Curt Flood was a wonderful fielder who hit .300 even if he didn't exhibit much power. Groat was a clutch hitter and a past National League MVP. Bill White was a slick fielder and hard hitter at first base. The pitching staff was short on depth, but besides Gibson, Ray Sadecki had a career year, winning 20 games, and Curt Simmons won 18.

The acquisition of Brock that June in a trade with the Chicago Cubs is regarded as perhaps the most one-sided swap in baseball history. The Cardinals gave up pitcher Ernie Broglio, who had been a 20-game winner. Brock was a young player who hadn't shown much besides potential at that time. Broglio suffered injuries and never pitched as well again, and Brock blossomed immediately. In 103 games for the Cards in 1964, Brock batted .348 with 33 stolen bases.

After retiring as a player, the revered Red Schoendienst returned to the Cardinals as a coach under Keane, just in time to be part of the World Series. "The 1964 season was one of the most exciting in Cardinals history," Schoendienst said. "We would not have won the pennant if had we not made the trade for Brock."[4]

While it took a long time during the summer of 1964 for the Cardinals to jell—and the addition of Brock was a big help—one constant throughout the year was Boyer. By then Boyer had an elder-statesman aura about him for the younger players. He not only was a clutch hitter who made big plays, he handled himself with authority and poise. The esteemed Pulitzer Prize-winning journalist and author David Halberstam wrote,

> Boyer, as far as the younger players on the Cardinals were concerned, was a great role model, a consummate professional who played hard every day and never lost sight of his essential purpose. It was as if he had a God-given instinct about what was real and what was not real in baseball. Once Boyer made a great play at third base, moving all the way to shortstop to reach a hard grounder, and Dusty Boggess, who was umpiring, turned to (Tim) McCarver and told him, "Take a good look, son, because you're not going to see anyone like him again."[5]

However, when McCarver relayed the compliment, Boyer shrugged it off. He always remained grounded.

The only interruption in Boyer's steadiness that season was the month of June. He played with a back injury and hit only .225 for the month, a figure that held his season's average below .300. Perhaps that gave popular announcer Harry Caray the opening he needed to criticize Boyer.

According to the Boyer sisters, who listened to the announcer on the radio, Caray at times seemed to have it in for Boyer, gratuitously insulting his fielding even though he was a perpetual Gold Glove Award winner. Boyer mostly ignored Caray's on-air gibes. Certainly the type of season he had in 1964 had to shut up Caray a bit. Caray just seemed to be harder on Boyer when he made a mistake than on others, and Caray's voice was influential. As popular as Boyer was in general in St. Louis, Caray's pecking away at him provoked some adverse reaction among fans. Caray would also disingenuously say, "I don't know why they're booing him."[6] Close listeners knew exactly why. Bob Gibson and other players took note of Caray's sniping about Boyer, and they felt it was unfounded.

Tim McCarver was still a young player in 1964, in the earlier days of a baseball career that spanned more than 50 years on the field and in the broadcast booth. Boyer acted as a mentor to him that year and showed McCarver that he could be a better player if he controlled his temper. McCarver considers Boyer one of the great idols in Cardinals history. "From Stan Musial to Bob Gibson, for me Kenny Boyer was at least as popular as anybody with the Cardinals from the Gas House Gang group through the next couple of generations," McCarver said.

Over the years, major league baseball has changed the timing of its announcement of the awarding of the biggest regular-season awards. However, voting for regular-season honors closes before post-season play begins, so how an athlete performs in the playoffs, or in the World Series, doesn't affect the balloting.

Once the Cardinals clinched the pennant, they were on the way to participation in the World Series, but the sport held off on making any announcements of the major awards until well after the Series concluded. The announcement of Boyer's selection as the majors' "Player of the Year" by The Sporting News came at the end of November, and the news that he was named the National League's Most Valuable Player was revealed shortly thereafter.

The Sporting News honor came first and Boyer was pleased to hear about it. It was one of the things that helped make 1964 so special for the player. "The season couldn't have been more satisfying," Boyer said. "I think I did just about everything I had hoped to do. Each spring, of course, you're always asked what your goals are for the season. I've always tried to avoid anything like that."[7] But this time all of his secret hopes and goals were realized.

It's quite possible that Boyer did not stop smiling from the beginning of October until spring training of 1965, the way good things kept happening for him.

Lynn Boyer holds a newspaper reporting on the 1964 St. Louis Cardinals achievements—his older brother Ken was the star third baseman for that squad (courtesy Cloyd and Nadine Boyer).

"This is an honor every baseball player dreams of winning," Boyer said of being officially anointed the NL's most valuable player. "To get it, you have to get a lot of breaks and have a fairly consistent year. But most important, you have to have teammates like I had—and they should feel they share in it."[8]

Fairly consistent? That was too self-effacing. Consistency alone does not pay off in MVP trophies. The MVP rewards excellence.

Boyer was actually not home when the telephone rang to inform him about being a winner of the MVP—he was on his way back from one of his favorite pastimes, a quail hunting trip. His wife Kathleen took the call and was the one who informed him when he opened the front door. After that the word got out and the telephone kept on ringing, with friends and family calling to offer congratulations.

The runner-up in the voting was the Phillies outfielder Johnny Callison. Cardinals teammates Bill White and Lou Brock got first-place votes, too.

"This award just about caps everything," said Boyer, who also was

Ken Boyer (right) with then–St. Louis Cardinals manager Johnny Keane (National Baseball Hall of Fame Library, Cooperstown, N.Y.).

recognized as the St. Louis area's "Outstanding Sports Figure."[9] "You know, my family and I are pretty pleased with this award," Boyer said. "But I think the relatives are even happier. We'll sure have a lot of questions to answer over Thanksgiving dinner Thursday."[10]

Conveniently, the MVP announcement occurred shortly before the annual Boyer Thanksgiving rendezvous in Missouri.

Boyer was right about that. There were going to be a large number of Boyers clustered in one place, and that year he was responsible for providing more thrills for them to talk about than any of the other baseball-playing brothers.

Boyer had turned in his finest season in the majors and led his team to the pennant, which automatically qualified the Cardinals for the World Series. What made the 1964 World Series so special was that St. Louis met the New York Yankees, and playing third base for the Yankees was brother Clete.

Not only was the Series New York vs. St. Louis, but Boyer vs. Boyer. That excited the Boyers of Alba, Missouri, more than any individual accomplishment. It was a pretty neat thing when the Cardinals, the hometown team, made it to the Series. And it was also a pretty neat thing when the Yankees made it because Clete was with them.

But to have both Boyer players reach the World Series at the same time? Wow. Who ever would have imagined that? The only problem that presented for Cloyd Boyer and all the other siblings, was whom to root for to become a world champion. It was a Solomonesque decision and one that would have to be kept quiet. Ken and Clete had their own little civil war going on the diamond in October of 1964. Nothing personal, but team versus team.

23

THE BOYER BROTHERS' WORLD SERIES
(Ken and Clete)

B y 1964 Clete Boyer was a 27-year-old veteran. He had been the Yankees' starting third baseman since 1960, and those early 1960s seasons were glory years indeed. When New York won the American League pennant in 1964, that qualified the Yanks for their fifth straight World Series appearance.

Clete already had two World Series rings, from victories over the Cincinnati Reds and the San Francisco Giants. He was looking to add to his ring collection when the 1964 opponent to decide the championship turned out to be his brother Ken's St. Louis Cardinals.

The Yankees finished 99–63 that season, but were chased to the finish line all of the way by the Chicago White Sox, who put up a 98–64 mark, and the Baltimore Orioles, who ended up 97–65. It was an extraordinary year in baseball for fans enduring the suspense of which team would claim the pennant in each league.

Although Clete Boyer played in 147 games that season and hit eight home runs with 52 runs batted in, it was the weakest season of his career for hitting safely. Boyer batted just .218.

Ken and Clete Boyer had both been in the majors for several years, but their careers had barely overlapped. There was no interleague play in the 1950s and 1960s except for the exhibition games of spring training, and both men had spent their entire playing time in opposite leagues. So when the regular season closed and the last two teams standing were the Cardinals and Yankees, the Boyer family was elated.

The Boyer brothers about to contend for the most coveted team prize in baseball made for a great story line for reporters, but an even bigger story line for the town of Alba, Missouri, and for anyone, anywhere, named Boyer. This was a very big deal. Sportswriters covering the World Series, which at the time was indisputably the biggest professional sporting event of the season, enjoyed writing about the situation—it was a natural angle for them. One sports columnist wrote of dad Vern and his gang of base-ball-playing sons,

> In Show Biz, they'd probably be billed as "Vern Boyer and the Seven Little Boyers." Only time pappy Vern Boyer gets his name in the sports pages is when one of his brood picks up a big-league bonus—which is just about every week or so. Or when one of the brood are competing against each other in a spotlighted attraction, such as the current World Series.[1]

The columnist made sure that all five of the other brothers were men-tioned, too, even quoting the youngest, Lenny, who was signed by St. Louis as a shortstop. "It's time someone in the family tried to do something besides play third base and pitch," Lenny said.[2]

Although dad Vern did not attend every game of the Series, he did find himself gaining attention amongst sportswriters. It was pointed out that this was the first time in 41 years that brothers had competed against one another in a Series. In 1923 Bob Meusel played for the New York Yan-kees and his brother Emil "Irish" Meusel played for the New York Giants. Both of them played left field.

Clete had become a fixture in the World Series with the perpetual pennant-winning Yankees. But Ken Boyer was making his October debut. This time it was sibling third basemen. Clete said he was informed of the Meusel historical precedent by a Yankees long-time clubhouse man. "Ken and I have talked about this for a long time," Clete Boyer said. "It's got to be the biggest thrill. I'm nervous. I just can't concentrate on anything."[3]

This was the type of thing the brothers talked about when they saw one another in the off-season. It was always speculative, comments made along the lines of: Wouldn't it be great if we got to the Series the same year? And then it became real.

"I've wanted Ken to get in every year," Clete Boyer said. "This is really a big thrill for me, as much as our winning it. He's 33 and he hasn't been in one yet. I'm really happy for him. I just hope they don't compare our records. Even in fielding he's probably better."[4]

These Boyer brothers were six years apart in age. That was a huge spread when they were growing up, making Ken a senior in high school when Clete was just finishing elementary school. "Ken's always been my idol as a ball player," Clete said. "They say my fielding was a little better in high school and I could hit a basket better—I was all-state two years—but he was a better all-around basketball player. We weren't very close as kids. I was too young for him. And when he signed with the Cardinals I was still in grammar school."[5]

Although Clete did not spell out why he felt that way, he said he thought most of the relatives from Missouri were going to be backing Ken in the Series. Part of that may have been because the Cardinals were their team and part of it may have been because Clete already had his World Series spoils and Ken did not.

"They'll probably be rooting for the Cardinals, too," Clete said. "That's why I'm going to let Ken pay for their tickets. He makes more money than I do, anyway." Referring to his parents and remembering those Cardinals games playing in the house on the radio, Clete said, "They live baseball and this is something they've thought about for a long time."[6]

Clete said he had been springing for family World Series tickets for a couple of years and now it was Ken's turn to pay as long as he was competing in the showcase. Some sportswriter asked Clete how he would handle a play if Ken hit a wicked shot down the third-base line, and of course he said he would give it his all. It was part of the that all's fair in love and war theme.

Even if this was a nice family story, it could not be forgotten that in a baseball series with the largest stakes, it was akin to sporting war. "If he hits a hard ground ball down the line it would be quite a thrill to take a double away from him," Clete said.[7]

Regardless of who sprang for the tickets, it was a Boyer festival at the World Series, with much of the clan attending games in St. Louis or New York or both. America was watching with intense interest because it was the championship of the National Pastime. The Boyers were watching with unusual interest because it was personal. Two of them were in the games, every game, going head-to-head for baseball supremacy.

It was not so important to other Boyers which team won each game, but that both Ken and Clete acquit themselves well. It was all about family pride. According to Ron Boyer,

> Mom and dad were there. My brother Len and his wife, too. But I got to go to the last two games of that Series. It was living our dream. I watched some of it on television, but saw some of it in person. I was still in the Yankees organization in 1964, but the Cardinals won it and I wasn't disappointed. I had grown up a Cardinals fan. Plus, it was Clete's fifth consecutive World Series and it was Kenton's only one. So I was more or less pulling for the Cardinals even though I was a Yankees organization player.

Ron Boyer and some family members found it easier to cheer for the Cardinals because of their long-time allegiance to the team, but chiefly because Ken Boyer had never been there before and Clete Boyer was on the big stage every year. At the time it seemed as if the Yankees' run of success would never end and they could well be back in the Series the next year, too. According to Ron,

> It was an awesome thing that it was Clete's fifth consecutive World Series. They lost three out of the five, but still they won two. It was pretty awesome that year to think that two of your brothers were playing in the World Series against each other. Even having one make it to the World Series was something, but to have two of them at once. That's as amazing as having seven brothers from the same family play professional baseball.

Ron Boyer wondered if there ever would be another family that sent seven players into professional ball. "You hear of families with three guys or four and maybe they just didn't have as big a family as we did," he said, "or more of them would have gone, too. But we had three of them play in the big leagues. That's something for the ages, I guess."

During practice leading up to the first game on October 7, Bob Uecker, who was then the back-up catcher for the Cardinals, but later became a Frick Award-winning broadcaster and a renowned comic genius when talking about the sport, was wandering about in left field. Some musicians with a Dixieland band who were going to play for the fans left their instruments unattended on the field, and Uecker picked up a tuba. He was going to give it a try. But just then a fly ball headed his way. Rather than toot the horn, Uecker decided the mouth of the instrument gave him a better chance than any old glove to catch the ball. He missed it, which in Uecker's own brand of self-deprecating humor, would have been predictable. However, after that he fielded a couple right down the pipe. The impromptu routine garnered lots of laughs.

The 1964 World Series opened at Busch Stadium, home of the National League champion St. Louis Cardinals, with Ray Sadecki pitching for the Cards and Whitey Ford hurling for the Yankees. For fans looking back in time with a fogged lens, they would be surprised that Johnny Keane started Sadecki over Bob Gibson. There were two logical reasons for that. Sadecki won 20 games that year, and Gibson had turned in yeoman efforts as September wound down and turned to October to enable St. Louis to pull out the pennant.

Ford was the mainstay of the Yankees rotation and was on his way to a Hall of Fame career. It seemed likely that he would control the St. Louis bats in a low-scoring game, but the contest did not turn out that way.

Actually, for several innings the game was close and fairly low-scoring. New York led 4–2 at the start of the sixth inning, but the Cardinals forced Yankees manager Yogi Berra to lift Ford.

Ken Boyer was at the root of the rally. He singled (his only hit of the game) and scored when Mike Shannon crashed a home run. Tim McCarver doubled to chase Ford, but after Carl Warwick singled, Curt Flood tripled. The Cardinals pecked away at Yankees relievers and won the opening game, 9–5. Shannon, who later opened a popular steakhouse in downtown St. Louis which is still operating, called the blow "my greatest thrill."[8]

Afterwards, Tom Tresh said he lost Flood's triple in the sun. "The Cardinals found the holes and we didn't," Berra said.[9]

Gibson started the second game and did not have his best stuff. The Yankees hit him hard and evened the Series at one game apiece with their 8–3 victory. Neither Boyer had a hit.

Right-hander Mel Stottlemyre stifled the Cardinals bats—Boyer was zero-for-four. "He never wavered," Ken Boyer said, praising Stottlemyre's sinker. "The few times he was in a jam he just worked a little harder and kept hitting the corners. He was great."[10]

For Game 3, the Series moved to New York and Yankee Stadium. The winning team had banged out numerous hits in the two games at Busch Stadium, but the third contest became a pitchers' duel. The final score was 2–1 Yankees, and they moved into the Series lead by the same 2–1 margin.

Mickey Mantle delivered the decisive blow, ending the game in the bottom of the ninth with a solo homer. Ken Boyer was handcuffed with no safeties, but Clete struck one hit. Righty Jim Bouton, later more famous for authoring the inside-the-locker room book *Ball Four*, pitched a complete-game six-hitter for New York.

The Yankees seemed on the verge of seizing control of the Series, but with a blast that delighted the Boyer family, Ken Boyer provided the key swing in the fourth game. Ken only had one hit in the game, but it was a huge one. The Yankees notched three runs in the first inning off of Sadecki. But in the sixth, Boyer strode to the plate with the bases loaded and crashed a grand slam homer off of Al Downing. There was one out when Carl Warwick, Curt Flood and Dick Groat filled the bases. The final score was 4–3, all of the runs coming across on that one hit. The bash traveled into the left field seats approximately 378 feet from home plate.

"I wasn't even trying to hit a homer when I came up with the bases loaded in the sixth," Ken Boyer said later. "I just wanted to get good wood on the ball."[11]

Ironically, the home-run ball was grabbed, though not without some difficulty in somewhat of a pig pile, by a young man who had long revered Boyer as his favorite player. Later, at a New York hotel he met Boyer and got the ball autographed as he and his fiancée posed for pictures with Boyer and his wife.

The grand slam killed the Yankees' momentum going into the fifth game, also at Yankee Stadium. Gibson got his second shot at the Bronx Bombers, who matched him with Stottlemyre, going after his second win of the Series. This time it was Gibson who was dominant, although Stottlemyre pitched well. After nine innings the game was knotted at 2–2 following a Yankees bottom-of-the-ninth rally. Until then Gibson was hurling a shutout, but with Mantle on base Tresh launched the tying homer with two out into the left-field stands. Stottlemyre was in the clubhouse, but Gibson was still on the mound.

Gibson's staying power was rewarded in the tenth inning when McCarver, his catcher, ripped a three-run homer off of Yankees reliever Pete Mikkelsen, clearing the right-field wall. "Mom asked me to hit a home run for her," McCarver said. "I promised her I would try."[12]

Cardinals first baseman Bill White started the rally with a walk and Ken Boyer fooled New York with a bunt for a hit—it was his first such safety of the year. Mikkelsen, who admitted he was not a good fielder, was definitely caught off guard. "He bunted it pretty hard and I couldn't change my direction to get to it," Mikkelsen said of the play.[13]

The Cardinals had slugged their way to a 3–2 lead in games as the Series shifted back to St. Louis. In the sixth game the Yankees showed why their power was so feared. First baseman Joe Pepitone smacked a grand slam, and Mantle and Maris also contributed homers in another 8–3 triumph over St. Louis. Starter Curt Simmons took the loss although he surrendered just three runs. More damage was accumulated against the bullpen.

That set up a seventh game, one of the most suspenseful scenarios in American sport. Interestingly, Ken Boyer had been signed up to pen a column of his thoughts during the Series for the *New York Journal-American*. One piece appeared in print on the cusp of the final game. Boyer wrote (or a sportswriter ghosted for him),

> I said all along this would be a seven-game Series. What it amounts to is that we played 200 games all year to play the one game today. Counting exhibition games we've played 200 games this year. Now it's the 201st that will decide whether or not we're the world champions. It also proves that we're evenly matched teams. What's happening in the Series is typical of both of

us. First we come back. Then they come back. Now we'll see who comes back today.[14]

Ken Boyer also said he was nursing a bad cold and to make sure he got a good night's rest before the big game, he took a sleeping pill. Meanwhile, reporters checked in with Vern Boyer on the scene to see how he was holding up with his sons locked in such a dramatic battle. "We couldn't stay in Alba," the senior Boyer said. "The excitement was too much."[15]

There it was, the grand World Series spectacle coming down to a deciding seventh game in St. Louis. It was Bob Gibson starting for the Cardinals and Mel Stottlemyre for the Yankees. It turned out to be neither a pitchers' duel nor a complete slugfest. For three innings the starters put up zeroes on the line score. Gibson did his part to keep those zeroes coming in the top of the fourth.

But then the Cardinals reached Stottlemyre for three runs in the bottom of the inning. Gibson was a strong man working on fumes after hurling ten innings just three days earlier. He struck out nine, but was hardly unhittable. This was one time his hitters bailed him out, and nobody had a bigger day than Ken Boyer. He collected three hits, including a home run and a double, and scored three runs as the Cardinals took a 3–0 lead in the fourth and added three more runs—enough—in the fifth.

New York was known for being hard to kill, though, and they touched Gibson for some hits and runs. Clete Boyer hit a ninth-inning homer as the Yankees tried to creep back into it. In the end Gibson, who pitched another complete game and was named the Series' outstanding player, held on for a 7–5 win.

The St. Louis Cardinals won the World Series 4–3 in games, making Ken Boyer a world champion for the first time. Although there had been a lot of hype about two brothers facing in each other in a Series, certainly a rarity, they were not the pivotal players. Clete did not hit particularly well. Ken Boyer's grand slam in the fourth game was huge and he hit particularly well in Games 6 and 7. But the Most Valuable Player of the regular season was not the Most Valuable Player of the Series. That honor, appropriately, went to Gibson.

"The '64 Series was like 'This Is Your Life,'" Clete Boyer said. "That was the most fun I ever had in a World Series. Those are times you just go out and play. You don't worry about winning and losing. You just go out and play and have fun."[16]

Ken and Clete spent most of their careers in different parts of the continent. They hardly ever saw one another on the field, and the World Series was a once-in-a-lifetime opportunity putting them together and

Clete Boyer was never a top hitter, but during his Yankees days his glove more than made up for it (National Baseball Hall of Fame Library, Cooperstown, N.Y.).

pitting them against one another. However, they did take advantage of the situation and spent time off together at meals during the midst of the Series. They may have been opponents on the diamond, but they were still brothers.

"We went out to eat together," Clete said. "My folks were in heaven in Missouri. We knew they were pulling for the Cardinals, being from Missouri. I remember Joe Garagiola (player turned broadcaster) asking who they were pulling for. My dad said, 'The third basemen.'"[17]

The fourth game was always a special memory for the Boyers, and even Clete, who was on the losing end, felt that way. He and Ken each stroked a homer in the seventh game, but Ken had that gargantuan blast of a grand slam in the fourth game.

"I was really happy for my brother," Clete said. "It really topped off a great career for him. It was his only World Series."[18]

24

BACK TO THE MAJORS
(Cloyd)

By that seminal family year of 1964, Cloyd Boyer was into his second baseball career as a coach and minor-league manager. One by one, members of the Boyer family took turns attending games of the World Series to watch Ken and Clete up close in the sport's biggest showdown. Some went to St. Louis. Some went to New York. Some went both places. "I think all of them made it to at least one game or another," Cloyd Boyer said.

Except him. He was working as a coach in Florida in the fall instructional league and did not make it to either big-league city. "I just stayed down there and watched it on TV," Cloyd said. "I worked the instructional league for years and years. I was dedicated to my work."

For quite some time Cloyd Boyer served the Yankees organization as a roving pitching coach, traveling around the country from team to team, evaluating prospects and tutoring young pitchers. He liked the role of teacher and enjoyed meeting the players.

Cloyd spent most of 13 years in the minors as a pitcher and he spent many years in the minors as a coach. That changed, if only temporarily, in 1975. That year Bill Virdon, the old Cardinals and Pirates outfielder, was in his second season managing the Yankees and he had Whitey Ford as his pitching coach. Ford, nicknamed the "Chairman of the Board" when he was a star hurler, was elected to the Baseball Hall of Fame in 1974. However, the next season he took ill partway through the season.

For the first time, Cloyd Boyer was summoned to the majors to coach. He filled in for Ford under Virdon's tutelage in 1975. While Cloyd enjoyed being back in the big-time, he knew it wouldn't last. In fact, Virdon did not last the entire season. Mercurial owner George Steinbrenner was putting his stamp on the team, and he fired Virdon and replaced him with Billy Martin. This was the first time Martin was put in charge, and thus began one of the great baseball soap operas of all time.

Steinbrenner picked away at Martin, inciting his temper. Martin drank hard, played hard, ran his team hard, and could not stand prosperity without sniping back at Steinbrenner. All of this petty bickering was highlighted in great big headlines on the back pages of the New York City tabloid newspapers.

After the 1975 season, Cloyd was ready to return to his standby job roaming the nation's minor-league outposts. But the Yankees wanted him to stay put as pitching coach of the AAA team in Syracuse. Clyde Kluttz was New York's scouting director at the time, and Boyer resisted the offer to locate to Syracuse. "I had been the traveling pitching coach for years and I balked on it a little bit," Boyer said. "Of course, when I was traveling I had all of my expenses paid, hotels, meals. I wouldn't get that in Syracuse."

Finally, the Yankees told Boyer that if he wanted to stay with the organization he had to go to Syracuse. Ownership sent the message to Kluttz, who relayed it to Boyer, saying, "Tell him he's going there or he's going home."

Boyer went to Syracuse. In the end that turned out to be a pretty good thing. Bobby Cox was the manager, and the two men formed a lifelong friendship. Being Cox's right-hand man paid off for Boyer later in his baseball career, too.

The Chiefs were a good team, going 82–57 in the International League and finishing second to Rochester. Among the pitchers Boyer worked with that year in AAA were Ron Guidry, Rick Sawyer, Jim Beattie, Ken Clay, Scott McGregor, Gil Patterson, Rick Anderson and Jim York, all of whom spent varying amounts of time in the majors, with varying amounts of success.

A year later, in 1977, Cloyd Boyer was back in the majors. He was now the volatile Billy Martin's pitching coach. That was not a match made in heaven. Although Martin, known for his aggressiveness and fisticuffs, and Steinbrenner warred with words in the press, Cloyd just didn't like Martin. That was a bit ironic because when his brother Clete served as a Martin coach, the men were drinking buddies. That just illustrated the differences in personal habits and personalities between Cloyd and Clete.

This may have been the high point of the Martin-Steinbrenner relationship, the honeymoon phase for as little time as that lasted. The Yankees went 100–62 that season, capturing the American League East. They disposed of the Kansas City Royals in the American League Championship Series, and they bested the Los Angeles Dodgers in six games in the World Series.

That was a loaded Yankees team. Reggie Jackson had been signed as a free agent after the 1976 season. Other position players included Cloyd Boyer's old protégé Thurman Munson, Willie Randolph, Chris Chambliss, Graig Nettles, Bucky Dent, Lou Piniella, Paul Blair, and Roy White.

Pitchers included Guidry, Clay and Patterson, who had apprenticed in Syracuse the year before, plus Mike Torrez, Sparky Lyle, Jim "Catfish" Hunter, Don Gullett, Dick Tidrow, and Ed Figueroa.

At the All-Star break, Cloyd got three days off, which he was ready for, and he always remembered Steinbrenner being generous enough to give the coaches $300 spending money for the break. At the time, Cloyd's overall salary was $20,000 a year.

Cloyd Boyer finally got his World Series ring, making it a sweep for all three brothers who reached the majors. Clete won a couple in the 1960s, Ken got his in 1964, and Cloyd earned his in 1977. It was a thrill for him to have that accomplishment on his resume, but it was not much fun. Cloyd detested working with Martin and being under the thumb of the meddling Steinbrenner. "I just couldn't get along with Billy," Cloyd said.

What disturbed him so much was how roughly Martin—sometimes at Steinbrenner's direct order—treated pitchers. As someone whose own career had been derailed because of arm problems, Cloyd was sensitive to the needs and health issues of young pitchers. In his mind, the way Martin and Steinbrenner handled some prized pitchers verged on abuse. Cloyd was particularly disdainful of how Tidrow, Patterson and Hunter were thrown into the fire when they should have been rested.

There was tremendous internal friction on that team, and rarely in baseball history has a ball club been gossiped about, analyzed, or picked apart as much as the inner workings of the 1977 Yankees. "We had so much frustration in the clubhouse," Cloyd said. "Guys were arguing and fighting. One time I spoke up and said, 'We don't have anybody in here that's happy anymore.'"

The Yankees were run by a manager under siege, overseen by an owner with no patience, who bellowed from his throne regularly with no tact. Cloyd said that about mid-season Steinbrenner was going to ship Martin into exile and promote coach Dick Howser. "Dick and I lived pretty close together and we rode back and forth to the ball park together every day," Cloyd said. "Our wives rode together in another car. One day Dick said, 'CB, George called me in today to talk and I went in.' I said, 'What did he want?' Howser replied, 'He said he wants me to take over the club as manager.'"

Such a change would have made Boyer happy, but he sensed Howser's hesitancy and tried to convince him to take the job.

> I said, "Well, I give you my word on it. If you take over, we'll win it. I think we can win it. We've got the club to do it. Everybody's pissed off at Billy. None of the pitchers like him anymore." But Dick said, "I can't do it." He didn't want to see Billy get fired. I was kind of proud of him for doing that. But I was wishing he would, from my standpoint.

Martin remained manager and the Yankees won the pennant and World Series anyway, albeit with large amounts of tension.

If Howser had taken command, Cloyd knew his opinion on the pitchers would have been respected more, and rather than being stuck in the bullpen during games he would have spent his time in the dugout. Once, Martin was thrown out of a game and Howser ran the team for the rest of the day. Howser summoned Boyer to his side, moving him from the bullpen to the bench. "Dick said, 'I'll do the managing. You take care of the pitching,'" Cloyd recalled. "I said, 'Damn, I haven't been able to do that all year. Are you sure you want to do that?'"

That year the workhorse out of the bullpen was southpaw Sparky Lyle. In the mid–1970s, relievers were not simply on call for one inning or a single out. The best guys regularly tossed two or three innings. The Yankees got into trouble and Lyle was inserted into the game. However, by the ninth inning he had thrown about 50 pitches and in Boyer's judgment he was gassed. "I said, 'Dick, he's had enough, I'd get him out of there.' Howser asked, 'Who do you want to warm up?' I said, '"Well, Billy ain't gonna like this, but I'd warm Tidrow up.' Dick said, 'Well, that's good enough for me.'"

Martin was in the clubhouse listening on the radio, and he sent a message that he wanted to see Elston Howard, another coach. Martin asked why Tidrow was warming up, and Howard told him that Boyer felt Lyle had had enough. Martin instructed Howard, "You go down there and tell those guys I'll decide when he's had enough pitches." So in accordance with Martin's orders, Howser and Boyer kept Lyle in the game.

> I mean, he's still the boss, even though he's in the clubhouse. Well, Sparky went back out there to the mound and got beat in the tenth inning. That didn't really tickle me because I don't like to lose. I may not show it, but I'm a hard loser. But that time it did tickle me and I was laughing into my sleeve. Of course nobody knew it but the coaches and Billy. It didn't get into the papers.

Here he was part of the management team of a World Series champion, the culmination of his long years of paying dues as a minor-league manager and coach, and he didn't want to work for the pinstriped gang anymore. The team president and general manager was Gabe Paul, a respected baseball man with a long track record in the game. As the end of the 1977 season came into sight, Cloyd informed Paul that was it for him. "I told Gabe I wasn't going back," Cloyd said. "I couldn't see hurting pitchers' arms when you didn't have to."

As it so happened, which Boyer was unaware of, Paul had had enough, too. He left the Yankees after that season as well.

But Boyer had his World Series ring. It was something he coveted, though not for the sake of owning spiffy jewelry.

"Clete and Ken had both done it," Cloyd said. "Now I was kind of in their class. Not the same way, but at least I got a ring. I was pretty proud. I didn't even stay for the party that night after we won. I immediately got my bags, and Nadine and I went to the motel, got into bed and at 3:30 in the morning we were up and headed home."

Not only were the Boyers quite ready to vacate New York, it turned out that was the end of Cloyd's long association with the Yankees. He had been to and worked in every outpost connected to Yankees baseball, and his time with the team ended with a moment of glory.

Cloyd Boyer was pleased to be in possession of a World Series ring, but he never wore it. He said he got it for Nadine. It was no fit for her smaller fingers, but the championship ring was shaped into a necklace. Nadine was Cloyd Boyer's world champion, and he made sure she was rewarded for all of the years on the go and all of the time spent in out-of-the-way baseball towns.

25

QUICK FALL
(Ken)

The 1964 World Series triumph, capped off by being named Most Valuable Player in the National League, was the high point of Ken Boyer's career. Surprisingly, though, the drop-off in performance as he turned 34 came about rather quickly.

Boyer's average fell 35 points in 1965. His home run total declined from 24 to 13, and after posting a league-leading 119 RBI in 1964, he knocked in 75 runs the next season. After being named to six straight All-Star teams (seven in all), he was not chosen to play in the game in 1965. In fact, he was never chosen for an All-Star team again.

The captain of the team, the leader of the St. Louis Cardinals to World Series glory, just about the most popular player in the city, did not realize it yet, but he was on his way out, on the verge of ending his association with his favorite team.

For defending world champions, the Cardinals of 1965 went through some serious upheaval. In a move that shocked the baseball establishment, the American League pennant-winning Yankees fired Yogi Berra as manager. Then, as the Cardinals called a press conference to announce a contract extension for their manager, Johnny Keane, they were stunned when instead of participating, Keane handed them a letter of resignation. After all of his years of service in the minors and as leader of the club when it captured the Series, Keane had not felt respected. Soon after, the twist to the entire matter became clear—Keane became the Yankees' new manager.

There was an uproar on several fronts from those unhappy with the way Berra was treated and with Keane's disassociation from the Cardinals. The Cardinals' damage control effort was admirable in that they promoted

176

coach and long-time favorite Red Schoendienst to the managerial post. "I didn't know it, but I was pleased someone had put my name in the hopper," Schoendienst said after being tipped by a Cardinals executive while they worked together training hunting dogs.[1]

Everything that went right for Keane in 1964 went wrong for Schoendienst in 1965, and Boyer's comparative production merely mirrored the entire team's problems. St. Louis finished 80–81, in seventh place in the NL. "I learned a lot about managing in that first season," Schoendienst said, "lessons I was to apply the rest of the time I had the job."[2]

It was not a feel-good season and it was apparent early. By July, just about the halfway point of the season when traditionalists feel they have a reading on what will happen by season's close, the Cardinals were floundering. The Cardinals were visiting New York to play the Mets and some of the same reporters were on hand who about eight months earlier had watched St. Louis top the Yankees in the Series. "The game is never over until the last out," Ken Boyer said. "And I believe that."[3] It was the ball player's innate optimism speaking, but no one believed the Cardinals were going to catch fire that year.

A short while before, the Cardinals had engaged in a players-only meeting. No manager, no coaches in the locker room, just the men on the roster. Boyer presided as they talked over their woes, tried to analyze what was going wrong, and explore what they could do about it.

> We decided everyone had to sharpen his own axe, and not say it was this or that department's fault or passing the buck. Everyone had an opportunity to make his personal gripe—if he thought he wasn't playing enough or he was playing out of position. We were feeling sorry for ourselves. We were looking back at the losses, instead of ahead. We were waiting for things to happen to beat us. We got in a lull. We made base running blunders.[4]

The clearing-the-air discussion may have made everyone feel better, but it didn't mean the Cardinals were about to go on a tear and propel themselves back into the race. They did improve the quality of their play initially, though.

"Psychologically, we got a pickup," Boyer said. "I don't think we're sitting back and waiting for the other club to beat us."[5] Inspirational speeches and behind-the-scenes bonding didn't do it for the Cardinals that season. They talked, but they didn't hit.

Miserable as he struggled at the plate and watched his team underperform, Ken Boyer, a lifelong Cardinal, did not see the future coming at him with the same impact as a runaway truck on a pedestrian. He could not know as the 1965 season wound down with hopes for a better tomorrow in 1966 that he would be living nowhere near St. Louis during that next year.

On October 20, 1965, shortly after the World Series ended, the Cardinals traded Ken Boyer to the New York Mets. St. Louis obtained pitcher Al Jackson and third baseman Charlie Smith in the unexpected swap that set Cardinals fans to grumbling and dismayed Boyer. Boyer wished to be a career Cardinal, but after his comparative slump in 1965 the Cardinals decided they wanted and needed change.

At the time, Susie, one of Ken's daughters, was 12 years old, and she burst into tears when informed of the news. Since the Mets were founded in the early 1960s, they had pretty much been the laughingstock of baseball, and even the youngster knew the other key characteristic of the team, referring to them as "the last-place Mets."[6]

Ken Boyer had been associated with the Cardinals organization for 17 years, 11 of them in the big leagues. To some, he reacted with the type of stiff upper lip more closely associated with British butlers, with a certain stoicism. "I think I'll be able to help the Mets," he said. "I'll put my whole heart and soul into it, like I did for the Cardinals. The sentiment is gone for the Cardinals. It'll be a strictly business basis now."[7]

It depended which sportswriter reached Ken on the phone or when he conducted a press conference, but Ken was harder hit by his swap than some led fans to believe. "I realize it's part of baseball," he said, "and I've always said I wouldn't worry about being traded. But it really shook me up. They (the Cardinals) can do whatever they feel is for the best future of the club, right or wrong. You go along with it."[8]

In the mid–1960s no-trade contracts were almost unheard-of, and so were multi-year pacts. Players were at the mercy of the owners' whims. Boyer's old teammate Curt Flood was a pivotal figure in the beginning of the unraveling of the owners' monopoly on player movement. He refused to report to Philadelphia when the Cardinals traded him in 1969 and appealed all of the way to the Supreme Court. Although Flood did not win his case, it helped pave the way for future challenges. Ken Boyer was not one of the early protestors. He was not happy he was being sent to the Mets, but he didn't fight it either.

It seemed as if some of the sportswriters who spoke to Boyer immediately after the trade was announced expected stronger reactions from him, more visceral. But the Boyer brothers always said that Ken kept his feelings closely guarded. "There are a lot of worse things in life," Ken said. "What if nobody wanted you?"[9]

That is a player's biggest fear. Being traded may be uncomfortable, but being rejected from every team in the majors spells either demotion to the minors or the end of a career. That day comes for every player, too, but being traded to a team in the same league beats those other fates.

The furor over the controversial deal settled down over the winter, and by spring training Boyer was with the Mets, not reporting to the Cards as he had done near the end of each winter since the late 1940s. He was pretty big news in St. Petersburg, Florida, and a pretty big name being added to the roster of a woebegone franchise. Sportswriters wanted to hear Boyer's thoughts and flocked around him since a player's name and the word "All-Star" were not often linked on the Mets.

There was a general feeling that Boyer might offer critical leadership to a young team that had shown it needed all of the help it could get from any source. The Mets had been losers since the day they were founded, and in 1962 recorded the worst season since 1900 at 40–120. Manager Casey Stengel amused the sportswriters with fantastical stories and humorous remarks in the hopes they wouldn't notice all of the errors and strikeouts taking place on the diamond. They did anyway, although they enjoyed his company.

By 1966 the fans and the ownership thought the Mets needed to show some signs of improvement, and the addition of a player of Ken Boyer's stature was supposed to help the situation. One sportswriter noted that Boyer set a good example and was a good influence for the younger players because, among other things, he "takes extra batting practice after almost everyone else has gone sun-bathing or to the golf course."[10]

Whether it was playing minor league ball, playing for the Cardinals, or for the Mets, Ken Boyer displayed the same work habits. That meant if he had to devote extra time to his swing or scooping up grounders, he was willing to do so. "There's such a thing as self-pride," Ken said. "I'll get to know them and I'll have just as much pride in the team as I ever had. I'll be just as happy to win a game and just as sad when we lose. Naturally, there has to be some complexes about losing. But there are a lot of new players here. It's our duty to change that."[11]

Ken did say that he felt a sense of responsibility—along with other veterans—to play an elder statesman role for such a green club.

If I see a man not doing all I think he can for the club, I may have to say something even though I'd be completely out of order. They (management) make me feel they want me to, and I accept the responsibility. If someone doesn't tell a man he's made a mistake, he'll keep on doing it. I couldn't jump all over a guy, but I'll ask him why he did something and if he had no reason, I'll have to tell him.[12]

That was only spring training, before a game was played. It didn't take long mingling with the Mets in the early days of the season for Ken's style to be obvious. That work ethic and innate leadership stood out.

One writer observed his interaction with the other players and commented, "Ken Boyer is now the leader of the New York Mets. The players were willing to ascribe him that status in spring training. He earned it in three games of the regular season. Boyer made six hits in his first 12 swings for the Mets." Trying to seek an answer as to what Ken's qualities were that translated to helping others, the same author sought input from pitcher Jack Fisher. "It's an intangible thing," Fisher said. "I can't put it into words, and I'll bet you can't put it down on paper. All I can tell you is that he's a pro. What does that mean? It means that everything he does is for one thing—to win."[13]

Boyer may have been an important addition as a clubhouse leader, but at 35 his batting stats more resembled his final season in St. Louis than his All-Star seasons. He hit .266 with 14 home runs and 61 runs batted in. Whether he wished to admit it or not, he was closer to the end of his playing days than to his starring baseball days. The numbers added up to average production.

Boyer reported to the Mets for another season in 1967, but after 56 games, when he was batting .235, New York traded him to the Chicago White Sox for a player to be named later. As of July 22, 1967, Boyer, then 36, was an ex–Met. He played in 57 games for the White Sox and hit .261.

He also began the 1968 season with the White Sox, but things didn't go well for the club and there was a lot of disgruntlement. Fans booed the team and writers criticized the players. At 37, Boyer lasted just ten more games with Chicago in 1968 before Chicago asked waivers on Boyer for the purpose of giving him his unconditional release. About five weeks later, he was picked up by the Los Angeles Dodgers. LA general manager Buzzie Bavasi believed he still had enough pop left in his bat to help the Dodgers by pinch-hitting. Boyer did not view his time spent in Comiskey Park with any type of fondness.

"I'd estimate that playing in Comiskey Park costs any hitter from 20 to 25 points in his batting average from what he'd normally hit anywhere else," said Boyer, who hit just .125 in his brief 1968 time with the Sox.

Things are tough enough for the batter at Comiskey Park under normal conditions because of the dimensions of the park and the fact that the wind is usually blowing in. Even when the wind is blowing out it doesn't help you much because it's blocked off by the high stands and you don't get much of it down on the field. But then management does everything else they possibly can to make it even tough for the hitter. They wet down the infield in front of the plate and also let the grass grow long.[14]

By Ken Boyer's standards, his speech about the difficulties of hitting in old Comiskey Park, the one built in 1910, as compared to the more recent version, was the Gettysburg Address. He could make thoughtful statements when he wanted to, but he didn't often want to talk at great length on any subject. Being a hitter playing regularly in Comiskey got him going, though.

> You need a cannon to drive the ball through that infield, because the first thing is the sting is taken out of it by the soggy turf in front of the plate and then the grass slows the ball down even more. Only a lame infielder could miss those. I just don't think you'll ever see a .300 hitter at Comiskey Park as long as these conditions prevail. The only way a guy could hit .300 there is if he has a phenomenally lucky year when everything is falling in for him. From the White Sox owner on down to the casual fan, everybody keeps rapping the players for not hitting, but everything is done to help the pitcher.[15]

Bavasi was right about Boyer. The Dodgers used the aging player judiciously in 83 games from May on during the 1968 season, and he batted .271 with six homers and 41 RBI in 221 official at-bats.

Wherever Ken Boyer went, the story of him and his brothers followed. By then Clete was playing elsewhere, too, gone from the Yankees, but Ken always put the plug in for Cloyd and the other siblings.

> Actually, as some think, I'm not the oldest Boyer in the game. That's my brother Cloyd, who is managing in Binghamton, a Yankee farm. The second oldest brother, Wayne, is a dentist and maybe the smartest of the bunch. I'm next. Then there's Lynn, who was a good player until he broke his wrist and hurt a shoulder. He's now coaching prep ball. Then Clete. Ronnie is the youngster who still may make the major leagues. But the best one of all might be Lenny, who is at third and outfield for Little Rock.[16]

That season Boyer was with the Dodgers and Clete had moved to the Atlanta Braves. That meant the two brothers played regular season games against one another. In one game, Ken hit a home run and as he circled the bases, passing Clete at third, his brother threw dirt on him. Ken laughed about it later. "He was just getting even with me," Ken said. "I did that to him when he hit one against us in that '64 Series."[17]

As 1969 dawned, Ken Boyer was ready to continue with the Dodgers for what he felt could be a few more years. He was coming off a season where he had hit safely six times as a pinch-hitter and knocked in 11 runs in that role.

"He's a handy guy to have around and gives you a good feeling when you see him walk up to the plate," said Dodgers manager Walter Alston before the team embarked for spring training.[18]

But the 1969 season did not play out the way either man hoped. Ken Boyer was used in just 25 games with only 34 at-bats, hitting .206. He didn't appear at the plate after August, and although the Dodgers wanted him to return in 1970, he felt it was time to retire. In October the Dodgers released him, and that ended Ken Boyer's major league playing career.

After 15 years in the majors, Ken Boyer concluded his career with 282 home runs, 1,141 runs batted in, and a .287 batting average. But when he turned in his Dodgers uniform, he did not want it to be the last time he wore a big-league jersey. He wanted to get into coaching and start fresh on the sidelines.

Staying in baseball was all that Ken Boyer wanted to do, and he knew where he wanted to do it as well. He once again hooked up with the St. Louis Cardinals, and the organization that gave him his start as a player and for which he had his finest years, came through with a new opportunity for the 1970 season.

Ken Boyer was retired, but not fully retired.

26

SWAPPED TO ATLANTA
(Clete)

The 1964 World Series, when Clete Boyer and brother Ken played on opposite sides, was the last high point for the New York Yankees for some time. The end of the Yankees dynasty was nigh. After winning five straight pennants, the Yankees of 1965 finished in seventh place, and the team was worse in 1966, finishing tenth and last.

This was unheard-of for the New York Yankees. Once in a while they missed out on capturing a pennant, but they didn't record losing marks. The team got old, and management didn't find replacements with the ease that it had in the 1950s. The Yankees' tumble was swift. Breaking up the old gang came easily. Some players retired. Others were deemed expendable. But starting over again was paramount.

In 1965 Clete Boyer batted .251 with 18 home runs and 58 runs batted in. That was fairly typical offensive production for him. In 1966 he batted .240 with 14 home runs and 57 RBI, and he played in 144 games. That November, he was traded to the Atlanta Braves for Chi-Chi Olivo and Bill Robinson.

The long and happy run in New York was over for Clete. He had relished the spotlight in New York City and was enough of a party animal to test whether New York was a city that never slept. Atlanta was a big city, essentially the capital city of the South, but its lights weren't as bright as New York's. It was great if you wanted to eat hush puppies and grits.

The way Clete told of hearing about the transaction that shipped him to the Braves, it was a late-night phone call from a fellow he mistook for a famous movie director of the same last name. When the telephone rings close to midnight, it is seldom good news. It was difficult to discern good or bad in this case, but it was meaningful.

Boyer took the call from the Braves' manager, Billy Hitchcock, but after he introduced himself, Clete said, "Billy who?" Hitchcock replied with his full name again. And Boyer said, "Oh, the guy that makes all them crazy movies? You must be calling for Charles and he ain't no kin to me." Boyer thought he had the wrong number all figured out, that director Alfred Hitchcock was looking for Charles Boyer, the French actor.[1]

It was the right number all right, and Clete Boyer was a new member of the Braves, where he was expected to play third base instead of long-time incumbent and future Hall of Famer Eddie Mathews. It was not clear which third baseman was more startled by the maneuver. "I don't know Boyer, but they say he's a real glove man," Mathews said when informed of the acquisition of Clete. "He and I will be vying for the job and it'll be a glove man against a stick man. The best man will win, and I think I'm the best man."[2]

It turned out Mathews was wrong. When the 1967 season began, he was manning third base for the Houston Astros and Clete Boyer was the third baseman for the Braves. Even more surprising, however, was the way Clete hit that season. All of a sudden, after all of those years, he was a stick man, too. He appeared in 154 games and while he batted just .245, he swatted 26 home runs and drove in 96 runs, both career highs at age 30 by a large margin.

In West Palm Beach, Florida, spring training, where the Braves worked out, of course all of the talk was about Clete's glove and what his fielding would mean to the Atlanta infield. There was no reason to believe that his bat would make a difference since it rarely had during the entirety of his stay with the Yankees. Just a few exhibition games into the spring, Boyer stabbed a difficult-to-catch grounder and threw to second base to start a double play. "I don't think Eddie Mathews would have got it," Clete said.[3]

The Braves obtained Clete for two reasons. One was that Mathews was aging. The second was that they gave up 82 unearned runs during the 1966 season and needed to tighten up the fielding game. "Sometimes adding one piece can make you so much stronger at other positions," Hitchcock said.[4]

Boyer never complained about playing in Yankee Stadium when he was a Yankee regular, but almost in foreshadowing of the season he was about to have for the Braves, he talked about his career-long struggles with the dimensions of New York's home stadium and how his strength with the bat didn't fit well with the shape of the park.

> The Stadium bugged me a lot. I think Ralph (Houk, manager for part of the time) knew it, too. I hit a lot of balls that should have been hits and home

runs. That works on you mentally after a while. (I) hit .280 or .290 on the road the last two years and about .150 at home. Certain guys, you know, another team will take a chance with. I had to go. It was obvious.[5]

Although sportswriters of that era did not report on off-the-field, extracurricular activities, Clete Boyer was a known quantity in the sense that he drank and enjoyed hanging out in bars. But he vehemently denied that his after-hours habits had anything to do with his so-so hitting in New York. "No, that wasn't it. I'm no different, no worse than 90 percent of the guys in baseball. I did my job in the infield. I don't think I ever had a bad year in the field. I wasn't a great ball player. Mickey Mantle, Whitey Ford, Elston Howard—you don't trade them. I just wasn't in that category."[6]

When brother Ken Boyer was asked to analyze the impact of Clete going to the Braves, he thought it was a significant move and that Clete would hit better in Atlanta. According to Ken,

He's a good competitor, and a better hitter than that career average. And I believe he'll prove it over in our league. I've got a good arm, but I never saw the day I could do what I've seen Clete do. He is now (better), but I wouldn't say that he was better when I was younger. I always ran faster and I was a little quicker, I believe, and as a result could afford to play deeper, which is an advantage when ranging. As Cloyd and I agreed, Clete had a major league arm and hands from the time he was 15, but he and I played third base differently, partly because of the parks in which we played. Atlanta is a hitter's park. He'll make the Braves a better ball club and they'll like him in Dixie.[7]

Most of what Ken suggested proved true, although Clete's average didn't spike. He did hit better all-around for Atlanta and the fans liked him from the start.

It didn't take long during the 1967 season for Boyer to raise himself into a category where no one

After playing in five World Series as third baseman for the New York Yankees, Clete Boyer finished his major league career with the Atlanta Braves, where he won his only Gold Glove Award (National Baseball Hall of Fame Library, Cooperstown, N.Y.).

expected him to be. Not only did he perform his usual magic tricks in the field, he also hit better than ever before. It was startling to most baseball people. Clete was pleased, but less surprised since Atlanta's Fulton County Stadium was a much friendlier hitter's park. He became pals with Fulton County Stadium in a hurry.

Clete was not challenging for a National League batting championship, but he started the season by making the timeliest of hits and making them often. Hitchcock—Billy, not Alfred—was impressed. "I'll take that," the Braves manager said. "Now if can only get about 140 hits. Seriously, he has had some big hits for us already this season, and Clete is a much better hitter than a lot of people think he is."[8]

For all of those early indications that Clete was going to hit better in Atlanta than in New York, most of the talk still focused on his defense. His reputation with the glove carried over from the American League. "The guy is something," Hitchcock said. "He's doing a great job for us and he hasn't even showed us his specialty yet. Just wait until you see that diving play he makes to his left and then throws from his knees."[9]

Clete Boyer was an everyday player with the Braves, and it wasn't easy to get him out of the lineup. Not for a rest and not when he wasn't feeling well. Before a June game against the Philadelphia Phillies, he ate bad Chinese food that made him sick, yet he hit a crucial grand-slam home run off Larry Jackson onto the roof of Connie Mack Stadium. "It was a hanging slider," Boyer said. "I just want to look at the ball when I'm batting. He made a mistake. All I tried to do is get it into the air."[10]

The long shot occurred in the fourth inning after Boyer had skipped batting practice altogether to make sure his stomach would hold together and not send him running to the bathroom to vomit once play commenced.

"Don't ever eat Chinese food in a cafeteria," Boyer said with a self-serving sob story after being fined $250 by Hitchcock because he missed a 12:30 a.m. curfew telephone call. "Ever since I got fined I can't afford to eat at the good places. Have to save the meal money. It was awful stuff. I should not have got sick. I drink a fifth of scotch and I don't get sick. What kind of Chinese food was it? Cats and rats, I believe. Awful."[11]

Clete singled his next time up as the game turned into a rout, and Hitchcock sent in a pinch-runner for him, begging the question of whether the effects of the food were catching up to him. "I didn't take myself out," Boyer said.[12]

The big blast in the 16–7 victory, coupled with Boyer's intestinal ordeal, made him big news after the game. Once again reporters seemed surprised that he was hitting home runs. "I'm a streak home-run hitter," Clete said. "I'll hit three or four in a week, then I won't hit any for three weeks or a month. It's all mental. When you know you're swinging good, you know they're going to go out. The more you hit the mistakes, the better hitter you are. That's what makes (Hank) Aaron so great. He hits all the mistakes."[13]

It was funny that Clete mentioned Hank Aaron, who would ultimately become the career home run king for more than three decades with 755 dingers, because Clete was hot enough to be mentioned in the same paragraph as Aaron in some Atlanta newspaper stories. Suddenly, Clete Boyer was a power hitter who was outdoing Aaron, Felipe Alou, Joe Torre and Rico Carty, all teammates with much longer track records of success in the batter's box—at least for a little while. The hits just kept on coming. So did the RBI. He trailed only Aaron in that category a couple of months into the 1967 season.

"If you'd said before the season that I'd be second in RBIs at the end of June, the only guy who would have believed it would have been me," Clete said. He could also joke about his hitting prowess on a day he went three-for-three before leaving the late June game against the Mets. "That wasn't my first perfect day. I've been playing 13 years, you know. I think I already had one."[14]

Clete Boyer was not a button-down guy, and the Yankees were a conservative, formal team. That didn't prevent Clete from enjoying the high life in the big city and making friends who provided clothes, gifts and free food. Atlanta was not that kind of town. It was not as enamored with ball players as celebrities, but Clete was able to find other perks to being a Brave besides the closer fences. One day, he came to the park for a game wearing red shorts, thongs on his feet and no socks. There wasn't a pinstripe to be seen. It was obvious to those who knew him that this was the real Clete, not a Clete coming to work in a suit.

Later that season, another home run, a three-run job, was a significant blow, though not because it helped Atlanta win a game. It did not. The Braves lost that day, but the shot was Clete's career 1,000th hit. He said the hit would have felt more meaningful if it came in a victory. "But it's nice to get anyway. I'm only 30 years old, too. I should be able to play five or six more years. If I can average around 120 hits a season, maybe I can wind up with 1,700 or 1,800. That's not too bad. I'm playing in a good park to do it, too. But a lot of guys don't get 1,000. I'm happy."[15]

As the season wound down, Clete's contributions at the bat remained steady. His average did not veer much off track from his career path, but those homers and RBI kept mounting up, and many marveled at that success. One thing on Clete's mind most of the season was that he was replacing the revered Eddie Mathews at third base, a player who became a member of the 500-home run club and who had played for a franchise's World Series champ and pennant winners.

Although Mathews was slowing down at 35, not everyone was thrilled with his departure to Houston and Clete Boyer's arrival. But Clete more than made his mark with the trade. Matthews got into 101 games with the Astros that season. He hit just ten homers with 38 RBI and finished with a .238 average. The end was near for him. Clete topped him in homers and average, an unlikely scenario when spring training began.

"I wanted to make the trade look good," Clete said, not about being swapped for Olivo and Robinson, but for replacing Mathews.

> I wanted to do well because I was taking the place of a player like Mathews. You take the place of someone like him, then you feel the pressure. You have to, if you have feelings. Of course, I wasn't traded for Mathews, but I was taking his spot in the lineup. If I didn't do well the fans were going to be on me. That's all there was to it. And I would have heard them, too. And it would have bothered me.[16]

Clete Boyer was insightful and reflective as the end of the season approached. He had no idea what to expect when he joined the Braves, but he had turned the change of scene into a success, even if he never could get that batting average up to a more respectable level. "I've never hit for a high average and probably never will," he said. "Let's face it, I'm a .240 hitter. All you have to do is check the record. But when I'm on a hot streak I know I can help a club with the bat. I drove in my share of winning runs with the Yankees and I made a few plays. But I was known for my glove and I appreciated that."[17]

Those casual clothes that Boyer wore to Atlanta Fulton County Stadium were indicative of how he thought about the Deep South versus New York. Both he and his wardrobe were more chilled out than up north. "I'm more relaxed here," he said of Atlanta. "Here you can spend more time with your family because the pace is slower and you're not always rushed. Also, the fans have been just great. They have been behind us all season and they've been very nice to me personally."[18]

In those years before Greg Maddux, Tom Glavine and others, the Braves were not particularly good. They finished 77–85 that season. But Clete Boyer had a happy individual year and was ready for more in 1968. However, things did not go well that year. Boyer had injury problems, primarily a bone chip in his left hand near the wrist, and appeared in only

71 games. It was also a completely different kind of season at bat. Boyer batted just .227 with four homers and 17 RBI.

Just about everything went wrong. Actually, Clete was at the root of some of his own problems. Unlike the year before when he was the newcomer in Braves training camp just trying to fit in, leading up to 1968 training camp Clete unleashed a diatribe at some of his teammates. He was especially critical of outfielder Rico Carty. Carty hit a sub-par .255 in 1967.

> He loafs. He doesn't give it 100 percent out there and Hitchcock (manager Billy Hitchcock, who was fired) couldn't handle him. If I were manager of this club, I'd put Felipe Alou in left center, Hank Aaron in right center and Carty in the bullpen where he can chase foul balls. We don't have the talent. We don't have a stopper in the bullpen. We don't have enough complete players.[19]

Boyer's comments, made in a speech at the Chattanooga Quarterback Club, were ill-advised for a number of reasons. It is never good policy to attack teammates and the team in public. Naturally, the critique got back to Carty. Carty ended up needing sympathy more than harsh treatment that year because he missed the entire season with tuberculosis. Clete missed more than half the season and was an insignificant contributor to the 1968 Braves, who finished 81–81.

After the frustrating season, Boyer made it sound as if he was almost finished, as well.

> Next season might be my last one. If I don't have a good year and get to the point where I can't play the way I should, I'll quit. I just might hang 'em up after this season if things don't get better. I'm gonna give it the good shot. What the heck. I make a good salary ($35,000) and I'd hate to give it up. But I can't play if I don't do the job I think I should.[20]

By the middle of the 1969 season, playing in pain from his left hand, Clete mused again about upcoming retirement, maybe even before the season ended. Almost like magic, though, as soon as he began speaking like that Clete caught fire. That included hitting and fielding. He raised his average to .250, slammed 14 homers and knocked in 57 runs. He was back in the groove.

"Not the way I'm going now, I can't quit," Clete said in mid–July. "I'm swinging the bat as good as I ever have now." He was in the midst of a two-week stretch where he hit .400. "It looks like I'll wait the way I've been playing and the way I've been swinging the bat. It makes a lot of difference the way you feel. The hand's been feeling better since I've started hitting."[21]

The season began with speculation about Clete's immediate future.

In mid-season there were doubts about how long he would last. But at the end of the year, with those improved numbers at the plate, he received one of the favorite rewards of his career. At long last, out from under the shadow of Brooks Robinson in the American League, and with a solid gold symbol to support his reputation, Clete Boyer won the National League Gold Glove Award as the circuit's best third baseman. It was the first—and only—time that Boyer earned a Gold Glove Award.

After receiving that prize, Boyer was not about to retire following the 1969 season.

27

FROM ATLANTA
TO HONOLULU TO JAPAN
(Clete)

Winning a Gold Glove Award after so many years of playing (and being out from under the shadow of Brooks Robinson) made Clete Boyer feel good and made him believe he had a few more solid years in his 33-year-old body when the 1970 season began.

The Gold Glove Award was special to him, particularly since midway through the 1969 season he thought the end may be looming for him. Then he rebounded. "Clete Boyer is a man of immense pride," one writer noted after Boyer was awarded that long-sought Gold Glove Award. "He threatened to retire last season when he was having difficulty with the bat. But it didn't affect his fielding. The ten-year veteran has sure hands, a strong, accurate arm, can make the charging, barehanded play look easy, goes to his left well and is fearless in bunt situations."[1]

Clete Boyer remained Atlanta's starting third baseman for the 1970 season, and while he did not repeat as the Gold Glove Award selection, he turned in a typical year at the plate. Boyer smacked 16 home runs, drove in 62 runs, and batted .246. The home run and RBI totals were on the high average side for him. And in 134 games Boyer did not seem to be showing any drop-off in the field.

Certainly, Clete felt he was as good as he always was. In June, a few months into the season, his self-assessment provided that information. "I really believe I have played my position better this year than at any time during my career," he said.[2]

After a season or two of watching Clete handle every type of chance at third, his Braves teammates and bosses had developed a large degree of faith in him. There was nothing that could be hit his way that they felt he couldn't master. "Any time I see the ball hit toward Clete, I know it's a sure out," said pitcher Phil Niekro. "He's amazing."[3]

As a knuckleball specialist, Niekro, who won more than 300 games in his career and was voted into the Hall of Fame, needed all the help he could get in the field when opposing batsmen pounded his stuff into the ground. That was a winning play, if the infielder scooped it up, and Niekro realized Clete was going to scoop up virtually everything. That slickness with the glove made Clete one of Niekro's best friends.

Clete manned third base because of his grace with the glove, not because he was a bombardier with the bat. While Atlanta manager Luman Harris raved about Clete's glove work to the extent that he suggested his hitting didn't matter, he took it to extremes in his compliments. Luckily, Clete never tested the theory that Harris espoused. "I don't care if Boyer bats only .100," Harris said. "He is my third baseman. The way he plays the position, he has to be."[4]

While Clete was no accomplished batsman when it came to hitting for average, he was never as weak as all that, either. "I know I'm not a great hitter," Clete said, "but I'm no 'out' either. I just want to knock in the important runs when I have to. That is the big thing."[5]

When Clete actually made an error, that bothered him, and he seemed to take it as a personal affront. Once during the 1971 season, he refused to go on air to talk to a radio reporter because he was sure his fielding error was the only topic that would be raised, and he was busy trying to put it out of his mind.

What Clete Boyer did not anticipate when the 1971 season began, his fifth with the Braves, was that things that summer would go terribly wrong and it would be his final season in the big leagues. He hurt himself during this period, however, with his mouth and actions. After playing in 30 games, with six homers, 19 RBI, and a .245 average, the always quotable and always candid Boyer was quoted in an early June newspaper story as being highly critical of manager Harris and vice president in charge of baseball operations Paul Richards.

> This man (Richards) has been on my neck ever since I joined the club. I don't know why. Three years ago I got my hand busted by a pitch from Don Drysdale. Richards docked me $5,000. This spring he wanted to cut me $5,000 again. I asked him why. He gave no explanation. He just said there are reasons. He cut me $2,500, from $47,500 to $45,000. We understand each other. We just don't get along.[6]

Bashing Richards was the wrong move. Whether he saw the handwriting on the wall, or was privately tongue-lashed by management, Clete asked for his own unconditional release. He was 34 and the Braves obliged him. Theoretically, he was a free agent and said he had feelers from a few teams, including the Oakland A's. But no job materialized.

About a week later, he was in bigger trouble yet. Commissioner Bowie Kuhn announced that Clete was being fined $1,000 for betting on college and pro football games. He met with Kuhn, accompanied by Major League Players Association executive director Marvin Miller, but admitted that he had made the bets. While he said he was willing to pay the fine, Kuhn made the payment contingent on him signing with another big-league team.

While Clete was in limbo, removed from the Braves, but before he met with Kuhn, the commissioner had informed the teams looking into signing Boyer that his status had to be cleared up before any new club could sign him. Concurrent with that problem there was some murkiness about Clete's parting of ways with the Braves. The Braves said he owed the team money. Boyer suggested the team owed him money.

Baseball has been death on betting ever since the Black Sox Scandal of 1919. That year eight members of the heavily favored Chicago White Sox were accused of fixing the World Series so their team would lose to the Cincinnati Reds. Although the White Sox players were exonerated in court, new Commissioner Kenesaw Mountain Landis banned the eight players from the sport for life.

The cardinal sin of baseball was betting on baseball games, which there was no evidence Clete Boyer did, and which he denied doing. But betting and associating with unsavory characters is considered a punishable offense, too, as baseball attempted to maintain an image of a clean game and a family sport. On June 10, 1971, Kuhn imposed the fine on Boyer. It was believed to be the first time the commissioner's office had ever fined a player for betting on sports other than baseball. "It is true that a couple of years ago I made a few bets on football games with a man I thought was a friend," Clete said following his session with Kuhn in New York. "I have never bet on baseball, and I have never made any kind of bet with anyone I knew to be a bookmaker. In any event, the commissioner has imposed a relatively small fine and has assured me that there is no reason why I cannot continue playing major league baseball."[7]

This "friend" was a used car salesman in Atlanta from whom Clete's rental car company purchased automobiles.

Miller called the split between Clete Boyer and Atlanta "a clear violation" of the Basic Agreement between players and owners, and Miller had "no doubt he will get his money." At issue was $10,000 that was considered severance pay, which could not be waived.[8]

Clete Boyer also said that Kuhn told him that now that the matter was settled, the teams which had shown interest in him would be able to sign him. "I'm innocent," he told reporters. "But I don't see any sense fighting it. The commissioner has shown a very understanding attitude. There are parlay cards—college and pro football—all over the locker rooms, with guys putting up a buck here and a buck there. They are as guilty as I am."[9]

It was reported elsewhere, though not by Boyer, that his bets were of the $50, $100, or $150 variety—more than a buck or two, but not huge money, even at the time when baseball salaries were much lower. Later, he also specified that the bets were made in 1969, two years earlier.

After Clete had his say following the announcement of the fine, he seemed optimistic about his future with another team. He was a free agent for the moment, had been playing well during his stay in Atlanta, and didn't view himself as over the hill quite yet. He thought he would be signed by some team soon. "Right now I think I'll get a drink and go see a friend who owns a sweater business," Clete told New York writers as he hopped into a taxi cab. "I don't know what's ahead for me. I would like to play on the West Coast—San Francisco, Oakland, or San Diego."[10]

To his dismay, Clete discovered that what interest had been apparent before his meeting with Kuhn—and despite Kuhn's assurances that he would not be held back from resuming play—had evaporated. No one tried to sign him.

One aspect of Clete's being called on the carpet that rankled him was that Kuhn refused to announce the name of his accuser, and unlike in a court of law he was not permitted to face him. "It's no secret that at one time or another all ball players bet on other sports," Clete said. "How come I'm getting rapped for it when there are so many others who have done the same?"[11]

Prominent New York sportswriter Milton Gross predicted in his column that Clete Boyer would not be harmed in the long run by the betting incident, but would be signed by a pennant contender for as much money as he was making with Atlanta. Clete thought so, too, but that call did not come.

When a couple of weeks passed and his telephone remained silent, Clete became suspicious about what might be happening. Before being summoned to Kuhn's office he was in demand. After his fine no one wanted him. He did not think this was a coincidence.

> I haven't received any calls from baseball officials since the fine was announced. Previously, I had talked to Charlie Finley of the Athletics, who was interested. I also had a talk with Jack Quinn of the Hawaii club (AAA

minors) in the Coast league. I wish the Western Union strike would end so I could wire Japan. I'd go, but I can't speak Japanese. The commissioner's office is supposed to represent the players, and I may be the victim of blacklisting. No move has been made to protect me. On the contrary, I was fined as a result of the information I gave.[12]

Clete began to gain some sympathy in the sports writing fraternity and among fans because his "crime" was not seen as being so terrible, and it was acknowledged that with his fielding skills he could still play for any number of teams. In fact, unlike other news outlets that trumpeted that he had been fined for betting, the lead paragraph in the *New York Times* report of the situation highlighted that he had been cleared to continue playing major league ball.

During the period when Clete made headlines for his dispute with the Atlanta brass and, after being fined by Kuhn, was looking for a new team, he said he received a lot of mail from baseball fans, but recalled only two of them being critical of him. He didn't feel he had angered the populace. But he came to wonder about what major league owners thought of him.

About the same time he made public his fears about being blacklisted, he cut a deal with the Hawaii Islanders. If a player had to return to the minors it was felt that playing in Honolulu's self-proclaimed paradise couldn't be beat. His first appearance in an Islanders uniform was as a pinch-hitter. Given his personal playing history it might have made more sense for him to be a late-inning replacement in the field.

"Coming to Hawaii is like a new lease on life," Clete said after being a major leaguer since 1955 with the exception of a couple seasons in the minors when he became Yankees property. "I would like to return to another major league team, a team of my liking, or sign with a team in Japan. I feel that Hawaii offered me the best opportunity for both goals. I feel I have three or four good seasons left. I know Hawaii is Triple-A, and I haven't been in the minors since 1959, but I also know that Hawaii is run like a major league operation. My daughters want to live here."[13]

During that time period, Jack Quinn, Hawaii's GM, and the team had a reputation for putting ex-major leaguers to work and thriving on the field with them. So he was plenty content to ink Boyer in the midst of a season that the third baseman began playing pretty well in Atlanta. "I can't see how anyone would have any trouble dealing with Clete," Quinn said. "He is a gentleman in negotiating and a winning player on the field. You can't ask for any more than that."[14]

Clete Boyer's reputation did come into question as a full-fledged, around-the-clock gentleman not much later on an Islanders' road trip to Portland, Oregon. Boyer was arrested after a Pacific Coast League game at a hotel when police said he was slow to leave the scene of some kind of disturbance and was charged with using foul language. Boyer forfeited $53 bond and did not appear in a court to face a charge of "disorderly conduct by profanity." That was likely a charge that few residents of that community even knew existed. Few probably realized the threat of going to jail for swearing. The entire matter seemed to revolve around Islanders teammate Marv Staehle, who was on the disabled list, refusing to leave a hotel bar when asked. Clete faced no team discipline from Hawaii.

Clete finished the season with Hawaii and said returning to the minors, even in a high-class place like Honolulu, was a learning experience after spending so long at the top level of the sport.

> You learn a lot about people down here. The kind of things you wouldn't find out in the big leagues. It's different down here. Some players have problems. They let the game, the pressure, get to them. Little things make a difference. Maybe it's just a single scouting report. Maybe once somebody wrote, 'Can't hit the curve' by a man's name and it sticks with him. So he's here. Some guys might think they're too good for this, but heck, I've enjoyed it. The ability of the players isn't much different, and the pitchers throw as hard here. A lot of the young guys are ready to go up. They just need experience.[15]

Clete Boyer had some fun in the sun, working on his tan as well as his game, but didn't know what his baseball future held. He was 34 going on 35. "At my age it's hard to tell how much I have left," he said. "I'd like to get invited to a big-league camp and see if I can make it. I don't know if I'll be invited, though. These owners are kinda funny, I guess. Maybe next year I'll try the majors. But I'm tired now, running out of gas. I just want to rest for a while."[16]

When Clete recharged, he looked for a new team for 1972. As it so happened, he was not going to try the majors again that year. He signed a deal with the Taiyo Whales in Japan. It was a one-year contract—he said he was offered a three-year pact, but at 35 he really didn't know what he could do and just wanted to have the experience of playing baseball in a foreign country.

"I didn't come here to make money," Clete said, "but to face a challenge in a new land. I insisted on a one-year contract. I didn't want to take money from a Japanese ball club without proving my worth."[17]

He hit as usual, 5-for-21 for a .238 average to start the season, and fielded as usual, flawlessly. Boyer was residing in a hotel and planned to bring his teenaged daughters to Japan when school let out.

"It's different here," he said, sounding a theme not so different in itself from his minor league experience of the preceding season. "In the States, for instance, pitchers are usually tall and well-built and they throw a very fast ball. Japanese pitchers don't have much speed, but I've found they have extremely good control. Probably five or six pitchers in the United States throw sinkers. Here, they all pitch sinkers."[18]

Clete did well enough to be asked back and he had enough fun to want to return. He was also making about $97,000 a year. For a guy who just thought he'd sample Japanese baseball play for a season to wrap up his career, Clete spent nearly as much time overseas in the island nation as he did with the Braves. Playing until he was about 40, he spent four seasons with the Whales.

Under the rules in Japanese baseball, teams were allowed to have only two American players on their roster at any one time. Clete Boyer became quite popular in Kawasaki, the home of the Whales, located on Tokyo Bay. After a couple of years as a full-time player, he became a player-coach, and for a half-season he was also a manager, virtually unheard-of in Japanese ball, especially in the 1970s. Clete appeared in 419 games during his stay in Japan, and twice batted in the .280s, with an overall average of .257. His highest home-run total was 20, in 1975, and at the age of 35.

Clete Boyer spent enough time in Japan that he picked up a fair amount of the language, one that is regarded as challenging for any native English speaker to learn. For a time he roomed on the road with Sadaharu Oh, the greatest home run hitter of all time and widely viewed as the best player ever in Japanese baseball.

In 1973, Joe Pepitone, one of Clete Boyer's old New York Yankees teammates, also crossed the Pacific Ocean to play baseball in Japan. Generally, over the decades, there have been two types of American players who go to Japan—those who enthusiastically embrace the culture and pick up some of the language, like Boyer—and those like Pepitone who can't adjust to playing in a foreign country.

Pepitone hooked up with the Tokyo Yakumato Atoms and blasted a long home run in his first game. According to Clete,

> There was a standing room only crowd of something like 45,000 at the game, and Pepi was an instant hero. It was all downhill for Joe from then on. That's the only homer he hit and after playing for another dozen or so games he just quit playing because he claimed he had an ankle injury At about this time, he moved in with me at my Tokyo apartment. We all told him that he should have his ankle examined by a doctor, but he refused.
>
> Joe stayed with me for a few weeks before he went back home to Brooklyn,

and in that time he kept calling his wife and friends on my phone. I think the bill came to as much as $3,000. I'm still waiting for his check.[19]

Clete Boyer's big-league career ended in a frustrating manner, but his active playing career concluded in 1976 with a very satisfying chapter in Japan.

28

CARDS BOSS
(Ken)

K en Boyer concluded his active major league playing career with the
Los Angeles Dodgers in 1969 and then went right back to the St.
Louis Cardinals organization where he had spent the vast majority of his
baseball life.

In 1970, the Cardinals hired Ken Boyer as manager of their AA
Arkansas Travelers team, giving him his first taste of being a skipper. It
had long been suggested that Boyer possessed the tools to become a field
boss—and indeed that as captain of the Cardinals he already had shown
leadership qualities.

Ken, as always, was candid about his thoughts when asked if he
thought handling the Arkansas assignment was a prelude to becoming a
big-league manager. It wasn't strange territory for him being in Little Rock,
either, since he had played for the club on his way up the ladder to the
majors.

> If I didn't want to manage in the big leagues someday, do you think I'd be
> messing around like this? I realize there is little security in being a big league
> manager, but that's what makes this game interesting. My career as a ball
> player is over and I'm 38. I know baseball better than anything else and I've
> been close to it all my life. It just wouldn't seem right to leave it now. And
> more important, I've got to put food on my table. I have a wife and two boys.[1]

Although it seemed obvious to most baseball fans that Ken Boyer
would end up back working for the Cardinals if he wished to stay in the
game, it turned out they were not his only suitors. Other big-league teams
approached him to talk about leadership opportunities. He preferred
minor league managing over major league coaching at that time, he said,
because he wanted to learn what it was like to be the top guy. "I like the

199

Cardinal organization, but I had offers from a couple of other clubs. I just didn't want to be a coach in the majors. You get stereotyped and you get into a rut that is hard to get out of. You manage ahead of the game. You're an inning or so ahead all the time and your decision is already made before the thing happens."[2]

One twist in Ken Boyer's assignment was becoming manager of a team where one of his brothers, Lenny, was playing. They were both Arkansas Travelers. Different Boyers had overlapped with different teams, from the Cardinals to the Yankees to the Athletics, as players, managers and coaches over the years. This was another such case.

Lenny was 15 years younger than Ken, so they hardly knew one another growing up. As was true with Cloyd and some of his younger siblings, that age spread made them almost of completely different generations. Lenny was in his third season with the Travelers, and beyond a last name he had something else in common with Ken—he had moved from shortstop to third base by then.

"I don't think it's going to cause any problems," Ken Boyer said. "Actually, I asked for Lenny. For one thing, he doesn't have any military obligations and he can play anywhere. And with all the other kids in the infield having reserve meetings and all, he's going to be valuable to me."[3]

Being manager of the Arkansas Travelers turned out to be a one-year deal. Soon enough Ken Boyer was back in the majors, acting as a coach under his old friend Red Schoendienst, the current Cardinals manager. Ken spent two years in the dugout, working with Red for the 1970 and 1971 seasons, and then he returned to the minors to supervise other Cardinals farm clubs.

The tour of the minors as manager sent Ken Boyer to as many places as he had played in the St. Louis chain years earlier. In 1973 he managed the Gulf Coast League Cardinals in Florida. In 1974 he took over the Tulsa Oilers of the American Association and won a league title. He stayed in Tulsa through 1976 and then became boss of the Rochester Red Wings for 1977 and what was supposed to be the 1978 season.

Ken Boyer had been a candidate to ascend to the Cardinals' job once already in 1977, but had been overlooked when they tabbed Vern Rapp. "I thought it was my time when Vern Rapp got the job instead of me," he said. "People say it would be logical if I got it, but things don't always turn out that way."[4]

However, in 1978 the call that Boyer wished for came from the head office. It came early in the season, too, before the end of April. Rapp began his second year as manager, but was fired with a 6–11 record. After coach

Jack Krol handled the team for a few days as an interim leader, and as suspense about a permanent hire built, Ken Boyer—then 46—was installed as manager.

"I have a lot more ties there than anyplace else," he said upon being hired. "I know most of the personnel on the club really well. (It) was sort of a dream job for me. I love the city and I live there in the winter. I can't in my wildest imagination see how anyone would want to turn down a situation like that." He was a bit surprised, though, at how swiftly St. Louis gave up on Rapp and also because he was on the road with Rochester when he got the call from the higher-ups. "I'm still in a state of shock. It seems like I've been sitting around and nothing happened. Then, when it happened, it seemed like I should have been there yesterday."[5]

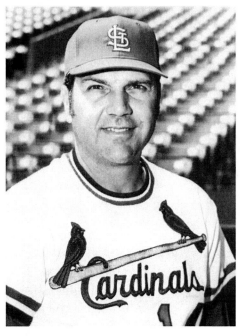

After retiring as a player, Ken Boyer served the Cardinals as a minor league manager and major league coach (here in 1972) and manager (National Baseball Hall of Fame Library, Cooperstown, N.Y.).

Rapp was viewed as a disciplinarian and was brought in following Schoendienst's 12-year run, and over Boyer, because his personality was very different from their live-and-let-live philosophy. Yet Rapp presided over a tumultuous year when the clubhouse was not a happy place. Ken Boyer did inform the owners, the players and the press that he was no martinet, but also said he could be firm and those who had played under him in the minors knew that.

"The players know me and I know them," Boyer said. "The players know how tough I am. When the game starts, it's all business. But hair codes and other stuff, that's not what I'm here for. You need discipline to know what to expect of one another on a club, but our rules will be simple."[6]

Rapp had irritated players by imposing numerous personal habit rules that many felt were unnecessary and annoying, and Ken Boyer said none of that stuff was on his priority list. He couldn't wait to get started and admitted he would be nervous in his first game in the new job.

All I want to do is get that first game over. It's just like opening day. It's been like that with me everywhere I've been. I have kids and brought them up to make their own decisions, and if they want a mustache or a beard or eyelashes, that's their decision. All I'm interested in is them playing baseball. What I want to do is treat them all like men. If they have a problem, we'll communicate.[7]

Perhaps Ken Boyer should not have been in such a hurry to reach St. Louis from Charleston, West Virginia. The Cardinals did not fare particularly well that season, going 62–81 on Boyer's watch, and 69–93 overall. His strategy was committing to a four-man pitching rotation and a lineup that was not frequently shuffled.

Among the best players on that Cardinals team was Lou Brock, at the tail end of his St. Louis career. Other top producers were Ken Reitz, George Hendrick, Keith Hernandez, Garry Templeton and Ted Simmons, some of whom Boyer had tutored in the minors. Templeton was a flashy shortstop with talent, but was erratic in the field for someone who was supposed to anchor the infield. He committed 39 errors that season.

"The one thing that will make this a better ball club is to take Garry Templeton and make him think defense first," Boyer said. "He's a great offensive player, but I don't think that he's fully got the impact of how important a shortstop is to a team."[8]

The best pitchers were John Denny, Bob Forsch and Pete Vuckovich. They were good, but the Cardinals didn't have enough of them. Given the slow start and shortage of talent, St. Louis did not blame Boyer for the finish and committed to bringing him back to run the team in 1979. "We are pleased with the job Ken Boyer has performed thus far and he certainly deserves the opportunity to begin in spring training with a program of his own choice," said Cardinals owner August A. Busch.[9]

It was apparent that Busch felt the Cardinals had more potential than their record indicated and he expected Boyer to bring the talent to the forefront. A blunt appraisal came from outfielder Bernie Carbo, a once and current Cardinal who took a look around at the roster he re-joined and said, "Those guys should have had their butts kicked for losing 94 games (93, actually)."[10]

Boyer did not want to hear what Carbo said. As Satchel Paige put it, "Never look back, something might be gaining on you." Boyer adopted that approach. "That was eons ago," Boyer said of 1978. "One thing we don't do is think or talk about last year."[11] That was not a bad idea since anyone examining those numbers might get depressed.

Ken Boyer being with the team from spring training on, and throughout the entire campaign, paid off in 1979 when the Cardinals improved to 86–76, finishing third in the National League East. Boyer also coaxed terrific years out of some of the same players who were merely solid the year previous. Hernandez batted .344. Brock at age 40 hit .304 in 120 games. Hendrick batted .300. Templeton stole 26 bases and finished with a .314 average.

The next season did not go nearly as smoothly, though it was not the hitters' fault. Simmons, Hernandez, Templeton, Ken Oberkfell, and Hendrick all hit .300 or better. However, the pitching was disastrous. Vuckovich's 12 victories led the team. There was no depth in the rotation and the bullpen was weak. Ken Boyer began the year as manager, but when the Cardinals were sitting on 18–33 he was canned. Before they reached the finishline with a 74–88 mark, St. Louis employed four managers that season.

Boyer was fired on June 8, between games of a doubleheader against the Montreal Expos. Not only were they 15 games under .500, they were sinking fast, having lost 21 out of their last 26 games when he was let go.

Boyer never saw his dismissal coming. When general manager John Claiborne came to town and entered the clubhouse in Montreal, Boyer thought it was because he wanted to talk about trade possibilities. Not quite. "If there had been internal problems and guys hadn't been busting their butts," he said, "people could point their finger and say, 'It's your fault.' But I don't think there was anything I could do."[12]

After his long journey to the majors as a player and a long journey back up to the majors as a manager, Ken Boyer was ousted, though the Cardinals wished to retain connections. But things were about to get a whole lot worse. Although he was slated to return to the minors to handle the Louisville Cardinals for the 1981 season, that never happened.

Ken Boyer was diagnosed with lung cancer and faced the biggest challenge of his life. He was only 50 years old. The shocking diagnosis occurred when he took a physical during spring training. But he didn't broadcast it, only stepped back from managing and began treatments. "He didn't really tell anybody," said Lynn Boyer. "That was just his way. It was terrible. It was like everything else with him, a big secret."

Initially, Ken did keep quiet because his father had just passed away from intestinal cancer and he didn't want to burden the rest of the family in its grief. At the funeral, however, brother Clete discovered what was going on. Ken had broken up with his wife and had a long-time girlfriend. When the woman approached Clete to talk, he thought she was going to confide that they were getting married. Instead, she informed him that Ken had cancer.

Clete was stunned, not only because Ken hadn't told him, but because he had recently seen him and nothing seemed amiss. "Ken looked great," Clete said. "But two weeks later he had some chest pains."[13]

The illness wasn't quite the secret Lynn thought it was because word of Ken Boyer's problem spread like wildfire around baseball. What Lynn meant was that Ken was taciturn on the topic—he didn't talk about it.

Others did. Billy Martin, who had been Clete Boyer's teammate in New York and knew most of the Boyer brothers, was managing the Oakland Athletics. Clete was one of Martin's coaches. Clete told Martin that not only was Ken Boyer's health prognosis dire, but his medical bills were growing at an astronomical rate. They had reached $10,000 and were climbing by $1,500 a week. Ken did not have the kind of insurance that covered his care. In addition, of his four children, three were in college.

Martin jump-started action, lending his name to a fund-raising dinner to cover Ken Boyer's medical bills. The dinner was scheduled for about three and a half weeks after Martin's announcement and was set for the Brown Derby Restaurant in Scottsdale, Arizona, one of the most popular spring training hangouts amongst players who trained in that area during the pre-season. It was also close to Oakland's spring training site.

A general invitation to come to the dinner (entertainment was planned and Bob Uecker, the old Ken Boyer teammate turned announcer, was to be the master of ceremonies) went out to baseball people around the country. Martin penned a note reading: "I have never asked in my lifetime for a favor for myself or anyone else. This will be my first, and sorry to say, my saddest. Whatever is in your heart to contribute on behalf of Ken Boyer, we would appreciate it."[14] Martin created The Ken Boyer Fund, asked for pledges via telephone or through the mail and signed the letter as chairman of the effort.

At about the same time Martin was making his appeal, Ken Boyer, desperate for a treatment that would slow the advance of the debilitating disease, traveled to Mexico to take laetrile, said his sister Delores. Clete was in constant long-distance phone contact with Ken while he was in Mexico. "The doctors in Tijuana don't want him to get too emotional," Clete said, "so I'm the only one in the family calling him. Everybody else goes through me. But last week when I told him about the dinner on the phone, he broke down and then Billy and I sat around and cried."[15]

At one point during spring training, Clete broke away from his coaching duties as Martin's third base coach to head to Mexico. "I went down to see him a few weeks ago," Clete said. "He's eating organic food and drinking a lot of juices—lettuce juice, spinach juice, carrot juice, mixed with liver juice. Maybe it'll work. There's a lady there who was given up for dead three years ago, but she's in good shape now."[16]

Once word was out about the dinner, Clete Boyer began talking it up to interested sportswriters, explaining Ken's condition and promoting the event. "It will take a miracle now," Clete said of Ken's odds of surviving, "but he's fighting like hell. My brother's always been a great competitor. In the beginning not a lot of people knew about it. Now everybody asks me about it. We are planning this fund-raising dinner for Ken and there is so much conversation about it. Billy has been great. He has also been very emotional. There are times we just look at each other and start crying. Mentally, Ken's fine. When they let him go, I want him to stay in my house in Oakland. I'll have to go down there and drive him home. He has my car."[17]

A few weeks later, the Ken Boyer dinner raised $100,000 for medical expenses. Mickey Mantle, Roger Maris, Billy Martin, and Clete Boyer were some of the baseball attendees. They were joined by Harmon Killebrew, Eddie Mathews, Ferguson Jenkins, Frank Robinson and Gaylord Perry. Joe Garagiola joined Uecker as a co–MC. Ken Boyer remained in Mexico, too tired to travel to the dinner. Howard Cosell, who knew Ken Boyer well, also spoke, recounting highlights of Ken's baseball career, and said he was a man of honor. Roughly 1,000 people came to the dinner held at the Ramada Safari Hotel.

Proceeds of an A's–California Angels exhibition game were turned over to the fund. The Association of Professional Baseball Players of America made a contribution. Solly Hemus, one-time Cardinals player and manager, donated $5,000. That was a very large amount at a time when former ball players were not nearly as wealthy as they are today.

Many were moved. Martin, who made the dinner happen, said, "I looked around at the room full of baseball people here and I was never so proud in my whole life."[18] He had every right to be because he was the author of a good deed. One speaker was Clete Boyer, who was not even sure he could handle standing at the podium to talk about his ill brother. He was nearly overcome.

"From Ken Boyer and all the Boyer family," Clete said, "I would just like to say I know how Lou Gehrig felt. I feel the Boyer family is the luckiest family in the world." His words echoed Gehrig's famous speech at Yankee Stadium in 1939 when he was stricken with amyotrophic lateral sclerosis. Away from the podium, Clete kept talking. "That was the toughest thing I ever had to do. You know, there are 110 people in the Boyer family, but now I've got 1,000 more brothers and sisters."[19]

Clete said Ken wanted to be present at the dinner. Plane tickets were purchased, but in a phone call a day or two before being scheduled to travel, Ken informed Clete that he was simply too weak to make the trip and then broke down crying.

The medicine available in Mexico was unable to arrest the advance of Ken Boyer's disease, and he eventually returned to St. Louis for more treatment. "We went back and forth to St. Louis to see him," sister Delores said. "He was gray-haired and his face looked weathered."

Over a period of months Ken's health deteriorated steadily. He spent most of his time in a hospital-nursing home. Lynn drove from the western part of the state to visit Ken in St. Louis. Cloyd was coaching and sometimes on trips he diverted to St. Louis to see Ken. Other times he was in Kansas City, and he and Lynn drove to St. Louis to see Ken. "When Cloyd was flying east somewhere I'd drive him to St. Louis from Kansas City and then take him to the airport in St. Louis when he had to leave," Lynn said. "I would go back and Kenny and I would visit some more."

Another regular visitor to Ken Boyer was old friend Red Schoendienst, who maintained his home in the St. Louis area and stopped by regularly to play cards. Relatives came and went, but Schoendienst lived in the area and it made it easier for him to spend time with Boyer.

Neither friendship nor love from family slowed down or cured the illness, and Ken Boyer passed away on September 7, 1982. He was only 51. Clete Boyer and Ken Boyer's four children, Susie, Janie, David and Danny, spent the last day of his life with him at the nursing home where he resided for several months.

Only the day before, Schoendienst visited Ken and found him harboring the same feisty attitude he maintained all along since diagnosed with cancer. "He was a real battler, not a showman like some players today," Schoendienst said. "Kenny said yesterday that he believed he could come back from this. He went down fighting."[20]

When Ken Boyer died, the New York Post called him the "greatest third baseman in Cardinal history." Clete also said Ken's battle for his life was a difficult one and that Ken endured a lot. "Knowing all that Kenny went through these past few months, all the pain and suffering he endured without ever bitching or feeling sorry for himself, I'm relieved now," Clete said. "I feel good that at last Kenny is resting. I'm so proud of him, the type of player he was, the type of brother he was. He was a super brother and a super athlete. I idolized him so much."[21]

The terrible illness took a very significant toll on Ken Boyer, shrinking his once powerful and athletic body. "If I hadn't known him, I wouldn't have recognized him," Clete said. "You know how he played at around 205 pounds? He was down to 120. The nurses told me Kenny never complained one time. He never let on."[22]

Words of praise flowed for Ken Boyer's courage in the face of disease, his All-Star baseball career, and about the type of man he was.

"He never complained about his illness, or sat around wondering, 'Why me?' said former Cardinals general manager Bing Devine. "That's the type of player he was. He went about his job and never complained."[23]

Red Schoendienst talked about admiring Ken Boyer's style of play and how much it hurt to see him laid low by his illness and watch him gradually physically diminish. "(Boyer) was a hard-nosed player who made 'em look easy in the field," Schoendienst said. "He didn't get the recognition he deserved until 1964. But to see him in failing health, after he was such a big, strong player, was tough to handle."[24]

When Ken passed away many sports writers sought out brother Clete, who had been a family spokesman, plus many former Cardinals teammates. Much of the talk centered on Ken's greatest year, the 1964 season when he led St. Louis to a World Series championship and won the National League Most Valuable Player Award.

One of those teammates, Mike Shannon, later a long-time broadcaster for the Cardinals, reminisced about that special season. According to Shannon,

> When you're going down the stretch in a pennant race you have to have a leader, a John Wayne. Somebody who can circle the wagons. That's what Kenny was to the St. Louis Cardinals. You gotta have somebody that you lean on, that you watch, who circles the wagons for you. And we really had a tremendously experienced ball club. But you always have to have one guy and that one guy was Kenny Boyer.[25]

The 1964 World Series was that famous two–Boyer championship competition. On the day his brother died, Clete Boyer slept at the nursing home. Ken's nurse woke Clete up at 7 a.m. and informed him that Ken had passed away at 6:15 a.m.

On that otherwise dismal day, Clete's thoughts raced back to the 1964 Series, too.

> We had so much fun in that Series. Both of us wanted our clubs to win, but we were still pulling for each other. We wrote notes to one another the whole Series. In one of the games in St. Louis, Mike Shannon hit a ball that went right through my legs and rolled all the way to the fence. Kenny wrote me a note saying, "Watch that infield of ours. It has a lot of bad hops in it." The next day he missed a little pop fly and I wrote him a note saying, "Watch the air out here, too. It's got a lot of bad pockets in it."[26]

One long-time St. Louis sportswriter took the trouble to look up some of the things Boyer told local reporters over the years as a player and manager in that town. He chose to highlight one telling passage— Ken Boyer talking about growing up in small-town Missouri in a house full of kids and the way he got his start in the game he loved.

"We never had trouble getting enough kids together for a game," Ken Boyer said, "and we played it until dark all summer. I don't think we will ever see anything like this again ... when the kids spend all their time playing ball. There are too many distractions now, mostly television. But when I was growing up all I wanted to do was play ball."[27]

And all Ken Boyer did for his entire life was play ball and coach ball. It was the perfect life for him.

29

Working on 50 Years
(Cloyd)

A fter the 1977 season ended and Cloyd Boyer earned his World Series ring as a coach on Billy Martin's staff, he refused to return to the Yankees. He wasn't enjoying working for either Martin or owner George Steinbrenner. Cloyd recounted his experience as a coach:

> One time Billy wanted to have a meeting with all of us coaches and feed us dinner. We all got down to the restaurant and sat around and waited for Billy for more than a half-hour and he didn't come. Bobby Cox and I got up and left. Billy didn't like that too well. He said, 'Here we are going to win a World Series and I'm the manager and my coaches run out on me.' Billy was that way. He would let you sit out there on the bus and wait while he drank a couple more beers.

That tried Cloyd Boyer's patience, and he also thought it was unprofessional. He believed it was time to find another major league club. He kept waiting for news to hit the papers and report that he was fired as a Yankees coach, or at least say that he had quit. But unlike the age of Twitter, ESPN and 24 hours of sports a day, he never heard a word about his status in the media. Or maybe, he thought, it was possible that he didn't pick up on things because he was in Missouri.

Cloyd knew Pat Gillick, who had just taken over as general manager of the Toronto Blue Jays, the first of four teams that Gillick served in that capacity on his way to being voted into the Baseball Hall of Fame. When Cloyd called Gillick, he was offered the managerial position in Syracuse, a place he was quite familiar with, but which had switched affiliations. "I said, 'Well, that's good enough for me,'" Cloyd said.

Boyer, Bobby Cox—recently named to the Hall of Fame as well—and Gillick were all close friends from time spent with the Yankees. All three were in new positions and worked to help one another whenever it was possible. Cox assumed the job as manager of the Atlanta Braves in 1978.

"I'd helped Bobby get to the big leagues as a coach," Boyer said. "I recommended him advancing through the Yankee organization."

It became payback time all around. Gillick offered Cloyd the managing job in AAA, but Cox came along and trumped that offer. Cox told Braves owner Ted Turner that he wanted Cloyd to be his pitching coach in Atlanta. Turner agreed reluctantly. He wanted to keep Johnny Sain as his pitching coach—and Sain was perhaps the best ever in that role. But Cox kept arguing for Boyer.

"Bobby wouldn't go for it (keeping Sain) because I'd fought for him a couple of times in the Yankee organization and he was returning the favor," Cloyd said. "So anyway he got me in down there."

Cloyd was back in the majors in the National League. There was only one problem. At that time, the Braves were a very bad team. In 1978, the Braves finished 69–93 and last in the National League West. In 1979, the Braves finished 66–94 and last in the National League West. This was a total rebuilding job. The Braves showed improvement in 1980 with an 81–80 record.

The 1981 season was supposed to be the great leap forward, but the season was cut short due to a strike. The Braves finished 50–56 in a season with 56 lost games. Turner was out of patience after four seasons of the Cox regime and fired him. Boyer went, too. Joe Torre came in and, in a normally played 1982 season, won the division title.

"I was there for four years," Cloyd Boyer said, "and we had a bad ball club for two of them. The last year, in 1981, we had a chance for the playoffs, but we had the strike that year. Even up to the last five games, when we went to San Francisco, Los Angeles and San Diego, we had a chance. But we ... played bad defense every game, and that knocked us right out of it."

And knocked him right out of a job, which was a shame because Cloyd Boyer was very pleased with his stay in Atlanta. It was more peaceful than New York in every way, from the owner on down to the clubhouse and to just walking down the street. "In New York there were crowds and it was hard getting to the park and back and fighting people all of the time," Cloyd said. "My wife loved it. She loved New York. She didn't like Atlanta because there weren't any people out. Heck, the crowds at the stadium sometimes were only a thousand. But we had a bad ball club."

The team was turning around. Dale Murphy was a catcher first, switched to center field and won two Most Valuable Player Awards. Slugger

Bob Horner came in from Arizona State and won the NL "Rookie of the Year" Award. But their maturation was too late to save the jobs of Cox (who later had a more spectacular run in Atlanta) and Boyer.

Another reason why Cloyd enjoyed Atlanta so much was that brother Clete was living in the city at the same time and went to work for the Braves as a minor league coach. For a time Clete also served the Braves as a major league coach tutoring young infielders on their fielding.

"We had a lot of dinners," Cloyd said. "We would go out to eat and talk a lot of baseball. He worked in Atlanta with the young kids before he became a coach with Billy Martin in Oakland. He was able to get along with him because they drank together. Billy liked somebody to drink with. Clete was a generous guy, but he drank too much."

Cloyd could read the tea leaves and was certain that Turner was going to fire Cox and the entire coaching staff. Clete had been a popular player for Atlanta in the 1960s, and Cloyd tipped him off that perhaps he should throw his name into consideration for the managing job.

Following a major league pitching career cut short by arm injuries, Cloyd Boyer embarked on a long coaching and managing career, including a stint coaching for the Atlanta Braves (National Baseball Hall of Fame Library, Cooperstown, N.Y.).

"I know Turner likes you and he's always spoke well of you in meetings and stuff," Cloyd said he informed Clete. "Job's going to be open here, I'm pretty sure." Clete initially balked at the idea because he felt the Braves had terrible pitching. Cloyd informed him he was out of date and that pitching was about to become the team's strength. "'Whether you believe it or not, it is.' I heard he never did call Turner, but his name was mentioned as a candidate. But Joe Torre got the job. He brought Bob Gibson in as pitching coach. But the pitchers didn't like him. Gibson would give them hell all of the time and say, 'You can't throw hard enough.' But they won the division the year after we left."

At the same time Cloyd Boyer was alerting Clete Boyer to a job prospect, he was trying to look out for himself. It was about a month before the regular season ended in 1982 and he was on the prowl. Another of Cloyd's best friends in the sport was Dick Howser. They had bonded together as coaches with the Yankees and developed a close friendship through work and driving back and forth to home games together.

Howser had accepted the Yankees managerial job and did it for one year in 1980. In the revolving door that George Steinbrenner spun, Howser was fired despite a 103–59 record. By 1981, Howser was in a better place, managing the Kansas City Royals. He led the Royals to some solid finishes and then in 1985 led the club to its only World Series championship. Howser had taken over in the middle of 1981, the strike year, and was building his own staff for 1982. He needed a pitching coach, and Cloyd lobbied for the job.

> I called him with a couple of weeks left in the 1981 season when he was in Anaheim and I told him what I thought was going to happen in Atlanta. I told him I was probably going to be looking for a job and that I had read in the paper that he was going to get his own coaches. "Have you got a pitching coach in mind?" Howser said he thought of me and Jerry Walker and another guy whose name I can't remember. And he said, "Why? You want the job?" I said, "Hell, I live just down the road from Kansas City. My wife could go to home games and go home while we're on the road. I'd love to do it." He said, "You got it." That was it. He gave me the job right there.

There was no more convenient big-league town to Alba, Missouri, than Kansas City. So Cloyd signed on as pitching coach for the 1982 season and worked with Howser through 1983. What should have been a terrific arrangement became strained fairly soon, not relations between Cloyd and Howser, but between Cloyd and the pitching staff. For some reason he did not connect with the pitchers the way he had in New York and Atlanta.

The team did well in 1982, finishing 90–72, but it was a difficult season for Boyer. Pitchers included Vida Blue, Bud Black, Paul Splittorff, Dan Quisenberry, Dennis Leonard and Larry Gura.

Leonard and Boyer got along famously and later, when they lived near one another, they became fishing buddies. Leonard had been a three-time 20-game-winner for the Royals by then, but had some injury problems both years he threw for Boyer. The second year, in particular, seemed jinxed. Leonard was 6–3 and Boyer was suspicious that Leonard was hurting, but refusing to admit it.

> I went up to him and said that I was pretty sure his knee was hurting him. I said, "You know what? I'm going to recommend that you don't pitch for

about ten days. Take some pills, antibiotics, or whatever, and have the trainer tell you what to do." He said, "No, I don't want to do that." I said, "Well, I think I'm going to talk to Dick about it. Dick will listen to me. I just don't think you should take a chance so early in the year." Leonard said, "I'll tell you what, CB. I haven't won a Cy Young Award. I'm gonna win the Cy Young this year." I said, "Well, if you feel that way about it, I won't say a word." Damn if he didn't go out and hurt his knee the next game and was out the rest of the year. And that was it. God, I couldn't sleep for a week. He could have maybe pitched us to a pennant. It would have made a difference.

Then a schism began to form within the organization. The general manager was John Schuerholz. One of his close friends in the game—a comparison made by Cloyd Boyer was that they were tight the way he and Gillick and Cox were tight—was Gary Blaylock, a team scout and minor league pitching instructor. Jose Martinez, another coach, was friends with Blaylock. After a while, Cloyd felt he was being undermined.

He said they "were working on me." That was despite Cloyd and Blaylock working together and being friends when they were both in the Yankees organization. "That's the only place (Kansas City) I ever got fired. I probably didn't do a good enough job there. I couldn't relate to that pitching staff like I could to the one in New York and the one in Atlanta, for some reason or another."

Cloyd Boyer started wondering about his long-term future with the Royals as early as spring training. One day Nadine and he went out for a steak dinner at a favorite place in Sarasota, and after the meal he said, "Enjoy yourself this year, because I won't be back here next year."

During the last week of the regular season in 1983, the Royals were on a road trip to Seattle when Howser asked Cloyd to come to his room for a talk. According to Howser,

"I've got bad news for you." I said, "Well, you don't have to tell me, I've got a pretty good idea." But I never said anything to him about what I thought about Blaylock and Jose. Never said a word about that. Dick said, "In the middle of the season I thought I had Schuerholz talked into bringing you back again." I said, "You know what, Dick? I know you don't like Gary and you didn't want him, but why don't you give him a chance?" Dick said, "Well, I don't really want him." I said, "Well, Schuerholz wants him. That's pretty obvious." So anyway, he did give him the job. I was always kind of proud of myself because sometimes I've got a big mouth and say things I know I shouldn't.

When the Royals won the World Series in 1985, Blaylock was the pitching coach.

As the manager of the American League pennant winner, Howser earned the honor of managing the AL team in the All-Star Game in 1986. However, before the game he felt sick and, after it he went to get checked out medically. Howser was diagnosed with a brain tumor. Despite surgery, he died from the illness in 1987. His No. 10 uniform jersey was the first number retired by the Royals.

After Cloyd Boyer's tenure expired in Kansas City, he hooked up with his friends Pat Gillick and Bobby Cox in the Toronto organization for the 1985 season. Soon after, Cox left Toronto to become general manager of the Braves. In 1990, Cox returned to his old job as Atlanta manager, and by then the Braves were a reborn team. Cox led Atlanta to the 1995 World Series title and repeated division titles on his way to 2013 election to the Hall of Fame.

In 1986, Cloyd Boyer managed the St. Catherines, Ontario, team in Canada for the Blue Jays and won the New York–Penn League championship. Then he moved to the Braves organization in 1987 and spent the remainder of his coaching and scouting career with that club, helping develop much of the young talent that kept producing winners for Atlanta.

During the 1988 season Cloyd managed the Pulaski Braves in the Appalachian League, and in 1989 he managed the Idaho Falls Braves in the Pioneer League. He remained in the Atlanta organization through the 1992 season, when he retired after roughly 48 years in professional baseball.

Cloyd Boyer was a minor league and major league player. He managed in the minors, and coached in the minors and majors. He scouted everywhere.

Some of his most satisfying work was done with young players between 1964 and 1974. He was a cross-checker who swooped in and studied young players recommended by other scouts. He was a roving pitching coach who helped innumerable young hurlers adjust to pro ball. One of the most famous was Ron Guidry, who won 170 games in the majors and who in 1978 recorded one of the greatest pitching seasons of the last half-century when he finished 25–3 with a 1.74 earned run average. All of that came after George Steinbrenner wanted to get rid of him and Cloyd Boyer argued to keep him with the Yankees.

At different times Cloyd Boyer helped Guidry regain his lost confidence and Jim "Catfish" Hunter regain his lost health.

Guidry was frustrated and once, when cut from the Yankees, sent to the minors again, he was about to quit baseball and return to Louisiana. His wife talked him out of it and Cloyd Boyer mentored him in Syracuse. A late bloomer, Guidry had a terrific fastball, but he wasn't yet consistent and Steinbrenner wanted to trade him. After a loss, Steinbrenner told Cloyd to meet with him.

"Well, everyone tells me how great a pitcher they think he's going to be. I don't think so." Cloyd told Steinbrenner he was wrong, which usually was a quick way to get fired from the Yankees. Steinbrenner said, "I don't think he's got any guts." Cloyd said, "He isn't scared of anything. He's a country boy from Louisiana and he's had his ups and downs, but that kid's got the chance to be a hell of a pitcher." Steinbrenner said, "I might just trade him off." Cloyd said, "That's up to you. You own the club and you're the boss, but I wouldn't trade him. He's struggling right now. A lot of people struggle." They kept arguing back and forth and Cloyd said, "Let me just say one thing and I'll get the hell out of here because I don't want to listen to you anymore, because I don't think you know what you're talking about."

Despite Steinbrenner's threats, he did not pull the trigger on a trade of Guidry, and Cloyd Boyer was vindicated. That was one time he was very proud of his judgment. At Cloyd's urging, Sparky Lyle and Dick Tidrow helped build up Guidry. "The next year he won 25," Cloyd said.

Many years later, in 2010, when the once terribly shy Guidry was well into a successful baseball broadcasting career, he telephoned Cloyd Boyer from Cooperstown, New York, during the week of the Hall of Fame induction ceremony to let Cloyd know he was thinking of him.

"He said, 'I'm sitting here with Yogi' and two or three other guys," Boyer said. "Yogi and I used to get up early and eat breakfast and drink coffee before anybody else thought about getting up. Guidry just said, 'You must have got me on the right track.' He was just telling me he appreciated it. I was so surprised. It was nice."

30

END OF THE LINE

Somehow it was appropriate that fun followed Clete Boyer on the diamond. During a May 1970, Braves game against the Chicago Cubs, Boyer was rushed on the field by a babe desiring to plant a kiss on him. Such shenanigans had been pioneered by Morganna, "The Kissing Bandit," who made her on-field debut that season by chasing after Pete Rose at Riverfront Stadium in Cincinnati to deliver her first wet one. The publicity was sensational. Taken aback, Rose let loose a stream of rough language. But the next day he sought out Morganna at a dance club where she performed and presented her with a dozen roses.

Morganna, whose outstanding physical characteristic was not her blonde hair, but her sensationally large chest measurement, began sneaking into ball parks all around the majors. It was documented that she kissed 37 big leaguers in such fashion, some of them twice. Morganna, who later posed for *Playboy* magazine, said she chased down Rose on a double dare from a friend.

Meanwhile, in Atlanta, Clete Boyer made a run for it when an anonymous babe jumped out of the stands and came after him. "This girl was better looking than Morganna," said Clete, who said he had a reason to out-run her smack at first. "That's because I had a wad of tobacco in my mouth. I told her I had to run until I could get rid of my tobacco and she said OK. Then I stopped running."[1]

The blonde young lady later said she ran onto the field for the kiss on a bet. There was no telling how Ken Boyer would have reacted if he was the target, but Clete somehow fit the profile of the scenario.

After Clete Boyer retired from playing in Japan, he became an infield coach for the Whales and then served as a coach with the New York Yankees and the Oakland Athletics. For a while he held down a job with Atlanta as a traveling infield coach, the way brother Cloyd used to be a

216

traveling pitching coach. Clete worked with Bob Horner, Dale Murphy, Jerry Royster and Glenn Hubbard on their fielding. One of Clete's old New York sports writing friends referred to the group as "The Infant Infield and Poppa Glove."[2]

The glove was still paying Clete's way in the game, and that was after he hit a high of .282 in Japan, which he rated equal to AA or AAA competition. If he had had to rely only on his bat for all of those years, he might have had a much shorter career in the big leagues.

"Remember when Ralph Houk used to call us his Million Dollar Infield?" Clete said. "Me, Tony Kubek, Bobby Richardson, and Joe Pepitone. I used to read all the nice things the sportswriters wrote about me in New York and swell up with pride."[3]

Boyer was 41 when he took on the task of tutoring that core group of Atlanta players and was a pleased observer during one game when he saw them pull off three double plays and a triple play. "I was sitting on the bench and I was so excited I couldn't believe it," Boyer said. "I never knew watching a game could be so much fun."[4]

The next season, 1979, Clete joined the Braves in spring training and got a good laugh out of the easy-going workouts in the sun. One thing always reported back from Japan when an American committed himself to playing ball in the Asian country was how challenging and regimented workouts were. There was little time for lollygagging in Japan when the manager and coaches sought to take up every minute of free time with training.

Japanese team leaders believed in sweating their players into shape, and Americans either adjusted or didn't last long. Back in the United States, Clete made the mental comparison and tried to tell his American cohorts how lucky they were to have it so easy.

> Everybody got up at 7:30. We did some stretching exercises and ran up and down 100 steps before we returned to our hotel for breakfast. Our regular spring training park was seven miles from the hotel. We'd dress at the hotel and have to carry our gear to and from the park every day. We'd go by bus to the park and get there about 9:30. We'd start off by jogging for 20 minutes and we'd play catch for about 15 minutes.
>
> After that, while the pitchers were throwing and the outfielders were shagging fly balls, the infielders would field ground balls—and we didn't stop until we'd handle 300 each, and after a while there would be about 500 baseballs scattered around the outfield. It looked like a snowstorm.[5]

Any young player listening to the requirements of that routine was probably goggle-eyed. In fact, he probably had to go lie down somewhere, just from hearing the details of the workout. And lying down is what the players on the Japanese teams felt like doing when they completed the day's efforts. "The Whales had a midnight curfew," Clete said from the vantage point of someone who believed midnight was a proper time to begin the evening's entertainment. "But there was no cabereting. Most of the players were so tired they went to bed about 10 o'clock. Baseball was their whole life."[6]

When Clete lived in Atlanta, Lenny Boyer spent a winter working at the rental car agency Clete owned and living in Clete's and wife Teri's home. Lenny was nine years younger and did not spend much time sharing a home in Missouri with Clete when they were youngsters. But this period of time brought them closer together.

"We spent every day together," Lenny said. The Braves started a charity basketball team, and Clete was one of the big scorers. Lenny watched him score 60 points in a game once. Ron Reed, who was both a major league pitcher and an NBA player, was on the same squad. "I really miss him because I did get close to him," Lenny said. "I think Clete really knew baseball. He could sit and talk game situations and baseball with anybody. He spent his whole life in baseball."

Indeed, baseball had been Clete Boyer's whole life, including in 1989, when he began a short-lived job as manager of the Bradenton Explorers of the Senior Professional Baseball Association. The league was founded for players 35-and-older, ostensibly to mimic the senior golf tour. The Explorers finished 38–34 during the circuit's debut season, but fled to Daytona Beach in 1990. The league went belly-up halfway through the second season because more seniors in the area played shuffleboard than watched age-group baseball players.

When Clete finally decided that he had had enough of the sidelines (after a 1992–1994 coaching stint with the Yankees), he still somehow wanted to stay close to the sport. He was one player who took advantage of the growth in nostalgia and public interest in collecting sports memorabilia, and he made appearances at sports card shows. Then he took things a step further. In 1998, he began spending summers in Cooperstown, New York, home of the Baseball Hall of Fame. He became a fixture at Mickey's Place, a sports memorabilia store located on the small town's main street. The establishment is run by Yankees fans and Clete regularly signed autographs there.

The distance from New York City to Cooperstown is about 200 miles by car, and although baseball fans flock to the Hall from all over the nation, likely more Yankees fans than those with allegiances to any other club make the trek to the remote community. Cooperstown has other charms,

Lynn (left) and Clete Boyer in 1997 at Stone Mountain, Georgia, after Clete had retired from the New York Yankees and Atlanta Braves (courtesy Cloyd and Nadine Boyer).

including lakes for fishing and boating, and is a vacation home mecca. Describing the place, Clete said that

> I love it up here. It's nice and quiet. I came up here for awhile last year and I liked it, so I decided to come up this year and just stay all summer. The way I feel about it is the fans only really get to see you one time, so if you go to a card show you may sit and sign for hours and not even hardly get to say hi to anybody. Here I can sit and talk to everybody. I go out to the Cooperstown Dreams Park and they're all baseball fans, and most of their dads or grand-parents know my name. I would like to be half as good as some of them think I was. If I was, I'd be enshrined down the street.[7]

In 1998, Boyer turned 61. He broke into the majors with the Athletics when he was 18, so he had covered a lot of miles representing several organizations while wearing a baseball uniform. In a sense he was still playing himself in this role as old Yankees hero, still on the periphery of baseball, at least, but not working quite as hard at it. "I don't miss the buses and eight months a year in a hotel," Clete said. "I was in it 41 years and I thought I'd take a year or two off. But I don't think they could get me back now. Everybody said I'd miss it, but I don't."[8]

Boyer became quite fond of Cooperstown and in 2000 moved his base of operation from Mickey's Place into his own place, a restaurant that he named "Clete Boyer's Hamburger Hall of Fame." It wasn't as difficult to gain entry there as it was to the real Hall of Fame, but getting on the menu at the popular eatery did take some pull with the owner. Clete applied the names of old Yankees teammates to the choices, such as "The Mickey Mantle Cheeseburger Deluxe" and "The Whitey Ford Blue Cheese Burger." Instead of hanging around at Mickey's Place, Clete hung around the restaurant and signed autographs on photos, napkins, you name it.

"He probably spent part of four or five years in Cooperstown," said brother Lewis Lynn Boyer. "He had one burger called 'The Clete Boyer Hall of Fame Burger.' He had a neat setup there and all of those Little League kids came in from those Dream Parks. They'd flock in there and he'd go out a couple of times a week and give free clinics to them. Thousands of kids came in. Every time a new busload came in he'd go out and give a free clinic. He always said, 'Kids are money.' And he loved to do it. He would give the kids autographs, but the parents would buy autographs and gloves. He just loved to be with those kids. He was a really good instructor."

After dabbling in the hamburger world for a couple of years, Clete Boyer once again became a regular at a different Cooperstown restaurant, T.J.'s. About 2005, he began to have health problems. He spent his off-seasons in Atlanta and returned there for medical treatment. Somewhat like his brother Ken, he was a bit reticent to talk about it at first when he received a diagnosis of colon cancer. According to Lenny,

After his playing days, Clete Boyer spent some time back with his old team as a coach (National Baseball Hall of Fame Library, Cooperstown, N.Y.).

He had cancer and he went with some treatments for a while, but I don't know how much good they were doing him. He was in Atlanta and we were in Missouri, and he didn't keep up all of the time. I think he got tired of doing the treatments. He kept going through cancer treatments for a year and a half and I know you can get to a point where you say, "When is enough?"

Lynn and Lyla Boyer did keep up. Part of Clete's colon was surgically removed in Atlanta, and they visited him in the hospital and stayed for two weeks during his recovery. Clete developed a hernia where the incision was made and had to undergo an additional operation. It was not an easy time.

After returning to Missouri, Lynn and Lyla remained the point of contact with Clete, who, in a phone call just a week before his death, reported feeling better. Still, "I think everybody knew that his health was getting worse," Lenny said. "Everybody was kind of ready for it (his death). Everybody knew that his health was deteriorating. It was a sad time, a real sad time. Clete was everybody's best friend. He was that kind of guy. He'd give you the shirt off his back. If he had a dollar, he'd give it to you. That's just the way he was. He was that way with his family, his friends, everybody."

One thing Lenny wished the family had done was save more of Clete's and Ken's baseball souvenirs. Nobody worked very hard at holding onto gloves, bats and balls. They are more interested in the sentimental value than the financial value, though none of them imagined the burgeoning interest in sports memorabilia either. At one time, when Clete was playing in the majors, he saved autographed balls from many of the guys who were teammates. The balls would be set aside and displayed at home in Missouri, yet young Lenny and young Ronnie didn't care a bit about that. They lived in the moment and played baseball every day in the summer. When they needed a new ball they just raided the house, purloining one of Clete's saved balls. "Ronnie and I used to go in the house, and if we didn't have an old baseball to play catch with, we'd get one of those autographed balls—there were so many of them around—and play catch with it," Lenny said. "Oh yeah, Ronnie and I played catch with a lot of autographed balls. It's not for the money value of it I wish we saved some of it. It's for the memories of it. I wanted to play catch. But I do have memories."

Lenny Boyer cherished those memories up until he died on June 12, 2013, in Missouri. He had outlived both Ken and Clete.

The end came for Clete Boyer on June 4, 2007, in an Atlanta hospital. Cancer had weakened Clete over a lengthy period of time; he was 70 years old when he passed away. Headlines in a variety of newspapers emphasized Clete's connection to the old Yankees championship teams, and several noted how famous he was for his fielding.

"He was a great Yankee and a tough guy," Yankees owner George Steinbrenner said. "He never talked too much, but he was extremely hardworking, a wonderful third baseman and had fire in his belly."[9]

Bobby Richardson, the second baseman in the same infield as Boyer for years with the Yankees, reminded inquirers about just how terrific Boyer was with the glove. "When I made the double play, I could just about close my eyes, put my glove up, and the ball would be there," he said. Richardson, who was known for his religious bent, accepted Clete Boyer for who he was, a drinker and partier more than a church-goer. "He was a hard liver. I don't think that's any secret. He lived life to the fullest."[10]

By the time Clete Boyer passed away, his older brother Ken had been deceased for a quarter of a century. Some felt that Ken's early death, at 51, cost him the opportunity to be elected to the Hall of Fame.

For some reason, third baseman have had a particularly difficult time being elected into the Hall of Fame, especially those who didn't bash 500 home runs or win so many Gold Glove Awards like Brooks Robinson. Ken Boyer first appeared on the Hall ballot to be considered by the members of the Baseball Writers Association of America in 1975. He received 2.5 percent of the vote. It takes 75 percent of those voting in a given year to be elected. Boyer received as much as 25.5 percent of the vote in 1988.

The 11 major league third basemen in the Hall of Fame are Frank "Home Run" Baker, Wade Boggs, George Brett, Jimmy Collins, George Kell, Freddie Lindstrom, Eddie Mathews, Brooks Robinson, Ron Santo, Mike Schmidt, and Pie Traynor.

Ken Boyer's lifetime stats include a .287 batting average, 1,141 runs batted in, and 282 home runs. He won the 1964 National League Most Valuable Player Award, won five Gold Glove Awards and was selected to All-Star teams in seven seasons, although some years two All Star Games took place, increasing his total of games played to ten.

Schmidt, Mathews, Santo and Brett have more home runs than Boyer. The others in the Hall do not. Six of the Hall third basemen have more RBI than Boyer. Seven have higher batting averages.

Remarkably, of the third basemen in the Hall, only Mike Schmidt has won an MVP award, something which he earned three times. Other third basemen besides Boyer have won MVPs, but have not been elected to the Hall.

Of the Hall of Fame third basemen who played in the Gold Glove Award era (which began in 1957), Brooks Robinson won 16 times, Schmidt 10 times, Santo five, Boggs two, Brett one, and Mathews zero. Ken Boyer won five Gold Glove Awards.

The third baseman in the Hall of Fame whose career Ken Boyer's most approximates is Santo's. Boyer's average was slightly higher. Santo hit more home runs and drove in more runs. Their All-Star selections are comparable. They won the same number of Gold Glove Awards. Boyer won an MVP and Santo did not. Boyer was part of a World Series champion and Santo was not.

While Ken Boyer passed away more than 30 years ago, Ron Santo remained in the limelight for decades after retirement, serving as a Chicago Cubs broadcaster. Even though in theory this admirable quality should have had nothing to do with his consideration, Santo also fought a courageous battle against diabetes as it gradually contributed to his death in 2010, a year before he was chosen for the Hall. Through charitable works, Santo also raised massive quantities of money to help fight the disease.

Santo was elected to the Hall of Fame by the Golden Era Committee. Ken Boyer was on the ballot of that committee, but received little support a few years ago and again in 2014. Boyer family members still think that one day Ken will be elected, and they look at Santo's election as supplying hope. Ken Boyer and Ron Santo played during the same era in the National League and had similar success.

"They are right there together," said Lewis Lynn Boyer. "Santo just left the game a couple of years ago. He was an announcer right up to the end. I think that might have helped him some. They're the same. I'm not saying Santo doesn't belong. No argument. I don't get a vote. In some ways it would be anticlimactic with him (Ken) gone. It would have been great if he was alive."

Ken's brothers may not have a vote, but someone else still around after all of these years believes that Ken Boyer should be in the Hall of Fame. That would be Hall of Famer Red Schoendienst, probably the player who knew Ken better than anyone except his siblings. "That's what I think," Schoendienst said of Ken Boyer belonging in the Hall of Fame. "You can look at Kenny's record."

Ron Boyer is one Boyer who still hopes that one day Ken Boyer will gain what he feels is his just due by being accepted in Cooperstown. He said it would be quite the clan gathering in the upstate New York town to celebrate the occasion on one of those typically hot summer days when Cooperstown lays out the red carpet. According to Ron Boyer,

I would be in Cooperstown that July, I know that. He's got four kids and all the grandkids and the brothers and sisters and nieces and nephews. I'd be there for Ken's induction if it ever happened. It would be a pretty awesome thing. He's in the Missouri Sports Hall of Fame and in the St. Louis Cardinals Hall of Fame. I think he's the only member of the Cardinals who has had his number retired who is not in the Baseball Hall of Fame.

Recent Hall of Fame voting made accurate Ron Boyer's comment about his brother's No. 14 jersey (except for the No. 85 retired for former owner August A. Busch Jr.). "It's still pretty awesome to have that, though," Ron Boyer said of Ken's retired number. "Not many guys' numbers are out there on that left-field wall in Busch Stadium and he's one of them."

The seven Boyer brothers from Alba, Missouri, who played professional baseball beat the odds against ever making it that far in the game, and the greater odds of reaching the majors. All seven brothers played for pay and three of them went all of the way to the top. Ken had the finest all-around playing career for the beloved St. Louis Cardinals. As a member of the New York Yankees, Clete won more than just about anyone.

Cloyd's tough luck seemed to wreck his big-league career at a young age, but he persevered, fought back from injury, absorbed and learned the game the way few have, and by doing so he spent 48 years in professional baseball. His time in baseball spanned 1945 to 1992.

"When Cloyd came to a town as a roving pitching coach he would be out there early in the morning working on the field, raking rocks and stuff out of the way," Ron Boyer said. "I remember that. He was a hard worker and I think the dedication paid off. Look at how many years he spent in pro baseball. He knew the game, but he was also a hard worker. That's what helped him stay in baseball as long as he did."

Cloyd Boyer turned 87 years old in September of 2014. He and his wife Nadine live in a comfortable home on a rural highway just a few miles from the Alba, Missouri, neighborhood where he grew up and which he left as a teenager to pursue his big-league dream.

Yes, Cloyd Boyer admits, he did work hard. But he was a good enough player to make it to the majors with the Cardinals, and when he couldn't pitch anymore he was a smart enough baseball man to stick around. What made him last as a scout and developer of young players was being a good judge of talent. Once Cloyd made up his mind, he stuck to his guns when others who he felt did not know as much insisted that a player couldn't make it. He was right about Ron Guidry. He was right about many other players in the Yankees farm system. He knew that his own brothers, Ken and Clete, had the right stuff to succeed.

He also got that World Series ring coaching for the Yankees, a most important souvenir of all the years spent in baseball—whether he ever wore it or not.

Cloyd Boyer continues to be a baseball fan, but from afar, mostly watching the games on TV—with few exceptions, he hasn't gone to the ball park in years. His baseball life gave him ties to the Yankees, the Braves, the Athletics, the Royals, the Blue Jays and the Cardinals. He doesn't root for all of them. There isn't room in any one fan's heart to encompass such a wide range of allegiances. He is not unhappy when St. Louis wins, but he enjoys it the most when Atlanta does well. In the American League he does root for the Yankees since he was associated with the team from 1962 to 1977, a big chunk of his professional life. Mostly, though, when Cloyd settles down in front of the television he just hopes to see a well-played game.

When he was a boy growing up in the same area, Cloyd was outside a lot, playing baseball for long hours on the closest field. He still spends time in the outdoors, though in a different way.

> I cut wood. I mow yards, raise a garden, rake leaves trying to keep the yard looking good. I cut my own wood, carry it in and burn it. Nadine helps me on that some. If I get in four hours a day, I've had a pretty good day. My family is always telling me I need to quit because I'm old now, that I don't know how old I am. I had some problems once and passed out and went to the doctor, and he told me I had to put my chainsaw up. I told him it was good advice, but I probably wasn't going to do it. Anyway, I just like to work. I don't know why. I'm an idiot. People in my family can't understand why I want to keep doing things like that. I just enjoy it.

It really was quite a baseball career, overlapping with so many fine teams, playing with so many terrific players, and coaching so many others.

"I don't go around bragging about anything," Cloyd Boyer said. "The way I figure it, the Lord's been good to me. I was lucky."

Lucky to some degree, but definitely fortunate to have such a long career in baseball and share the love of the game with six of his younger brothers. The likes of the seven Boyer brothers in the world of professional baseball will probably never be seen again.

CHAPTER NOTES

Unless otherwise noted, all quotations in this book come from interviews conducted by the author.

Chapter 4

1. Morris Frank and Addie Marks, *The Pecan Park Eagle*, 1948.

Chapter 5

1. Jack Zanger, *Ken Boyer: Guardian of the Hot Corner* (New York: Thomas Nelson & Sons, 1965), 32.
2. Ibid., 32.
3. Ibid., 20.
4. Ibid., 25.
5. Ibid., 27.
6. Brennan Stebbins, "Boyers' Baseball Legacy Began in SW Missouri," undated newspaper clipping, Baseball Hall of Fame archives.
7. Zanger, 30.
8. Ibid., 39.

Chapter 11

1. Dave Klein, *Great Infielders of the Major Leagues* (New York: Random House, 1972), 116.

Chapter 12

1. *Fowl Ball Magazine*, 1982; clipping from the Baseball Hall of Fame Archives.
2. Ibid.
3. Jack Zanger, *Ken Boyer: Guardian of the Hot Corner* (New York: Thomas Nelson & Sons, 1965), 42.

4. Ibid., 43.
5. Ibid., 46.
6. Ibid., 73.

Chapter 15

1. Bob Broeg, "Cards, Luke-Warm at Hot Sack, Boom Boyer as Best Ever," *St. Louis Post-Dispatch*, March 2, 1955.
2. Ibid.
3. Oscar Fraley, "Boyer Comes into Own," *United Press International*, July 12, 1956.
4. Broeg.
5. Jack Zanger, *Ken Boyer: Guardian of the Hot Corner* (New York: Thomas Nelson & Sons, 1965), 91.
6. Ibid., 92.
7. Red Schoendienst and Rob Rains, *RED: A Baseball Life* (Champaign, IL: Sports Publishing, 1998), 100.
8. Bob Broeg and Stan Musial, *Stan Musial: "The Man's" Own Story* (New York: Doubleday, 1964), 186.
9. Zanger, 94.
10. *Fowl Ball Magazine*, 1982, clipping in Baseball Hall of Fame Archives.

Chapter 16

1. Dave Klein, *Great Infielders of the Major Leagues* (New York: Random House, 1972), 119.
2. Rich Marazzi, "Turning Back the

Clock with Clete Boyer," *Sports Collectors Digest,* July 30, 1993.

3. Ibid.

4. Ibid.

5. Ibid.

6. Ibid.

7. Maury Allen, *You Could Look It Up* (New York: Times Books, 1979), 78.

8. Ibid., 182.

9. Andrew Marchand, "I Hate Casey Stengel," *New York Post,* October 18, 1998.

10. Ibid.

11. Allen, *You Could Look It Up,* 202.

12. Eric Ahlqvist, "Boyer Recalls Home Run Race During '61 Season," *Cooperstown Crier,* July 26, 2001.

13. "Boyer a Witness to History," *Atlanta Journal/Constitution,* September 14, 1994.

14. Joe King, "Boyer's Oh-Boy Plays Rate Yank Raves," *The Sporting News,* November 15, 1961.

15. Ibid.

16. Ibid.

Chapter 20

1. Maury Allen, *Yankees: Where Have You Gone?* (Champaign, IL: Sports Publishing, 2004), 161.

2. Ibid., 161.

3. Ibid., 161–162.

4. Til Ferdenzi, "Trio of Baseball Boyers Provide Family Touch to Yankees' Camp," *The Sporting News,* March 9, 1963.

5. Ibid.

6. Rich Marazzi, "Turning Back the Clock with Clete Boyer," *Sports Collectors Digest,* July 30, 1993.

7. Ibid.

8. Ibid.

9. "For The Record: Clete Boyer," *Sports Illustrated,* June 18, 2007.

10. Til Ferdenzi, "Clete Boyer in Class by Himself—Ferdenzi," *The Sporting News,* June 15, 1963.

11. Bobby Richardson with David Thomas, *Impact Player: A Memoir* (Carol Stream, IL: Tyndale House, 2012), 209.

12. Ibid., 217.

13. Maury Allen, *Roger Maris: A Man for All Seasons* (New York: Donald Fine, Inc., 1986), 24.

14. Ibid., 143.

15. Ibid., 190–191.

16. Ibid., 191.

17. Ralph Houk with Robert Creamer, *Season of Glory* (New York: Pocket Books, 1988), 159.

18. Mickey Mantle with Mickey Hershkowitz, *Mickey Mantle: All My Octobers* (New York: Harper Paperbacks, 1994), 133.

19. Tony Kubek and Terry Pluto, *Sixty-One: The Team, the Record, the Men* (New York: A Fireside Book, 1987), 7.

20. Ibid., 133.

21. Ibid., 133–134.

22. Jane Leavy, *The Last Boy: Mickey Mantle and the End of America's Childhood* (New York: HarperCollins, 2010), 198.

23. Kubek and Pluto, 147.

24. Leavy, 260.

25. Leavy, 135.

Chapter 21

1. Neal Russo, "Cards Name Boyer Team Captain, First Since Schoendienst," *St. Louis Post-Dispatch,* August 25, 1959.

2. Neal Russo, "Boyer Given Two-Year Contract," *St. Louis Post-Dispatch,* February 9, 1961.

3. Jack Zanger, *Ken Boyer: Guardian of the Hot Corner* (New York: Thomas Nelson & Sons, 1965), 96.

4. Ibid., 100.

5. Bob Broeg, "Boyer: 7 Years of Plenty After Trade Was Squelched," *St. Louis Post-Dispatch,* July 5, 1967.

6. Bob Broeg, "Dean Compares Boyer to Traynor," *St. Louis Post-Dispatch,* June 2, 1964.

7. Ibid.

8. George Vecsey, *Stan Musial: An American Life* (New York: Ballantine, 2011), 251.

Chapter 22

1. Jack Zanger, *Ken Boyer: Guardian of the Hot Corner* (New York: Thomas Nelson & Sons, 1965), 103.
2. Bob Gibson with Lonnie Wheeler, *Stranger to the Game: The Autobiography of Bob Gibson* (New York: Viking Penguin, 1994), 91.
3. Zanger, 113.
4. Red Schoendienst with Rob Rains, *RED: A Baseball Life* (Champaign, IL: Sports Publishing, 1998), 130.
5. David Halberstam, *October 1964* (New York: Villard, 1994), 257.
6. Ibid., 259.
7. Ed Wilks, "Boyer Crowned Majors' Player of Year," *The Sporting News*, November 14, 1964.
8. United Press International, "'Team Helped Me'—Boyer," *Cincinnati Enquirer*, November 25, 1964.
9. Neal Russo, "'This Caps It All,' Excited Ken Says of His MVP Prize," *The Sporting News*, December 5, 1964.
10. United Press International, "'Team Helped Me'—Boyer," *Cincinnati Enquirer*, November 25, 1964.

Chapter 23

1. Joe Williams, "Boyer Brothers Rewriting the Script," *New York World-Telegram*, October 12, 1964.
2. Ibid.
3. Maury Allen, "Brother vs. Brother," *New York Post*, October 5, 1964.
4. Larry Fox, "Oh, Brother! Boyers' Dad on Hot Seat," *New York World-Telegram*, October 5, 1964.
5. Ibid.
6. Ibid.
7. Maury Allen, "Brother Vs. Brother," *New York Post*, October 5, 1964.
8. United Press International, "Shannon's Home Run Was 'Turning Point,'" *Cincinnati Enquirer*, October 8, 1964.
9. United Press International, "Flood's 3-Bagger Lost in Sun—Tresh," *Cincinnati Enquirer*, October 8, 1964.
10. Bob Burnes, "Stottlemyre Stifles Cards, Gives Bombers Big Lift," *The Sporting News*, October 24, 1964.

11. Ibid.
12. Ibid.
13. Ibid.
14. Ken Boyer, "If Only Ellie Didn't Get Hit," *New York Journal-American*, October 15, 1964.
15. Bob Burnes, "Stottlemyre Stifles Cards, Gives Bombers Big Lift," *The Sporting News*, October 24, 1964.
16. Rich Marazzi, "Turning Back the Clock with Clete Boyer," *Sports Collectors Digest*, July 30, 1983.
17. Ibid.
18. Ibid.

Chapter 25

1. Red Schoendienst with Rob Rains, *RED: A Baseball Life* (Champaign, IL: Sports Publishing, 1998), 133.
2. Ibid.
3. Steve Jacobson, "Cards' Talk Is Brave—It's Also in Private," *Newsday*, July 6, 1965.
4. Ibid.
5. Ibid.
6. "Trade Shocks Ken; Al, Charlie Elated," *New York Daily News*, October 21, 1965.
7. Ibid.
8. "17 Years—Then a Phone Call," *St. Louis Post-Dispatch*, October 21, 1965.
9. Maury Allen, "Surprise! Boyer's Not Bitter," *New York Post*, October 21, 1965.
10. Steve Jacobson, "Boyer Could Lead, If Mets Can Follow," *Newsday*, March 10, 1966.
11. Ibid.
12. Ibid.
13. George Vecsey, "Ken Boyer Gives Mets an Intangible Thing," *New York Times*, April 19, 1966.
14. Edgar Munzel, "Sox Bosses Partly to Blame for Low Bat Marks—Boyer," *The Sporting News*, June 1, 1968.
15. Ibid.
16. "Ken Boyer Just One of Long Line," *Los Angeles Times*, July 30, 1968.
17. Ibid.
18. Bob Hunter, "Boyer Adds a Clutch

Bat to L.A.'s Anemic Attack," *Los Angeles Examiner,* January 18, 1969.

Chapter 26

1. Furman Bisher, "Third Base Is Mine," *Atlanta Journal*, December 1, 1966.
2. Ibid.
3. Steve Jacobson, "Braves Wild About Clete Boyer's Glove," *Newsday*, March 15, 1967.
4. Ibid.
5. Ibid.
6. Ibid.
7. Bob Broeg, "Ken Boyer on Brother Clete: 'He'll Swing in Dixie,'" *St. Louis Post-Dispatch*, April 2, 1967.
8. Wayne Minshew, "Braves Clap Hands Over Clete's Feats," *The Sporting News*, May 27, 1967.
9. Ibid.
10. Frank Bilovsky, "'Awful' Chinese Food Couldn't Upset Clete Boyer," *Philadelphia Bulletin*, June 15, 1967.
11. Ibid.
12. Ibid.
13. Ibid.
14. Steve Jacobson, "Braves' Boyer Is Not Like the Old Days," *Newsday*, June 26, 1967.
15. Wayne Minshew, "Clete Clouts His No. 1000 Hit—But a Defeat Removes the Gloss," *Atlanta Constitution*, August 5, 1967.
16. Wayne Minshew, "Mathews' Braves Hardly Miss Him, Thanks to Clete," *The Sporting News*, September 2, 1967.
17. Ibid.
18. Ibid.
19. Jay Searcy, "Clete Takes Verbal Jab at Rico; 'He Loafs,' Claims Third Sacker," *Chattanooga Lookout*, February 24, 1968.
20. Wayne Minshew, "Another Bad Year Would Cause Clete to Call It a Career," *The Sporting News*, November 23, 1968.
21. Wilt Browning, "Streaking Clete Cancels Early Retirement Plans," *Atlanta Journal*, July 10, 1969.

Chapter 27

1. Wayne Minshew, "Clemente Tops N.L. Defensive Unit," *The Sporting News*, November 29, 1969.
2. Wayne Minshew, "Clete's Hits Are Scarce—But His Glove Is Great," *The Sporting News*, June 13, 1970.
3. Ibid.
4. Ibid.
5. Ibid.
6. Associated Press/United Press International, "$1,000 Fine for Boyer—Betting," *San Francisco Chronicle*, June 11, 1971.
7. Associated Press/United Press International, "Boyer Fined $1,000 for Betting," *San Francisco Examiner*, June 10, 1971.
8. Ibid.
9. Associated Press/United Press International, "$1,000 Fine for Boyer—Betting," *San Francisco Chronicle*, June 11, 1971.
10. Ibid.
11. Milton Gross, "Things Are Looking Up," *New York Post*, June 11, 1971.
12. Wayne Minshew, "Boyer Says He Suspects a Blacklisting," *The Sporting News*, June 26, 1971.
13. Ferd Borsch, "'A New Lease on Life'—Boyer in Hawaii," *Honolulu Star-Advertiser*, July 3, 1971.
14. Ibid.
15. Jan Petranek, "Minor League Baseball an Education for Boyer," *The Sporting News*, September 18, 1971.
16. Ibid.
17. Mash Yoshimi, "Boyer's Enjoying Baseball in Japan," *Associated Press*, April 19, 1972.
18. Ibid.
19. Robert Obojski, "Ex-Yankee, Brave Clete Boyer Interview," *Sports Collectors Digest*, August 14, 1998.

Chapter 28

1. Bill E. Burk, "Boyer Finds Pilot Must Think Ahead on Moves," *The Sporting News*, May 9, 1970.
2. Ibid.

3. Ibid.

4. United Press International, "Ken Boyer Back as Card Manager," *New York Daily News*, April 29, 1978.

5. Ibid.

6. Neal Russo, "Boyer's Cardinal Strategy: Set Lineup, 4-Man Rotation," *The Sporting News*, May 13, 1978.

7. Associated Press and United Press International, "Cardinals Ask Boyer to Manage—Finally," *Chicago Tribune*, April 29, 1978.

8. Neal Russo, "Boyer Rehired for Fresh Start with Cardinals," *The Sporting News*, October 14, 1978.

9. Ibid.

10. Rick Hummel, "Year of the Cardinals? Birds Pack Real Wallop," *The Sporting News*, June 23, 1979.

11. Ibid.

12. Rick Hummel, "Boyer Out—Can Herzog Revive Redbirds?" *The Sporting News*, June 21, 1980.

13. Dave Anderson, "The Dinner for Ken Boyer," *New York Times*, March 2, 1982.

14. Ibid.

15. Ibid.

16. Ibid.

17. Maury Allen, "Clete Goes to Bat for Brother Ken," *New York Post*, March 3, 1982.

18. Phil Pepe, "Baseball Goes to Bat for Ken Boyer," *New York Daily News*, March 30, 1982.

19. Ibid.

20. Associated Press, "Ken Boyer Succumbs to Cancer," September 8, 1982.

21. Henry Hecht, "Ken Boyer Succumbs to Cancer at 51," *New York Post*, September 8, 1982.

22. Ibid.

23. Ibid.

24. Ibid.

25. *Fowl Ball Magazine*, 1982, clipping in Baseball Hall of Fame Archives.

26. Milton Richman, "Undying Love Bound Boyers," United Press International, *New York Post*, September 8, 1962.

27. Robert L. Burnes, "Ken Boyer (1931–1982), Greatest Third Baseman in Cardinal History," *St. Louis Globe-Democrat*, September 8, 1982.

Chapter 30

1. Wilt Browning, "Another Kiss Revives Clete," *Atlanta Journal*, May 2, 1970.

2. Maury Allen, "Clete Conducts Infield Class," *New York Post*, July 19, 1978.

3. Ibid.

4. Ibid.

5. C. Johnson Spink, "We Believe," *The Sporting News*, March 10, 1979.

6. Ibid.

7. Bill Francis, "Former Yankee Clete Boyer Calls Cooperstown Home for Summer," *Freeman's Journal*, July 3, 1998.

8. Ibid.

9. Ben Walker, "Clete Boyer, at 70; 3d Baseman for Yanks Was Brilliant Fielder," Associated Press, *Boston Globe*, June 5, 2007.

10. Ibid.

Bibliography

Interviews

Boyer, Cloyd, December 13–15, 2011; January 15, 2014.
Boyer, Lenny, December 14, 2011.
Boyer, Lewis Lynn, December 15, 2011.
Boyer, Nadine, December 13, 2011.
Boyer, Ron, December 14, 2011.
Boyer, Wayne, January 10, 2012.
Groat, Dick, September 18, 2012.
Lockhart, Shirley Boyer, September 17, 2012.
McCarver, Tim, November 27, 2012.
Schell, Pansy Boyer, December 14, 2011.
Schoendienst, Red, August 31, 2012.
Virdon, Bill, September 18, 2012.
Webb, Dolores Boyer, August 31, 2012.
Woodmansee, Juanita Boyer, December 14, 2011.

Books

Allen, Maury. *Roger Maris: A Man for All Seasons*. New York: Donald Fine, 1986.
_____. *Yankees: Where Have You Gone?* Champaign, IL: Sports Publishing, 2004.
_____. *You Could Look It Up*. New York: Times Books, 1979.
Broeg, Bob, and Stan Musial. *Stan Musial: "The Man's" Own Story*. New York: Doubleday, 1964.
Frank, Morris, and Addie Marks. *Your 1948 Houston Buffs, Dixie Champions: Brief Biographies*. Autograph book. Pecan Park, TX: Pecan Park Eagle, 1948.
Gibson, Bob, with Lonnie Wheeler. *Stranger to the Game: The Autobiography of Bob Gibson*. New York: Viking Penguin, 1994.
Halberstam, David. *October 1964*. New York: Villard, 1994.
Houk, Ralph, and Robert Creamer. *Season of Glory*. New York: Pocket Books, 1988.
Klein, Dave. *Great Infielders of the Major Leagues*. New York: Random House, 1972.
Kubek, Tony, and Terry Pluto. *Sixty-One: The Team, the Record, the Men*. New York: A Fireside Book, 1987.
Leavy, Jane. *The Last Boy: Mickey Mantle and the End of America's Childhood*. New York: HarperCollins, 2010.
Mantle, Mickey, with Mickey Hershkowitz. *Mickey Mantle: All My Octobers*. New York: HarperCollins, 1994.

Richardson, Bobby, with David Thomas. *Impact Player: A Memoir.* Carol Stream, IL: Tyndale House, 2012.

Schoendienst, Red, with Rob Rains. *Red: A Baseball Life.* Champaign, IL: Sports Publishing, 1998.

Vecsey, George. *Stan Musial: An American Life.* New York: Ballantine, 2011.

Zanger, Jack. *Ken Boyer: Guardian of the Hot Corner.* New York: Thomas Nelson, 1965.

Magazine Articles

Burk, Bill E. "Boyer Finds Pilot Must Think Ahead on Moves." *The Sporting News,* May 9, 1970.

Burnes, Bob. "Stottlemyre Stifles Cards, Gives Bombers Big Lift." *The Sporting News,* October 24, 1964.

Ferdenzi, Til. "Clete Boyer in Class by Himself—Ferdenzi." *The Sporting News,* June 15, 1963.

_____. "Trio of Baseball Boyers Provide Family Touch to Yankees' Camp." *The Sporting News,* March 9, 1963.

"For the Record: Clete Boyer." *Sports Illustrated,* June 18, 2007.

Fowl Ball Magazine, 1982. Clipping from the Baseball Hall of Fame Archives.

Hummel, Rick. "Boyer Out—Can Herzog Revive Redbirds?" *The Sporting News,* June 21, 1980.

_____. "Year of the Cardinals? Birds Pack Real Wallop." *The Sporting News,* June 23, 1979.

King, Joe. "Boyer's Oh-Boy Plays Rate Yank Raves." *The Sporting News,* November 15, 1961.

Marazzi, Rich. "Turning Back the Clock with Clete Boyer." *Sports Collectors Digest,* July 30, 1993.

Minshew, Wayne. "Another Bad Year Would Cause Clete to Call It a Career." *The Sporting News,* November 23, 1968.

_____. "Boyer Says He Suspects a Blacklisting." *The Sporting News,* June 26, 1971.

_____. "Braves Clap Hands Over Clete's Feats." *The Sporting News,* May 27, 1967.

_____. "Clemente Tops N.L. Defensive Unit." *The Sporting News,* November 29, 1969.

_____. "Clete's Hits Are Scarce—But His Glove Is Great." *The Sporting News,* June 13, 1970.

_____. "Mathews? Braves Hardly Miss Him, Thanks to Clete." *The Sporting News,* September 2, 1967.

Munzel, Edgar. "Sox Bosses Partly to Blame for Low Bat Marks—Boyer." *The Sporting News,* June 1, 1968.

Obojski, Robert. "Ex-Yankee, Brave Clete Boyer Interview." *Sports Collectors Digest,* August 14, 1998.

Petranek, Jan. "Minor League Baseball an Education for Boyer." *The Sporting News,* September 18, 1971.

Russo, Neal. "Boyer's Cardinal Strategy: Set Lineup, 4-Man Rotation." *The Sporting News,* May 13, 1978.

_____. "Boyer Rehired for Fresh Start with Cardinals." *The Sporting News,* October 14, 1978.

_____. "'This Caps It All,' Excited Ken Says of His MVP Prize." *The Sporting News,* December 5, 1964.

Spink, C. Johnson. "We Believe." *The Sporting News,* March 10, 1979.

Wilks, Ed. "Boyer Crowned Majors' Player of Year." *The Sporting News,* November 14, 1964.

Wire Services

Associated Press. "Ken Boyer Succumbs to Cancer." September 8, 1982.

Associated Press and United Press International. "$1,000 Fine for Boyer—Betting." *San Francisco Chronicle*, June 11, 1971.

Associated Press and United Press International. "Boyer Fined $1,000 for Betting." *San Francisco Examiner*, June 10, 1971.

Associated Press and United Press International. "Cardinals Ask Boyer to Manage—Finally." *Chicago Tribune*, April 29, 1978.

Fraley, Oscar. "Boyer Comes Into Own." United Press International, July 12, 1956.

Richman, Milton. "Undying Love Bound Boyers." United Press International, *New York Post*, September 8, 1962.

United Press International. "Flood's 3-Bagger Lost in Sun—Tresh." *Cincinnati Enquirer*, October 8, 1964.

United Press International. "Ken Boyer Back as Cards Manager." *New York Daily News*, April 29, 1978.

United Press International. "Shannon's Home Run Was 'Turning Point.'" *Cincinnati Enquirer*, October 8, 1964.

United Press International. "'Team Helped Me'—Boyer." *Cincinnati Enquirer*, November 25, 1964.

Walker, Ben. "Clete Boyer, at 70; 3d Baseman for Yanks Was Brilliant Fielder." Associated Press, *Boston Globe*, June 5, 2007.

Yoshimi, Mash. "Boyer's Enjoying Baseball in Japan." Associated Press, April 19, 1972.

Newspaper Articles

Ahlqvist, Eric. "Boyer Recalls Home Run Race During '61 Season." *Cooperstown Crier*, July 26, 2001.

Allen, Maury. "Brother vs. Brother." *New York Post*, October 5, 1964.

_____. "Clete Conducts Infield Class." *New York Post*, July 19, 1978.

_____. "Clete Goes to Bat for Brother Ken." *New York Post*, March 3, 1982.

_____. "Surprise! Boyer's Not Bitter." *New York Post*, October 21, 1965.

Anderson, Dave. "The Dinner for Ken Boyer." *New York Times*, March 2, 1982.

Bilovsky, Frank. "'Awful' Chinese Food Couldn't Upset Clete Boyer." *Philadelphia Bulletin*, June 15, 1967.

Bisher, Furman. "Third Base Is Mine." *Atlanta Journal*, December 1, 1966.

Borsch, Ferd. "'A New Lease on Life'—Boyer in Hawaii." *Honolulu Star-Advertiser*, July 3, 1971.

"Boyer a Witness to History." *Atlanta Journal-Constitution*, September 14, 1994.

Boyer, Ken. "If Only Ellie Didn't Get Hit." *New York Journal-American*, October 15, 1964

Broeg, Bob. "Boyer: 7 Years of Plenty After Trade Was Squelched." *St. Louis Post-Dispatch*, July 5, 1967.

_____. "Cards, Luke-Warm at Hot Sack, Boom Boyer as Best Ever." *St. Louis Post-Dispatch*, March 2, 1955.

_____. "Dean Compares Boyer to Traynor." *St. Louis Post-Dispatch*, June 2, 1964.

_____. "Ken Boyer on Brother Clete: 'He'll Swing in Dixie.'" *St. Louis Post-Dispatch*, April 2, 1967.

Browning, Wilt. "Another Kiss Revives Clete." *Atlanta Journal*, May 2, 1970.

_____. "Streaking Clete Cancels Early Retirement Plans." *Atlanta Journal*, July 10, 1969.

Burnes, Robert L. "Ken Boyer (1931–1982), Greatest Third Baseman in Cardinal History." *St. Louis Globe-Democrat*, September 8, 1982.

Fox, Larry. "Oh, Brother! Boyers' Dad on Hot Seat." *New York World-Telegram*, October 5, 1964.

Francis, Bill. "Former Yankee Clete Boyer Calls Cooperstown Home for Summer." *Freeman's Journal*, July 3, 1998.

Gross, Milton. "Things Are Looking Up." *New York Post*, June 11, 1971.

Hecht, Henry. "Ken Boyer Succumbs to Cancer at 51." *New York Post*, September 8, 1982.

Hunter, Bob. "Boyer Adds a Clutch Bat to L.A.'s Anemic Attack." *Los Angeles Examiner*, January 18, 1969.

Jacobson, Steve. "Boyer Could Lead, If Mets Can Follow." *Newsday*, March 10, 1966.

_____. "Braves' Boyer Is Not Like the Old Days." *Newsday*, June 26, 1967.

_____. "Braves Wild About Clete Boyer's Glove." *Newsday*, March 15, 1967.

_____. "Cards' Talk Is Brave—It's Also in Private." *Newsday*, July 6, 1965.

"Ken Boyer Just One of Long Line." *Los Angeles Times*, July 30, 1968.

Marchand, Andrew. "I Hate Casey Stengel." *New York Post*, October 18, 1998.

Minshew, Wayne. "Clete Clouts His No. 1000 Hit—But a Defeat Removes the Gloss." *Atlanta Constitution*, August 5, 1967.

Pepe, Phil. "Baseball Goes to Bat for Ken Boyer." *New York Daily News*, March 30, 1982.

Russo, Neal. "Boyer Given Two-Year Contract." *St. Louis Post-Dispatch*, February 9, 1961.

_____. "Cards Name Boyer Team Captain, First Since Schoendienst." *St. Louis Post-Dispatch*, August 25, 1959.

Searcy, Jay. "Clete Takes Verbal Jab at Rico; 'He Loafs,' Claims Third Sacker." *Chattanooga Lookout*, February 24, 1968.

"17 Years—Then a Phone Call." *St. Louis Post-Dispatch*, October 21, 1965.

Stebbins, Brennan. "Boyers' Baseball Legacy Began in SW Missouri." *Carthage (MO) Press*, no date.

"Trade Shocks Ken; Al, Charlie Elated." *New York Daily News*, October 21, 1965.

Vecsey, George. "Ken Boyer Gives Mets an Intangible Thing." *New York Times*, April 19, 1966.

Williams, Joe. "Boyer Brothers Rewriting the Script." *New York World-Telegram*, October 12, 1964.

INDEX